Dollhouse & Miniature Dolls

1840 to 1990

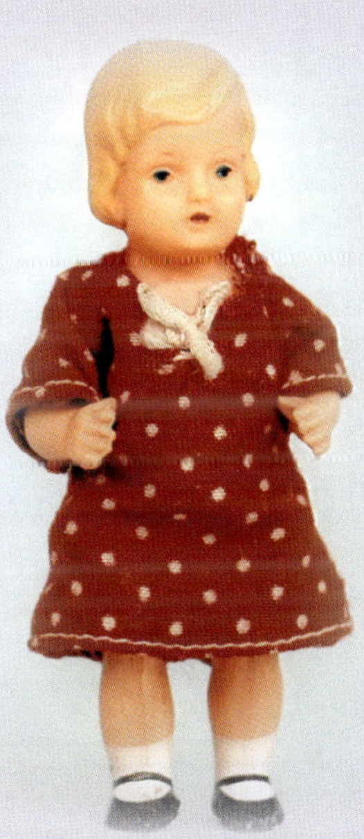

Marcie and Bob Tubbs
with Dian Zillner

Schiffer Publishing Ltd®

4880 Lower Valley Road, Atglen, Pennsylvania 19310

Dedication

All collectors of vintage, commercially made dollhouses and miniatures owe a huge debt of gratitude to a woman who opened the door for us to gain real knowledge of the hobby. In 1995, when more complete and accurate information about the subject was just coming to light, this former librarian published *American Dollhouses & Furniture*. Over the next decade she continued to dig into the subject, authoring or co-authoring five books on such topics as antique, furnished, and international dollhouses, and vintage toy buildings. To further aid research, a sixth book addressed the historical advertising pictured in old magazines, trade journals, and company brochures. In writing her books she called upon others to share their collections and knowledge, creating a community around the hobby. We were always on the lookout for a special dollhouse, unique furnishing, or new fact that could be added to her next publication. She allotted room whether you collected Bliss or Brumberger. Her enthusiasm was catching! When the time came to add dollhouse inhabitants to the body of growing knowledge she became my muse, teacher, friend, and co-author. Without her encouragement and guidance this book would never have become a reality. Her books have made education a continual process that never ends.

Thank you, Dian Zillner.

This book is dedicated to you.

Valuation

Market values of collectibles vary first and foremost by their condition and rarity. It is not enough to say that a doll is "good considering its age." Pristine dolls exist in nearly every type pictured in this book. Unless otherwise noted, pricing is for a doll in excellent condition, unrepaired, of original clothing. Dolls found in their original box generally are worth at least 50% more than toys of like condition without a box. Repairs or replacements, if minor, will cause dolls to lose at least 10-20% of their value. Significant repair or restoration will result in a reduction in value of 50% or more. Dolls in heavily played with condition are worth 20-30% of the value of those in excellent condition. Market values in recent years have fluctuated greatly. Dolls that were considered rare fifteen years ago are now frequently found on online auctions, and prices have dropped by as much as 50% or more. Rare dolls in excellent condition continue to rise in value. There is a premium for things that are truly special. Dolls of the immediate post World War II years are now more than sixty years old and have already achieved vintage status on their way to becoming antiques. Pricing for unique dolls of that era is now creeping up as people recognize their quality.

Values listed in the captions are intended only as a guide, and should not be used to set prices for dolls. Retail prices vary from country to country, from one section of the United States to another, and from dealer to dealer. The values listed here are the best estimates the authors can give at the time of publication, but prices can change quickly. Neither the authors nor the publisher assume responsibility for any losses that might be incurred as a result of consulting this price guide.

A Note About Scale

Throughout this book we talk about "scale." To make calculation of actual sizes more universal, today's common 1" to 1' scale is listed as 1:12; 1 cm to 10 cm scale, common in early and European dolls, is 1:10; ¾" to 1' scale of the post World War II era is shown throughout as 1:18; half-scale is 1:24; 2" to 1' scale is 1:6. All measurements have been converted to decimal fractions but appear as inches and not metric length.

Notice: All items in this book are from private collections and museums. Grateful acknowledgement is given to the original producers of the materials photographed. The copyright or ownership has been identified for each item whenever possible. If any omission or incorrect information is found, please notify the authors or publisher, and it will be amended in any future edition of the book.

Other Schiffer Books on Related Subjects:
Cloth Dolls from Ancient to Modern. Linda Edward.
ISBN: 0-7643-0213-2. $29.95
American Dollhouses and Furniture from the 20th century. Dian Zillner.
ISBN: 0-88740-768-4. $59.95
International Dollhouses & Accessories, 1880s to 1980s. Dian Zillner.
ISBN: 0-7643-1725-3. $59.95
Antique & Collectible Dollhouses and Their Furnishings. Dian Zillner and Patty Cooper. ISBN: 0-7643-0120-9. $59.95
Furnished Dollhouses 1880s-1980s. Dian Zillner with Patty Cooper.
ISBN: 0-7643-1188-3. $59.95

Library of Congress Control Number: 2008943518

Designed by Mark David Bowyer
Type set in Caslon224 Bk BT / Zurich BT

ISBN: 978-0-7643-3264-7
Printed in China

Schiffer Books are available at special discounts for bulk purchases for sales promotions or premiums. Special editions, including personalized covers, corporate imprints, and excerpts can be created in large quantities for special needs. For more information contact the publisher:

Published by Schiffer Publishing Ltd.
4880 Lower Valley Road
Atglen, PA 19310
Phone: (610) 593-1777; Fax: (610) 593-2002
E-mail: Info@schifferbooks.com

For the largest selection of fine reference books on this and related subjects, please visit our web site at **www.schifferbooks.com**
We are always looking for people to write books on new and related subjects. If you have an idea for a book please contact us at the above address.

This book may be purchased from the publisher.
Include $5.00 for shipping.
Please try your bookstore first.
You may write for a free catalog.

In Europe, Schiffer books are distributed by
Bushwood Books
6 Marksbury Ave.
Kew Gardens
Surrey TW9 4JF England
Phone: 44 (0) 20 8392-8585; Fax: 44 (0) 20 8392-9876
E-mail: info@bushwoodbooks.co.uk
Website: www.bushwoodbooks.co.uk
Free postage in the U.K., Europe; air mail at cost.

Contents

Preface and Acknowledgments

I am a Baby Boomer and collector of dollhouses and miniatures of the 1920s-1960s. In one of many chats with my friend, noted author Dian Zillner, she urged me to write a book to help fill a void in published information on miniature dolls of the Depression, War years, and Baby Boomer era. She knew that this was the current focus of my collection and promised to help me by sharing her wealth of information on small dolls of the early years.

At first the book was only meant to focus on the time period that I knew well. Dian suggested that in order to understand more modern dolls, it would be necessary to understand how they have historically evolved. Many scholarly books have been written on miniature dolls of the 19th and early 20th centuries and I couldn't have hoped to cover those periods with as much depth. No one book can hope to do justice to the broad area of collecting dollhouse and miniature dolls over many centuries. Small dolls have been made for over a thousand years. But the story starting in 1920 needed to be researched and told before basic information was lost and memories dimmed. Without apologizing, I realize that the book is "heavy" on material of the mid 20th century.

Once the focus of the book was decided, it was necessary to establish the parameters. For the most part, I tried to restrict the book to dolls less than 7". Sometimes taller dolls would sneak in to illustrate a point, but for the most part I chose to write about dolls that fit "in a dollhouse." Some dolls were excluded even if they met the height requirement, because they weren't proportioned for a dollhouse. I chose to include fairytale dolls, especially those made in Europe, because they were part of a doll maker's complete line of miniature dolls. In the last twenty-five years of the 20th century, many small dolls have been made as collectible toys, and I have not given them in-depth coverage.

I chose to start around 1840 because that was roughly the beginning of commercially made dollhouse dolls. I stopped before the end of the 20th century because trends in doll making were creating changes significantly different than in prior years. Information on this period is still fresh and others will be able to research and write about it. One of the directions in the last part of the century was toward artist-made miniature dolls. I could not do justice to artist dolls in this book and chose not to cover them at all. It is a story that needs to be told with an eye towards including as many of today's fine artists as possible. There are some beautiful creations out there!

When I began collecting Baby Boomer dollhouses in 1991, I knew little about them. Memories of my childhood Marx "Disney" dollhouse frustrated me as I began to research the hobby. There was very little published information about dollhouses, miniatures and their makers. Finally, in 1993 Bill Hanlon's book *Plastic Toys, Dimestore Dreams of the 40s & 50s* was published and gave Baby Boomers a beginning. Mary Brett's *Tomart's Price Guide to Tin Litho Doll Houses & Plastic Doll House Furniture* soon followed, and by that time I had gathered enough of a collection to submit photos for her very well researched, but underappreciated, book on the dollhouses and miniatures of my childhood. While attending a collectors' club conference, I met Dian, who was working on her first book about dollhouses, and she invited my input. Since that time, Dian Zillner, often with the thoughtful and gifted Patty Cooper, has published six informative books on dollhouses. Chuck Donovan published an authoritative work, now in its third printing, on Renwal, based in part on his collection of Renwal catalogs. Due to the influence and encouragement of these authors and the helpful, well informed community listed below, this book on miniature dolls has come to pass. Some participants were happy sharing photos from their own collections; others gave of their time in researching historical information. Dealers found dolls needed for the book or allowed dolls they were offering to be photographed. Some contributors were witnesses to the actual making of the dolls. As I began researching miniature dolls, I discovered authors new to me, who provided an incredible wealth of information on dolls, large and small. Many of them are listed in the bibliography, and their superior knowledge and research requires praise and acknowledgement. Some of these authors are not alive to witness the results of their cumulative research. Special mention needs to be given to Dee Snyder, who, for years, wrote the "In A Nutshell" column for *Nutshell News* and Janet Pagter Johl, who wrote several books about dolls in general at the beginning of the Baby Boomer Era, often providing the only contemporary written history on that period's doll makers. Their research has come alive once again, serving as a launching point for much of this book.

A significant amount of the new information for this book came from those who "lived it" or who were fortunate to know the doll makers that we discuss. Gathering and preserving their "oral histories" has been one of the most rewarding aspects of writing this book. Special thanks for all the time the following people gave: Lee Forsythe (Ethyl Strong), Prudence Zedler and Colleen Coffen (Joan Beringer Pripps), Gabriele John von Freyend (Erna Meyer), Mary P., Malcolm C., and Christopher Winsor, Jessie Tramutolo, Joel Pratt (Marion Winsor), Leslie Flagg Reynolds (Sheila and Charles Flagg), Mette Markes Jepsen (Anne Beate Design), Joy Sorensen Reis (Tiny Town Dolls), Janet and Robert, grandchildren of Alice T. Shields (Alice Shields Dolls), Louis Charpentier (Dolls of the World and Twinky Dolls), Jim Miller, Marketing Coordinator of Story Land Theme Park (Baps Dolls).

Heartfelt thanks is due to my fellow collectors: Patty Cooper, Sue Grabill Morse, Lettie Schwarz, Gail Carey, Geraldine Scott, Jeannie Beaumont, Sheryl Leisure, Diane Hogan, Hilda Pitman, Christine Wolf, Lois Freeman, and Sally Bovill. Special thanks to Suzanne Silverthorne and my husband, Bob, for capturing the beauty and playfulness of the dolls in their photography.

Dealers who were extremely helpful in sharing their dolls and their knowledge include: Ann Meehan, Jo and Les Payne, Zelma and Jules Fink, Penny Hadfield of A Quiet Place Dolls, Joy Kelleher of Special Joys, Cynthia Orgeron, Nancy A. Smith, Kathy Evans of Kathy's and Terry's Dolls, Sue Sizemore, T.J.Geppert, Lucy Morgan and Susan Singer of Lucy's Doll House.

Fellow authors who were not afraid to share their knowledge, hoping to build the most accurate and complete base of information possible for all collectors include: Swantje Köhler, Marion Osborne, Dave L. Leopard, Mary Young, and Marian H. Schmuhl.

In writing a book like this you try to read everything you can find. You want to locate as much primary source material as possible to take speculation and supposition out of the writing. A lot of material has been lost. Some has been stored on microfilm but not indexed. Thank goodness we live in a digital world, however. The internet gives us access to original records, articles, and web sites of people wanting to share information about our hobby. Newspapers, historical societies, academic institutions, and governments have now started to create digital indexes giving researchers greater practical access to stored information. With all of that, you still can't be sure that you have found everything and I'll be happy to receive any corrections or additions that collectors submit.

We sometimes forget that libraries are still the greatest storehouse of information available to the public. Librarians aren't there to simply "check out a book", but take real pleasure in unlocking the door to stored information. Special praise is given to the Bridgeport, Connecticut, Public Library and its wonderful staff of research librarians. It is an "old time city library" full of treasures. Unfortunately it suffers from lack of funding, and it is feared that much of their trove will soon be lost. I hope that doesn't happen. Special mention is also due: Lois Holly, Interloan Librarian at the Fairfield, Connecticut, Public Library; Susan at the Reference Desk of Stratford, Connecticut, Public Library; Terri Nelson, Special Collections Librarian at the Princeton, New Jersey, Public Library; Chicago, Illinois, Public Library; Boston, Massachusetts, Public Library; San Francisco, California, Public Library; Mary K.B. Carter, of the Pasadena, California, Public Library; Gayle Walsh, Reference Librarian at the Paul Pratt Memorial Library in Cohasset, Massachusetts; Carol A. Brach, Engineering Librarian at the University of Notre Dame Library, South Bend, Indiana.

Museums and historical societies serve the dual purpose of preserving our heritage and aiding in the dissemination of our history. Special thanks is given to: Tracey Crawley, Principal Keeper of the Stamford Museum in Lincolnshire, United Kingdom; Kristie Dobbins, Curator, and Mary Wheeler, Collections Manager, Toy & Miniature Museum of Kansas City, Missouri; Adrienne E. Saint-Pierre, Curator of the Fairfield, Connecticut, Historical Society; Lynne DeGiacomo, Executive Director of the Cohasset, Massachusetts, Historical Society; Carol Sandler, Library Director, Strong Museum, Rochester, New York; Rachel Rails, Membership Services, United Federation of Doll Clubs, Inc., Kansas City, Missouri.

I would also like to mention my children, Brian and Carly, who, on every family vacation, tolerated stops at passing antique shops, malls, and flea markets. The memory of their groans, occasional good humor, and helpful searching made me smile as I wrote this book.

The book reads somewhat as a history text. I hope you will find it interesting and informative. It is the author's belief that toys, in general, and dolls, in particular, reflect social and economic trends of the time in which they were made. To understand the context of dolls, you need to understand the history of their times. The book is written as a compendium to the wonderful books of Dian Zillner, including those co-authored with Patty Cooper. Hopefully, it fills the gap that Dian identified.

Section One

An Age of Finery, Industrialization, and Prosperity

1840-1915

The last half of the 19th century and the first decade of the 20th century witnessed great social, economic and political change throughout the world, but particularly in Europe and the United States. The Industrial Revolution not only introduced concepts of mass production, which made goods more available and affordable, but also generated wealth for the middle and lower classes. Fine goods and leisure time were no longer solely available to the aristocracy. Democracy, the most important tenet of the French Revolution, had been spread throughout Western Europe by Napoleon, further blurring class lines.

Until the beginning of mass production around 1850, toys and dolls were generally hand-made. They were made of readily available materials: wood, clay, stone, cloth, bone, or wax. In ancient times dolls served many purposes besides being playthings. They were religious statuary, christening tokens, after-life possessions, and homes for spirits. By the mid 19th century, childhood was recognized as a unique period of a person's life. Children were still expected to share the family burdens, but as formal education became more available, so did the concept of "free time" that could be filled, in part, with play. Play dolls became more common, although many were fashioned as adults, not children. One of the first commercial "baby dolls" was made in Japan and shown at the London Exhibition in 1851.

Dollhouses were typically owned only by the rich and royal. In Europe the vogue started around the mid-16th century with houses like one made for Albert V, the Duke of Bavaria. They were originally not conceived as playthings, but rather as displays of interior design and art. They were to be looked at and admired. Some writers suggest that women married in their early teens, and that play with small houses may have been a natural source of diversion and homemaking education for immature minds. Early display houses were generally of large scale and quite detailed, so as to better show off their furnishings and accessories. Since houses were not for play, there was little need for them to be inhabited. By the mid 1800s, however, dolls had found their way into dollhouses.

Just as dollhouses were meant as displays of interior design, their inhabitants were often purchased to model the fashions of the times. Hairstyles of dolls, as well as their clothes, were modified to remain up-to-date. In fact, one of the surer ways to identify an antique doll's age is to study its hairstyle. Dollhouse dolls soon began to be made in both genders, of different generations, and of different classes. The dollhouse of an aristocrat needed a full retinue of household help.

The concept of mass production meant that dolls could be made to be sold. Artisans joined together in England, Germany, and France to make dolls from wood, wax, *papier mâché*, and clay. Cottage artists, utilizing a central distribution source, did much of the work, but as the need for kilns and other specialized equipment increased, more work was performed in factories, with finishing being outsourced to home workers. It was a production method that was seen throughout the next 100 years, and is still used today.

In order for dolls to be mass-produced the material from which they were made had to change. Toy makers became specialists, and certain geographic regions began to dominate the production of toys. The center of the toy industry shifted from the craft fairs of England to Southern Germany. France continued to develop its doll industry and successfully competed with the Germans, especially with their fine fashion dolls. American manufacturers did not really participate in the market, especially for small dolls.

During the relatively peaceful period of the Concert Of Europe, between 1871 and 1914, the middle class grew and prospered. Wealth was not just centered in the hereditary aristocracy. A new class of economic aristocrats had the money to spend trying to emulate the lifestyles of the nobility. It was this setting that produced a golden era of dollhouses.

Chapter 1

Victorians & the Belle Époque

The last twenty years of the 19th century was a time of peace and prosperity that coincided with the end of the Victorian Era. It is often referred to in Europe as "the Beautiful Era." Victorians preferred heavily decorated homes, furnishings, and fashions, but the trend began to change as the Art Nouveau period spread through Europe. The Impressionists replaced realistic painting styles. Classical music gave way to "salon music," short pieces that could be played in a parlor or in small gatherings. The Industrial Revolution was well established. Wealth spread down through the rigid class system of the time, but there was real exploitation of the working classes by the wealthy. This period was also a time of colonial expansion by the European powers and the United States. Westerners were re-introduced to the seemingly exotic settings and peoples of Africa, Asia, and the Caribbean.

In North America, the Civil War and Reconstruction periods had ended and industrialism was firmly established. America was fast becoming the world's leading industrial producer. The United States did not have the rigid class system found in Europe, although there was great disparity in wealth, and the working class faced exploitation like their European counterparts. There was opportunity, however, to escape poverty, receive an education, and change one's position in life. America still had an open door immigration policy, except for China, and the customs of many countries were assimilated and adopted into the every day life of Americans. Little contribution was made in cultural fields. Mark Twain, somewhat ironically, referred to the time as a "Gilded Age," shiny on the surface, but without much substance.

European dollhouses had become fixtures in the homes of the noble and wealthy. They were generally hand-made, although commercial mass-produced dollhouses by firms such as Christian Hacker, Moritz Gottschalk, and G&J Lines became prevalent in the last two decades of the century. Smaller than many display houses, they were affordable to the middle class. America was introduced to the German and English dollhouses through toys stores like FAO Schwarz.

Until the 1850s, a dollhouse might well have been inhabited by small dolls, not specially made to fit inside. By the 1880s, however, dolls were being made to reside in dollhouses. They were still made from the traditional materials of wood, cloth, wax, and *papier mâché*, but by this time china and bisque began to dominate. They could be inexpensively mass-produced. Small dolls were not, at first, gender-specific, but rather dressed to be male or female. By the late 1800s, families of dolls were being made in different sizes with decorated mothers, fathers, and children. Dolls, like dollhouses, were miniature fashion plates.

It was not uncommon for the head and limbs of a doll to be made by one manufacturer, and be joined to a body of a different media made by another, with clothes made by an artist, a seamstress, or "the woman of the house." Dolls of one manufacturer resembled those of another as each strived to produce a doll representing current hair and dress style. Tracing unmarked dolls by their manufacturer is difficult, although a noted collector and author, Mary Krumbholz, has written excellent articles and books to aid in identification. Most components were not marked until the industry began to consolidate and the McKinley Tariff required, after 1891, that the country of origin be marked on all articles imported to the United States. The best way to understand the dolls of the late 19th century is to separate them by the material from which they were made.

Wooden Dolls

Among the first dolls to be commercially produced were the turned wood dolls known as "Queen Anne's." Made in England from the beginning of the 18th century through the early 19th century, dolls had one-piece bodies and painted heads with limbs generally attached by nail and leather hinge. They were dressed in the fashions of the times either as males or females. They fit into the large scaled dollhouses of the period. In fact, Queen Victoria's childhood dollhouse contained examples of such dolls that she and her governess, Louise Lehzen, had dressed.

The earliest wooden dolls of the 18th and 19th century were generally carved from a single piece of wood and had limbs attached by peg or leather hinges. Pictured in the inset on the right is a carved 4.5" doll originally attached to a small dowel, allowing it to be used like a puppet. The larger doll is an 18th century 16" Queen Anne doll in original clothing. She was "turned" from a single piece of wood. *From the collection of Lucy's Dollhouse.* Small doll, $650. Large doll, $25,000.

Toy makers of Southern Germany were blessed with abundant forests for material, and imperial roads and rivers that allowed for distribution of their products. Wooden crèche figures had been carved for many years, and the skill was translated into doll making. Dolls were carved with ball and socket joints. Small dolls might only have shoulder and hip joints, but larger dolls had elbow, knee, and neck joints as well. Hairstyles were carved into the heads, and feet did not show a raised heel. Fingers and thumbs might have been indicated in the carving. As Barbara Rand pointed out in her April 1988 *Doll Reader* article, there was a very strict guild system in Germany so it was unlikely that an early doll maker painted the doll. It wasn't until the early 1800s that a doll maker in Nuremberg began painting his own dolls in defiance of the guild system.

Wood was the medium of choice of the Grödner Tal, then part of Austria, now part of Italy's Trentino region. Dolls, hand carved during this period, became known as "peg-wooden dolls." They were easily mass-produced by more than 300 artisans working in a cooperative cottage industry from the early 1800s through the first decade of the 20th century. The dolls were gathered to be decorated and then sold by cooperatives to German and Dutch traders who then distributed them throughout the world. They could range in size from 2" to 25", but most are in the 4" to 9" range. Their articulated joints, pinned with wooden pegs that give them their name, make them well suited for dollhouse play. They could be posed in any position. The peg-wooden style was used throughout the world from the earliest of times. It was relatively simple to carve for an experienced whittler, so the source is not easily verified. Detail and craftsmanship set the Grödner Tal dolls apart.

By the mid-1800s peg-wooden doll bodies were combined with molded plaster heads. The plaster enabled the molding of more elaborate hairstyles and even bonnets and hats. Some dolls were bald, allowing for a hair wig to be added. *Papier mâché* heads were also used on peg-wooden bodies giving similar design flexibility.

Most peg wooden dolls were decorated as females although male dolls are found. The 3" doll, pictured on the left from the early to mid-1800s, was a converted female with tuck comb covered by a hat. Heads of earlier dolls, such as very early 19th century 2.25" sailor on the right, were somewhat cartoonish, but as time progressed, they became more realistic in carving and decoration, as the boy pictured on the left. *Courtesy of Cynthia Orgeron*. Doll on left, $750. Doll on right, $650.

A very early 9" peg-wooden doll from the Grödner Tal. Many of the dolls had high foreheads, making it easier to hand paint the elaborate hairstyles of the times. Dolls' heads might have had tuck-combs or even carved braids, curls and knots. Leggings of the pictured doll were elaborately intertwined ribbon. *Courtesy of Cynthia Orgeron*. $1150.

9" tall all wood doll c.1890. She had carved black painted hair, painted features, and a red painted torso with leather joints at the shoulders and hips. Leather "joints" were nailed to the shoulders and the lower leather piece was attached to the torso and legs with glue. She has been redressed in a c. early 1900s doll dress. Pictured with the doll are walnut furniture pieces and accessories that would be suitable for use in a larger dollhouse. *From the collection of Dian Zillner. Photo courtesy of Suzanne Silverthorne.* $125+.

Wax Dolls

Wax was an obvious choice as a material for doll heads. It gave a beautiful, smooth, translucent quality and tone to skin. In its liquid state it could be poured into finely sculpted molds with intricate details either part of the mold or added later. Wax dolls were the province of the English who had long used the medium to make crèche figures, although the Germans participated in the low end of the market and the French later made wax dolls as fashion models. English families such as Marsh, Pierotti, and Montanari refined the art throughout the 18th century, with examples by Madame Augusta Montanari being displayed at London's Great Exhibition of 1851 and again in Paris in 1855.

The making of a thick-wax doll was a labor-intensive process with specialists dedicated to each discrete step: molding, placement of eyes, painting, making models, and attachment of the hair. A modeler would sculpt a head and limbs from wax and then cast three-part molds in plaster. Wax, generally a mixture of beeswax and paraffin, would then be poured in the mold. On the fanciest of dolls, eye sockets were cut into cooled heads and glass eyes made in Germany were placed into the heads and attached with a small drop of molten wax. Eyes of less expensive dolls were molded. Earrings could likewise be added to pierced ears. Teeth were commonly molded into doll's heads, a first in doll making. Real hair or mohair could be tediously inserted by needle or knife into heads of the most expensive dolls, although elaborate hairstyles of the times were easily molded as part of the head. Doll bodies were generally sawdust or straw stuffed cloth made by home workers paid on piece-work. Lower arms and legs were most often made from wax, although kid leather was also used. Assembling dolls was done by the doll maker's firm, which then packed and shipped the dolls to market. Melissa Haug's wonderful online article, "The English Poured Wax Doll," carefully details the entire process. She states that many of the English thick-wax dolls were shipped overseas and sold at retail from 25¢ to $10.

The other major form of wax doll is the "thin-wax" or reinforced wax doll, generally a painted composition or *papier mâché* doll head that had been dipped in wax or occasionally inserted in a plaster mold before wax was poured around it. These thin wax dolls generally had fully molded features and embellishments. The most popular hairstyle of many wax dolls was the center part with side curls worn by Queen Victoria, although pompadours, known as "Squash-Head" or "Pumpkin Head" and other popular hairstyles were not uncommon.

Eventually, the susceptibility of wax dolls to heat damage, scratching, chipping, and loss of paint, led to their decline in popularity as playthings. They did, however, rival porcelain head dolls in popularity until the turn of the 20th century.

A pair of 14" and 16" molded wax sisters with inset glass eyes. The original owner of the dolls assembled a wardrobe of matching outfits for the "big" and "little" sister. They were likely made in the United Kingdom in the last half of the 19th century. *From the collection of Joy Kelleher of Special Joys.* $9000/pr.

While wax dolls were generally larger than dollhouse scale, small English dolls were often cast in scenes, covered with a glass globe and given as Valentines. *From the collection of Joy Kelleher of Special Joys.* $225.

Papier Mâché Dolls

Papier mâché, a combination of mashed paper pulp, strengthening filler, and binding agent had been used for centuries, especially in Asia to make various products, but in the early 1800s it became a media in Europe for doll heads. It could be molded into the styles of the day. Easily finished and painted, it was very strong and lightweight – perfect for play and easy to ship. Production was at first centered in England and Germany, but German manufacturers, primarily in the paper mill town of Sonneberg, began to dominate the market by the 1820s. One of the few early contributions of an American to doll making was the process developed in 1858 by Ludwig Greiner of Philadelphia. His use of linen as a fill layer to strengthen the paper made heads almost unbreakable. By the 1880s *papier mâché* would give way to ceramics.

Papier mâché heads were most often attached to slim kid leather bodies with wooden lower arms and legs. Dolls found a unique use as "milliners' models." A "milliner" in the mid-19th century supplied women's clothing. Dolls became their advertising medium. They were shipped all over the world wearing miniature examples of the latest clothing. Their *papier mâché* shoulder heads included a variety of molded black hair styles and painted features. Hair styles included the very plain "Covered Wagon" design, long curls around the head, braided buns and knots in the back, coiled braids at the ears, and dolls with molded bonnets. These dolls can be found in sizes from 6" to 26" tall; the smaller ones were well scaled for most early dollhouses.

10" tall *papier mâché* shoulder head doll made in Germany c.1850s. She had black painted hair with a center part and a molded braided bun in the back. Her eyes were painted blue. She is a different version of a milliner's model with wood lower arms and lower legs and painted shoes that have no heels. *From the collection of Ann Meehan. Photograph courtesy of Ann Meehan.* $750.

10" tall *papier mâché* shoulder head doll made in Germany c.1860s. She had black painted hair parted in the middle featuring molded long curls. She had blue painted eyes. Her lower arms and legs were wood with painted shoes. These dolls are sometimes called milliner's models and generally include kid bodies. Although these dolls were not produced to be used as dollhouse dolls, some collectors with very large old dollhouses use them for that purpose. *From the collection of Ann Meehan. Photograph courtesy of Ann Meehan.* $750.

Male *papier mâché* dolls were not common. *Papier mâché* dolls, such as the one pictured, often had kid leather bodies to which were attached wooden arms and legs. This very unusual 5.75" male was dressed as a carriage driver with molded hat and full moustache. A feather was inserted in his hat during molding. All his features were hand-painted. *From the collection of Lucy's Dollhouse.* $1050.

Porcelain Dolls

When discussing basic materials of doll making, it is necessary to understand the concept of ceramics. A ceramic is a clay object that has been heated to drive out its water content. Heating can be done by leaving an object in the hot sun or by placing it in an oven. The amount of heat applied and the basic components of the clay determine the characteristics of a finished piece. There are four basic types of clays and more than thirty subclasses, each made up of rocks that have been worn away into extremely small particles through natural forces. Clay that is of concern in discussing modern doll making is called *kaolinite*, or *kaolin*, an aluminum silicate mineral produced when rocks, like feldspar, weather. Kaolin is fine white clay from southern China that was used to make imported ceramic pieces enjoyed by Europe's wealthy. It became known by the French as porcelain and by the English as chinaware. Kaolin is found all over the world, and where it was found, porcelain industries flourished: Limoge, France; Staffordshire, Great Britain; and Colditz near Meissen, Germany.

The Chinese had developed porcelain, clay mixtures fired at very hot temperatures, by 1000 BC. They used trial and error to determine correct firing temperatures and the right combination of ingredients mixed with kaolin. A search for the magic combination started in Europe in the mid 1600s, but it wasn't until January 1708 that two Germans from Meissen were successful. Ehrenfried Walther von Tschirnhaus and Johann Friedrich Böttger combined Colditz clay, alabaster, and quartz and heated it to temperatures over 1350°C (approximately 2500°F) and produced the first translucent white porcelain. Their discovery led to the birth of the European porcelain industry, first centered near Dresden, Germany, and later spreading to Austria, France, and England.

10" tall German china shoulder head doll c.1840-1860 with black painted hair, molded long curls on each side, and a molded braided bun on the back of her head. She had a wood jointed body with wood arms and legs and painted shoes. *From the collection of Ann Meehan. Photograph courtesy of Ann Meehan.* $1500.

8.5" tall pink tinted china shoulder head c.1850s. Her painted hair included a middle part and a molded bun in the back. Her features were painted and included red eyelid lines above her blue eyes. She had porcelain lower arms and legs, a wood jointed body, and painted shoes. Dolls of this style were offered in the catalogues of Franz Carl Weber, the Zurich toy seller. Dolls were jointed at the shoulders, elbows, hips, and knees. *From the collection of Ann Meehan. Photograph courtesy of Ann Meehan.* $2000.

6" tall German china shoulder head doll that may have been made in the A.W. Fr. Kister factory. Collectors have called this style of wigged china head doll Biedermeyer for many years. Her lower arms and legs were also made of china and she had a cloth body. Her eyes were painted blue with red eyelid lines over eyes. Because of her small size, she is very rare. *Doll from the collection of Ann Meehan. Photograph courtesy of Ann Meehan.* $2,000.

Porcelain is produced in many stages. First clay is mixed with water and other minerals such as feldspar rock, quartz, and ash to form a semi liquid paste or "slip." Slip is poured into a mold of plaster of paris. It begins to solidify from the outside in. When a thin dry layer has set up, the remaining wet slip is poured off, leaving a hollow piece that is removed from the mold. When thoroughly dry, now known as "greenware," all unwanted dry slip is trimmed, sanded, and wet polished. Small details can be added or embellished. Fine dust is removed in a bath. The doll maker now has a choice to make that will determine how his work will be characterized – china or bisque.

The first porcelain doll heads appeared in the early 1800s, but were not produced in commercial quantity until around the 1820s, probably as sidelines by the German porzellanwërks. These early examples are called "china heads." Porcelain makers applied a coating or glaze to the "greenware" doll heads and then heated the pieces in kilns. The glaze gave a shiny finish to the dolls that is the determining factor in labeling a doll "china." Tints, enamels, and various colored glazes could be applied before or after the first high temperature firing to highlight facial and hair details and then set by one or more subsequent low temperature firings. Although, each step and additional detail added time and cost to the process. Glazes were relatively thick liquids that made the molded and incised details less distinct. Bisque, on the other hand, is unglazed porcelain made from a blend of kaolin and other materials. It has various tints and colors applied to the surface before firing, but not glazes. Because it lacks china's heavy glass-like finish, which obscures details, it has a more realistic and refined look.

7" tall German rare china male doll that may also have come from the Kister factory. His shoulder head featured painted black hair with brush marks around the sides, blue eyes with red eyelid lines, and red dots at the inside corners of the eyes. His lower arms and legs were china and his body was cloth. Shoes were painted, and his feet were flat. His leggings appear to be made of some kind of oilcloth type material and his trousers were white leather. *Doll from the collection of Ann Meehan. Photograph courtesy of Ann Meehan.* $950.

7" tall German rare pink tint china male doll with a different hairstyle. He also had black painted hair with brush marks around the front of his hair. Eyes were painted blue and included red eyelid lines over his eyes. He had china lower arms and legs and a cloth body. Both of these male dolls are the perfect size for many of the antique dollhouses. *From the collection of Ann Meehan. Photograph courtesy of Ann Meehan.* $1800.

China dolls competed with wood, wax, and *papier mâché.* Like their competitive counterparts, they followed the hair, dress, and shoe fashions of the day. The heyday of china shoulder heads was 1840 through the 1860s. In the 1840s, heads reflected the center part bun style favored by young Queen Victoria. Covered Wagon heads of the1850s had center parts, flat tops, and side curls. Alice In Wonderland with a molded headband was seen in the 1860s, and by the 1870s, doll heads had high top-knots or elaborate curls. Finer dolls had brush stroke feathering around the hairline and at the temples to add realism and often had a pink tinted underglaze. There are rare examples of women molded with bonnets, or produced bald, ready to accept a wig. Distinctly male dolls were rare, although some were produced with moustaches and hats.

Throughout most of the 1800s china dolls had black hair and blue eyes, with blond and brown hair only produced in the last 20 years of the century. All china molded dolls known as "frozen charlottes" were introduced in mid-century and continued thereafter. Porcelain makers, however, made china lower arms and legs for dolls that were then attached to cloth, kid, or the most desirable, peg wood bodies. Shoes on leg pieces indicate age. Until around 1860 shoes or low boots did not have heels. When low heels were added to women's shoes, dolls were molded in the same way. High heels became fashionable by 1870. China dolls were eventually replaced in the market place by alternatives with finer detail and lower cost.

7" tall china shoulder head male featured painted black hair with a middle part and an unusual mustache and small goatee. He had a wood jointed body including wood arms and legs. Very rare and unusual doll. *From the collection of Ann Meehan. Photograph courtesy of Ann Meehan.* $2000.

A fine couple of mid-18th century china dolls prepare to entertain in their parlor. The 8.25" woman with flat top hairstyle was dressed in a full hoop skirt with applied bows. The pink tint 9" china head man was dressed in the symbols of his peerage – campaign medals, sash, watch chain, and fob. His hands have been repaired. *From the collection of Lucy's Dollhouse.* Woman, $1000. Man, $500.

6″ tall china shoulder head unusual woman doll. She had grey-black molded and painted hair, blue painted eyes, and red eyelid liner. Her hair had a molded bun in the back. Most of these china head dolls came in a variety of sizes. This doll has been seen in a 13″ tall example. Both this doll and the 13″ example wore painted shoes with no heels indicating their earlier origin. *From the collection of Ann Meehan. Photograph courtesy of Ann Meehan.* $1600.

5.75″ tall German china head doll perfect for dollhouse use. The flat top hairstyle with middle part was made for several decades beginning in the 1860s. This doll had boots with heels, which indicated she was one of the later models c.1880s. The back of her shoulder plate was marked with the size number "7." She had a china shoulder plate, black molded hair, painted features, lower china arms and legs, and a cloth body. She has been redressed. The doll is pictured with pieces of a German 1:12 scale parlor dating from the early 1900s set in a McLoughlin Bros. Folding Doll House. *From the collection of Dian Zillner. Photo courtesy of Suzanne Silverthorne.* Doll, $125+.

3″ tall tiny German china head doll dressed as a bride. She wears an old dress and underwear made for her many ears ago. She had molded black painted hair and painted features. Her body and lower untinted bisque arms and legs are original. *From the collection of Dian Zillner. Photo courtesy of Suzanne Silverthorne.* $50+.

The porcelain doll that eventually dominated the market was the bisque or biscuit doll. Writers have suggested that the recipe for a bisque doll was developed between 1854 and 1860 in the German region of Thuringia, a toy center that later became the capital of German porcelain doll production. The recipe appears to be a slight variation of the normal bisque mixtures available for decades, but it may have been well suited for doll making. Mary Krumbholz in her authoritative *Identifying German Parian Dolls*, introduces an interesting element in the process. One firm, the forerunner to Alt, Beck, and Gottschalk, could not afford a large water powered Masse mill to grind the ingredients for their slip. Instead they ground their material by hand, resulting in a finer textured blend. When heated, the material produced extremely smooth surfaced bisque that was very desirable. Apparently, however, hand grinding was not the norm, but might explain bisque's early acceptance and quality variation over time.

A variation of bisque, "Parian," appeared sometime after 1842, named after the very finely textured white marble found on the Greek island, Paros. While the English firm owned by William Taylor Copeland and Thomas Garrett claimed its invention, it wasn't until the Crystal Palace Exhibition in 1851 that parian gained popularity. A small copy of Hiram Power's *The Captive Slave* was produced in fine bisque by Thomas Battan, and set a trend copied by many English and Irish potteries. The German doll makers soon picked up the term, although there is no indication that they adopted the mixtures used by the English. Genevieve Angione in her book, *All-Bisque & Half-Bisque Dolls,* argues that true Parian-ware had a smooth soapy feel that she had not seen in dolls. Frances K. Bowen in her 1951 article, "Biscuit Porcelain Dolls" appearing in *The Doll World,* provides an excellent working definition: "The term 'parian' is used to describe the bisque head of unusual whiteness or delicate pink hued biscuit of exceptional fineness with lustrous transparency, no visible glaze, yet to the touch suggests a dull polish as though the granular marble-like surface had been rubbed down." Probably the correct term for fine-bisque dolls is "parian-like" and refers to dolls made before bisque texture became coarser at the end of the 1800s.

Bisque shoulder heads generally followed the hairstyles found on china and *papier mâché.* In fact, many of the same molds were used. Because bisque dolls showed far more detail than their china and *papier mâché* counterparts, hair decoration could be more elaborate. Curls flowed down the back in ringlets. Curls and pompadours added height to the front. Snoods or netting held hair in place in the back, and flowers, beads, and combs were added for decoration. Women sported bonnets and hats of prevailing style. Jewelry was molded to necklines. Bodices were decorated with lace, ribbons, and ruffles. Ears were pierced so earrings could be added. Male dolls were less common, but brush stroke detail was added to their hairlines and temples. Porcelain shrinks as it is fired, and small heads are made by creating new, progressively smaller molds each time a new size head leaves the kiln. Unless time is taken to re-incise the detail, a smaller head will not be as sharp as its larger siblings. Nonetheless, the detail added to the dolls made them exquisite and highly desired.

Blonde became the hair color of choice through the end of the century. Female dolls with glazed black hair are found less often, a fact resulting from the idealized fashion of the day, but also from the nature of tints used on bisque. Creating an even color over a bisque surface was difficult, and the most senior artists did the final daubing of color. Tints were very thin, and it took successive coats and firings to create dark colors. Each step added cost to the process, and blond was easier to achieve. When black or dark brown is found, it is generally a glossy glaze as used in making a china head.

8" tall German parian type shoulder head doll with an unusual swivel head. She had beautifully painted eyes and eyelashes and molded hair with a molded hair ribbon. Her body was cloth with bisque lower arms and legs. Many different German firms produced these dolls made of fine, white bisque. *From the collection of Ann Meehan. Photograph courtesy of Ann Meehan.* $1750.

6.5" tall German parian type shoulder head doll also featured a swivel head, unusual on such a small doll. In her molded hair was a molded hair band with unusual comb markings in front of the band. She had large painted eyes with red eyelid lines. Her lower arms and legs were bisque and her body was cloth. Several different German factories made these types of dolls including C.F. Kling & Co. and Alt, Beck and Gottschalck. *From the collection of Ann Meehan. Photograph courtesy of Ann Meehan.* $1200.

6" tall untinted bisque shoulder head doll with molded hair decorated with a molded black hair band. The front of her hair featured comb marks. Collectors sometimes refer to these "hair band" dolls as Alice in Wonderland style dolls, but different companies made them in a variety of styles. She had painted features including blue painted eyes with no red eyelid lines. Lower limbs were also made of untinted bisque. *From the collection of Ann Meehan. Photograph courtesy of Ann Meehan.* $1500.

6" tall German parian type shoulder head lady doll. She had a very fancy molded hairstyle, trimmed with a molded gold ribbon. Features, including blue eyes, were painted. Lower arms and legs were bisque attached to a cloth body. *From the collection of Ann Meehan. Photograph courtesy of Ann Meehan.* $1000.

6" tall untinted bisque shoulder head lady doll had a "flat top" molded hair style. She had painted features with blue eyes. Lower limbs were also made of untinted bisque. *From the collection of Ann Meehan. Photograph courtesy of Ann Meehan.* $850.

The Doll Makers

With some exception, Germans dominated the manufacture of dolls throughout the last 70 years of the 19th century. The "Toy Road" that wends it way north from the Bavarian town of Nuremberg into Thuringia with its famous towns of Walterhausen, Ohrdruf, and Sonneberg, housed many of the artisan toy makers who worked in wood for over 300 years. As time progressed, with ample natural resources, successive generations embraced the other media being used to produce dolls: *papier mâché*, thin wax, and porcelain.

Porcelain lent itself to factory, as opposed to cottage, production and there was sufficient capital in Germany during this time to fund new factories. Labor was very cheap and abundant, and not controlled by unions or guilds. Coal and wood was available to heat kilns and numerous rivers provided water power to run the grinding mills that powdered ingredients. Storage facilities were needed to house large inventories of raw materials used to make heads and molds. Kilns, larger than a room, allowed production of huge quantities, offsetting any waste from inconsistencies in the raw material or firing temperature. At first German doll makers made dolls of a quality equal to that of any in the world, but as competition increased, pricing became an important issue. Less detailed finishing on rougher textured clays became common. Lower costs resulting from economies of scale, enabled lower prices that often justified the lower quality.

J.D. Kestner Spilewarenfabrik

There were many companies that formed the German doll industry during its glory years of the 19th century. One of the best known was Walterhausen's J.D. Kestner Spilewarenfabrik founded in 1805 by Johannes Daniel Kestner, Jr., to make *papier mâché* products. He expanded into doll making in 1845 with *papier mâché* and thin wax heads and bodies of all types: wood, cloth, and kid. In 1860 the company, by then under the direction of his wife and son, purchased a porcelain factory in Ohrdruf. It gave them the ability to make an entire doll, perhaps the only German mass producer to have that capacity. During this time, Walterhausen also housed the famous Heinrich Handwerck Puppenfabrick, founded in 1885, and Kämmer and Reinhardt, founded in 1885.

4.75" tall all-bisque German made boy with jointed arms and stationary legs. He wore molded two-strap bootines and shirred stockings. He had molded blond hair, blue painted eyes, and a closed mouth. He has been redressed. These pieces of Bliss furniture, usually called the ABC furniture, are c.1900. *From the collection of Dian Zillner. Photo courtesy of Suzanne Silverthorne.* Doll, $125.

4.25" tall all-bisque early doll made in Germany with the number 73 on her back. She had a wig, painted features and was jointed only at the shoulders. Her feet seem rather large and she is quite chunky in appearance. Shoes were painted and socks were molded with an overall pattern. She has been redressed. The doll was probably originally sold nude c.1890-1900. *From the collection of Dian Zillner. Photo courtesy of Suzanne Silverthorne.* Doll, $75.

3.5" tall all-bisque little boy and little girl both made in Germany. The boy had a wig, painted features, and was jointed at the shoulders and hips. He had wonderful molded and painted boots. They were blue trimmed in black with black heels and toes. He has been redressed. He once belonged to Olive de Luce, a well-known Midwest art professor, when she was a child over 100 years ago. The little girl wore a wig, had painted features and wire jointed limbs and painted shoes. She has also been redressed. Furniture made in Germany for the French trade is pictured with the dolls. *From the collection of Dian Zillner. Photo courtesy of Suzanne Silverthorne.* Dolls, $75/each.

Hertwig & Co.

The German porcelain firm, Hertwig & Co., founded by Christoph Hertwig, Carl Birkner, and Nikolaus and Benjamin Beyerman in the Thuringian town of Katzhütte, was producing doll heads by 1865. After the death of Benjamin Beyerman in 1865 and Birkner's and Nikolaus' departures, it became a Hertwig family business in 1868 when Christoph's three sons joined. Operating at first with cottage workers making doll bodies and attaching them to Hertwig factory produced heads, it soon expanded to bring all operations under one roof. Throughout the next 70 years, Hertwig & Co. was a major producer willing to innovate and keep up with the latest trends and styles: dolls with names, all-bisque, stone bisque, molded clothing, and hats. Grandsons entered the business just before 1920, keeping management continuity and philosophy that continued until the East German government nationalized the company in 1953. Luckily, many of the company's records and samples were retrieved after the reunification of Germany and sold at auction in 2002. Florence Theriault detailed the auction in her book, *Hertwig & Co. Archives 1890-1937*. The documentation has allowed many collectors to determine the origin of many previously unidentified dolls. Unfortunately the records of other Thuringian companies expropriated by the Communists have been lost.

6" tall Hertwig doll with a bisque shoulder head that was made by the firm for many years beginning in the 1880s. Hertwig produced this head in at least five sizes ranging in size from 1.25" to 2" tall. This head measured approximately 1.5" in height. These heads were meant to represent children, but since they were attached to cloth bodies with lower bisque limbs most of the dolls look like women when assembled. Head was mounted on a cloth body with lower bisque arms and lower white bisque legs with black painted boots and shirred white stockings. Hair was molded and features painted. Although the body is an old one, it is a replacement. She has been redressed. She is pictured with iron furniture pieces made by J. & E. Stevens Co. of Cromwell, Connecticut c.1880s. *From the collection of Dian Zillner. Photo courtesy of Suzanne Silverthorne.* Dolls, $100+.

C. F. Kling, Simon & Halbig, Kister

The firm of C.F. Kling, formed in 1837, began making doll heads in the 1850s. It passed through successive generations of ownership after the 1870 death of Christian Friedrich Kling, and is thought by many, including Mary Krumbholz, to be the maker of some of the highest quality parian-like heads ever produced. They also continued to make china heads through the end of the century. Kling spawned the very successful and innovative firm of Alt, Beck, and Gottschalck, when four of its skilled workmen left and formed a new porcelain factory in 1854 in Nauendorf. Legend suggests that Theodor Gottschalk and Gottlieb Beck invented the recipe for bisque, although, since it was after the 1848 development of Parianware, it is more likely that they found a variation that worked well for porcelain doll head production. The firm founded by Carl Halbig and Wilhelm Simon in 1869 was located in the Thuringian town of Grafenhain. Simon & Halbig, like Kestner, produced many of the fine doll heads used by other doll makers, including some of the better known French firms. The town of Rudolstadt and nearby villages housed the firm of Kister & Co., founded by Louis Oels in 1835, and later known as A.W. Fr. Kister after it was purchased in 1876 by August Wilhelm Friedolin. In all, there were more than 300 doll making companies in Germany during this time. Some, such as those just mentioned, made contributions to the beginnings of this period of mass production. Others, to be discussed, contributed to its ongoing success in the 20th century.

English and Danish Makers

The Germans were, by no means, the only doll makers of the late 19th century. English wax head firms were still producing, although the popularity of the medium was waning. The Royal Manufactory of Copenhagen produced fine china doll heads from 1843 until 1888. Meant to compete with German dolls, the tints and glazes used were thinner and gave a finer quality to the heads. There were at least 13 styles made in 6 sizes, but all hairstyles date from the 1840-1850 time frame. Doll heads were marked with three wavy blue lines inside the shoulder plate.

Pair of 5.5" and 6" tall Hertwig Bonnet dolls c.1890s-1910. These dolls also come in a variety of sizes but the small dolls are harder to find than larger examples. Dolls had white bisque shoulder heads with molded bonnets and hair and painted features. Their original cloth bodies had lower limbs of white bisque and brown glazed boots. Some of the larger Hertwig Bonnet head dolls included gold necklaces or molded collars. Both dolls have been redressed. *From the collection of Dian Zillner. Photo courtesy of Suzanne Silverthorne.* Dolls, $150+ each.

4.75" tall Hertwig doll, c. late 1890s. This head is pictured on a sample card of china and bisque doll shoulder heads in the Hertwig & Co. Archives book. It came in a variety of sizes ranging from 1" to 2.5" tall. She had a bisque shoulder head with molded hair, a black hair band, and painted features. Her original cloth body had cloth upper limbs and lower arms and legs of tinted bisque. Doll's boots were painted black and her garters were pink. She has been redressed. A black metal vintage bulldog is pictured with her. *From the collection of Dian Zillner. Photo courtesy of Suzanne Silverthorne.* Dolls, $100+.

The French Makers: Jumeau and Bru

Among the most exquisite of all porcelain dolls were those made by French firms. Interestingly, French porcelain workers often disdained the production of dolls, feeling them below their artistic abilities. Many French dolls, in fact, had heads made by German firms. What made them distinctively French was their elaborate dress as fashion dolls, or *poupées*. Dolls smaller than 9" are rare, but are often found matched with room-boxes beautifully finished with the high decoration of the day.

Pierre Francois Jumeau established a Parisian doll making business in 1845, after being exposed to the business by his in-laws. *Papier mâché* heads were imported from Germany and wax heads from England. Jumeau's firm dressed and wigged the dolls, as the French market did not favor painted hair. By 1872, Jumeau had opened a porcelain factory to make doll heads. The firm made *poupées* and children, *bébés*, generally larger than dollhouse scale. While heads of the *poupées* changed with the fashion, *bébés* changed little. Despite the firm's high quality , it suffered from an undersized kiln. The Germans benefited from large-scale production.

Dolls by doll maker Bru Jne. & Cie, founded by Leon Casimir Bru, are among the most sought after of all French fashion dolls, although they are usually oversized for dollhouse play. The company is best known for its distinctive "pudgy cheeked" *bébés.* Françoise Gaultier made porcelain doll heads that were used by many French doll makers. The firm held the patent for a method of inserting glass eyes into porcelain heads, another hallmark of the French style. Firms like Schmitt & Fils, Barrois, and Rohmer all competed in a crowded field, constantly battling the Germans.

The century saw the beginning of mass production of dolls, a trend that would become more important over successive decades. Germans grew to dominate all toy production, and especially doll production. The 20th century and two world wars saw that dominance end. Good quality dolls were no longer solely owned by rich children. They were becoming affordable to all, albeit made and dressed to emulate the styles and fashions of the rich and privileged.

6.5" tall Hertwig "Low Brow" china head doll which the firm produced for decades from the 1890s until 1930. China shoulder heads were made with black or blonde painted and molded hair on cloth bodies with either china or untinted bisque lower limbs. Dolls came in 17 sizes from 3.5" to 17.5" tall. The pictured doll holds a small "Frozen Charlotte" (no moving parts) china doll as her "baby." She has been redressed. Many of the firms' larger dolls, using this basic head design, included a name on the front of the doll including Ethel, Bertha, and other similar old fashioned names. *From the collection of Dian Zillner. Photo courtesy of Suzanne Silverthorne.* Doll, $75.

Chapter 2

The Edwardian Era and Doll Reform

When Queen Victoria died in January 1901, the era that followed was far more complicated socially, scientifically, economically, and politically. Edward VII ascended to the British throne and became a beacon for the social and economic elite throughout Europe and even in the United States. He gave his name to an era that saw the invention of the radio and the airplane, the women's universal suffrage movement, increased industrialization, Socialist political thought, increased military production, music halls catering to the tastes of the masses, and the simplified designs of the Arts and Crafts Movement. The Edwardian Era was also a time of leisure activity for the privileged classes.

Economic trends accelerated after the turn of the century. Industrialization created wealth for the "captains of industry," but social injustice and unrest among the working classes. Competition increased in all industries, as low-cost mass-produced goods were readily available in every market of the world. Restrictive tariffs in every country raised consumer prices, but manufacturers in the exporting countries simply produced less costly products to offset protectionist duties. In the doll and toy industry this favored countries like Germany that had moved away from artisan production.

Fashions changed during the period to allow women greater ease of movement. The American illustrator Charles Dana Gibson's ideal *Gibson Girl* found its way back to Europe and helped create the style of the early part of the 20th century. Women not only wore beautiful gowns and dresses, but layered skirts and shirtwaists. Gibson's S-curve look gave way to long, close fitting, but less corseted skirts, often worn with suit jackets. Large hats were popular throughout the time. Men were idealized as well, with blond hair and closely trimmed moustaches, wearing well tailored suits and formal wear appropriate to the time of day and event.

The decorative excess of the previous Victorian Era was challenged by the Arts and Crafts Movement, which favored simplified lines, geometric shapes, and stylized nature motifs. William Morris, Charles Rennie Macintosh, and Gustav Stickley set new styles of architecture, home furnishing, and decoration that were adopted throughout Europe and the United States. This same movement spawned "Puppen Reform" in Germany and France. Artisan doll makers reacted against the "idealized" dolls of the previous century and began to produce dolls that had more realistic faces and clothing. The term "character doll" was coined to describe these figures. Not only were the dolls' faces less serene and more expressive, but realistic family groupings began to appear. Differentiated parents and grandparents, as well as children, toddlers, and babies were produced. Maids, cooks, chefs, butlers, nursemaids, chauffeurs, and military men were added to the lines. The early movement started in Germany and soon spread to France. The American market embraced the change as it more reflected less aristocratic American ideals.

The Doll Industry

German Doll Making

Dolls were now made especially for dollhouses, and could be purchased either dressed or undressed. Although some low-priced china heads were still produced, most dolls were made with bisque heads, usually painted eyes, (fewer with glass eyes), and with either molded and painted hair or fitted with wigs. Most dolls had cloth bodies and bisque arms and lower legs. Less expensive dolls only had bisque lower arms but more expensive dolls had full bisque arms. Household help and military men might have molded caps, helmets, or bonnets reflecting their jobs and station in life. Early male dolls wore mustaches, beards, or mutton chops. The most expensive of these dolls are the soldiers in their original uniforms and the African Heritage dolls who were stereotypically depicted as cooks, butlers, maids or other household helpers. In the early part of the 1900s, women's dresses were the long Gibson Girl style, and their molded hairstyle usually included a bun or a topknot. Most of these dollhouse women had molded hair and painted features, but some wore mohair wigs and fewer yet had glass eyes. The German firm, J.D. Kestner, quickly picked up the style producing its own Gibson Girl in a range of sizes as small as 10." Kestner's Gibson Girl had a bisque shoulder head with a cloth body and lower bisque limbs. The prolific Thuringian company, Armand Marseille, manufactured a lady doll with a bisque head and five-piece body in a 9" size.

Original clothing is desirable for the collectors of these dolls but since many of the dolls were sold nude, most dolls were dressed at home. Factory clothing can be easily identified because it was usually machine sewn. Sometimes added belts or decorations were glued to outfits on machine made clothing.

Dolls were usually not marked with a maker's name or initials. Most dolls included only a model number and a size number on the backs of the shoulder plates. At the end of the 1890s both England and the United States required country of origin marking, which suggests the conclusion that most of the dolls were made in Germany. An exception to unmarked dolls were Simon & Halbig "Little Women" dolls, marked "S&H 1160." They were made with glass eyes and wigs. Since these dolls were produced in a variety of larger sizes as well as dollhouse size, they were probably not meant to be dollhouse dolls. The same firm also made another bisque shoulder head doll 7.5" tall marked "S 3/0 H." She had longer bisque arms, molded with a bend at the elbows, along with bare feet on her lower bisque legs. She also had glass eyes, a closed mouth, and an applied wig. A third doll, which was marked "S H," is pictured in Patricia Smith's *Doll Values Fifth Series*. She was approximately 6.5" tall and had a mohair wig and painted features. It is assumed that she was also a Simon & Halbig product. C.F. Kling also produced a 6.5" bisque shoulder head doll with molded hair, bisque lower arms and legs, and a cloth body with upper arms and legs, pictured in the Colemans' *The Collector's Encyclopedia of Dolls Volume I.* Her molded shoes included three straps. Kling's marking was a drawing of a bell with a "K" inside. Nora Earnshaw in *Collecting Dolls Houses and Miniatures* pictures three bisque shoulder head military dolls, which she attributed to Kling. These dolls had their hats molded on their heads. They were made with lower arms and legs of bisque and bodies and upper limbs of cloth.

7.5" china shoulder head doll with more unusual blonde painted hair in the "low brow" style c. early 1900s. Her features were painted and she had white bisque lower arms and legs on her original red cloth body. Her boots were painted brown. She is pictured with Star furniture standing mirror and a more recent metal dog. *From the collection of Dian Zillner. Photo courtesy of Suzanne Silverthorne.* Doll, $50+.

As the 20th century began, china head dolls became less popular, but the "low brow" hair styled dolls continued to be made by different companies for several decades. This example, 5.5" tall had lower limbs of white bisque attached to a cloth body and upper limbs. Shoes were painted brown. She is pictured in a McLoughlin Brothers Folding Doll House with German furniture c. early 1900s. *From the collection of Dian Zillner. Photo courtesy of Suzanne Silverthorne.* Doll, $50.

Bisque shoulder head dollhouse dolls wore a variety of molded footwear through their years of popularity. Pictured are five examples. All of the styles include heels. Pictured are two strap boot type footwear sometimes referred to as bootines, boots with no straps, two strapped shoes, one strap shoes, and slipper type shoes (similar shoes painted gold were used in fancier dolls). *From the collection of Dian Zillner. Photo courtesy of Suzanne Silverthorne.*

An exquisite 7.25"glass-eyed parian dressed in her original clothing. The wigged mother is pictured in the nursery of her 1860's American Fretwork dollhouse with her two small babies. The mother has a deep bisque shoulder plate and full-length, slender, jointed arms. The canopied cradle is a rare Rock and Graner of faux-burled walnut tin, and holds a German all-bisque baby, wire-jointed at the shoulders and hips. The tin buggy, with frozen bisque baby, is by Rock and Graner, as well. *From the collection of the Toy and Miniature Museum of Kansas City. Photo courtesy of the Toy and Miniature Museum of Kansas City.* Doll, $500.

Pair of older dollhouse dolls with glass eyes and wigs. The 6.25" tall doll on the left was made by the German Simon & Halbig firm. She was marked "S&H/1160". These dolls were usually referred to as "Little Women" and are c. 1900. They were also made in sizes of 7", 10", and 14". Her body included wires in her cloth upper arms and legs to allow her to bend. Her molded shoes were black with two straps. Her wig originally had curls on each side but they are missing. She has been redressed. The other doll is also 6.25" tall. She was numbered 409-9/10 on the back of her shoulder plate. Her wig was similar to those worn by large dolls that are thought to represent the Gibson girl image c. 1900. *From the collection of Dian Zillner. Photo courtesy of Suzanne Silverthorne.* S& H doll, $250+; other $200+.

Simon & Halbig produced small all-bisque dolls suitable for dollhouse use. This 4" pair of African heritage glass-eyed, wigged dolls was uniquely dressed and quite rare. *From the collection of Penny Hadfield of A Quiet Place Dolls.* $895/pr.

5" all original German dollhouse chef. He had molded hair, painted features, and a large mustache. As do most of the painted eye German dollhouse dolls, this doll had a bisque shoulder head, lower bisque arms and legs, and a cloth body and upper limbs. He wears his original chef's hat, apron, and other chef clothing. These types of dolls were made for decades. A similar doll was still being advertised in Kammer & Reinhardt's doll catalog in 1927. *From the collection of Gail and Ray Carey. Photograph courtesy of Gail Carey.* $200+.

Very few advertisements for early dollhouse dolls are available for study. In the United States, Sears and Montgomery Ward catalogs did carry these more elaborate dolls. Only high-end stores like FAO Schwarz, Marshall Field, and other similar department stores appeared to sell these dolls on a regular basis, perhaps because dollhouses were expensive in the early 1900s, and few children owned large dollhouses that would accommodate a family of dolls 5" to 7" tall. A 1913 FAO Schwarz ad, reproduced in Flora Gill Jacobs' *Dolls' Houses in America,* pictured dollhouse dolls representing a maid in a long apron and cap, a nursemaid with a baby, a butler, a lady in a fancy gown, a man wearing a suit and hat, and a man wearing a top hat and tuxedo. The 5"-7" dolls were priced from 50 cents to $1.50 each.

A Kestner ad for dollhouse dolls is pictured in *Identifying German Parian Dolls* by Mary Gorham Krumbholz. Twenty-one nude dolls are shown, including fourteen female dolls and seven male examples. Four of the female dolls wore wigs and the rest had molded hair. One of the dolls represented a grandmother. Four of the male dolls had muttonchops or mustaches. One of the males wore a chauffeur's molded hat and what appear to be glasses. The other male may be intended to be a grandfather.

French Consolidation

Firms like Armand Marseille, founded in Sonneberg in 1884, fine-tuned the concept of mass production, making 1000 or more doll heads a day after the turn of the century. Faced with such competition from Marseille and the traditional and newer German firms centered in Walterhausen, the French could not compete. A German, Salomon Fleischmann, a major supplier of parts to the French doll market from his French factories, proposed that major doll makers merge their assets and form one major doll making company in France. It would enable them to rationalize their product lines and manufacturing facilities to obtain competitive costs. Just before 1900, the Société Française de Fabrication de Bébés et Jouets, S.F.B.J., was formed, combining Fleischmann with Jumeau, Bru, Gaultier, and others. For the most part, Jumeau dolls survived, although the most competitive products of each manufacturer were kept. The merger allowed the French doll industry to survive.

6" German dollhouse doll being used as a butler. These types of dolls were usually holding a towel as part of their clothing to indicate their status. This example is an older man with balding hair, wearing his original clothing. A German dollhouse grandfather clock is behind the butler. His duties must also include dog care as he is surrounded by a china mother dog and her puppies. *From the collection of Gail and Ray Carey. Photograph courtesy of Gail Carey.* $200+.

Many dollhouse residences needed a chauffeur in the early days. This 4.75" chauffeur wears his original felt uniform with black leatherette boots. He is missing his hat. His 4.5" tall female passenger on the left is all original. She wore a molded bisque hat, molded goggles, and original motoring costume. These dolls probably date from the teens. They were originally in the collection of the Washington Dolls' House and Toy Museum. *From the collection of Gail and Ray Carey. Photograph courtesy of Gail Carey.* $450 +/ pair.

7″ tall German dollhouse doll dressed in his livery. He had molded hair, painted features, and boots made as part of his legs. His uniform and hat (on the chair) are all original. The red, gold, and black outfit was similar to those still being pictured on dollhouse dolls in the 1927 German Kammer & Reinhardt catalog. Boots made as part of the leg, shorter pants, and flat hats similar to this one are on two of the pictured dolls. The number in the catalog for these dolls indicates they are from the "All other professions" series. This doll is pictured in front of a German red desk and chair accompanied by a vintage bulldog. *From the collection of Gail and Ray Carey. Photograph courtesy of Gail Carey.* $250+.

Three 5″ dollhouse maids made before the 1920s. All three dolls wear their original long dresses and aprons. Each had a different hair style. A German metal cart holds a decorated cake. *From the collection of Gail and Ray Carey. Photograph courtesy of Gail Carey.* $200 +/each.

A 6″ all bisque, wire-jointed nursemaid holds a small 1.125″ baby dressed in a christening gown. Dolls of this design were dressed to denote their status: maid, nursemaid, nurse, or mother. A 1913 Schwarz advertisement pictured a nursemaid holding a similar all bisque baby. The china "frozen" toddler sits in a German metal padded three-wheel Rock and Graner perambulator. Running water had not yet found its way into the home, judging from the wall-mounted lavabo, also by Rock and Graner. *From the collection of the Toy and Miniature Museum of Kansas City. Photo courtesy of the Toy and Miniature Museum of Kansas City.* Nursemaid, $200+. Babies, $50-75+.

A similar 6.125″ cloth bisque, cloth-bodied doll with bisque lower arms and legs was dressed as a nurse. She tends a similarly sized invalid, painted to be a grandmother, wearing her original, simple clothing. By this time, lower priced dolls would not have been molded with facial lines suggesting age. Dolls, $175-200/each.

Three grandmother dolls with slightly different bisque shoulder heads. The largest doll measured 7.25" tall. She was marked on her back "225" along with another number not visible. She had grey hair with a bun in the back and has been redressed. The doll on the right was 6.25" tall. Her arms included wires to make them bend. This doll had a molded ribbon in the back of her hair and has been nicely redressed. The smallest grandmother doll measured 6" tall. Her grey hair also included a bun in the back. Her shoulder plate was marked "Germany/650/8/0". The "Germany" was written in script as was done with some dolls made by Kestner. This doll had a less expressive face than the other two dolls. All three dolls wore molded black one strap shoes. *From the collection of Dian Zillner. Photo courtesy of Suzanne Silverthorne.* $150-200 each.

7" tall man and 6.5" woman dollhouse dolls, both with molded hair. The man had a small mustache and wears his original clothing, including a long suit jacket. It is similar to the one shown wearing a removable top hat in a 1913 FAO Schwarz advertisement. The woman doll also wears her original clothing. *From the collection of Gail and Ray Carey. Photograph courtesy of Gail Carey.* $225 +.

6.25" tall early 1900s male dollhouse doll represented a grandfather or an older business man. This doll was probably a more highly priced doll as his face was molded with wrinkles and a solemn expression. He has a balding head with grey hair and whiskers on each side of his face. *From the collection of Gail and Ray Carey. Photograph courtesy of Gail Carey.* $225 +.

7" tall man and women dollhouse dolls shown on the right. The man had molded hair and mustache. He wears a black felt tux with a tie and vest that may be a replacement. The woman had an applied wig, painted features, and what appears to be her original dress with a short train in the back. The sleeves are leg of mutton style, which would date to c. 1900. The upper front of the dress has been padded to indicate a grown woman's figure. A 7.25" man and 6.75" woman are also formally dressed. The male doll had molded hair with painted features, including a large mustache. He wore a black felt tuxedo with a vest, tie, shirt front, and watch chain. The woman had a mohair wig braided around the top of her head. Both of the dolls had wires in their upper arms to allow them to bend. *From the collection of Dian Zillner. Photo courtesy of Suzanne Silverthorne.* Dolls on right $450/pr. Dolls on left, $425/pr.

6″ tall man and woman dollhouse dolls. The man had a molded top hat, molded hair, and painted features with a wide mustache. His shirt is original but his felt suit has probably been replaced. The lady doll had a slightly different molded hairstyle. This hairdo is shown on one of the childhood dolls of Dorothy Coleman pictured in *Collectors Encyclopedia of Dolls*. The author stated that her dollhouse dolls were purchased shortly after World War I but she believed some of them were old store stock. *From the collection of Dian Zillner. Photo courtesy of Suzanne Silverthorne.* Man, $275+. Woman, $150+.

6.25″ tall doll representing an older man with a large mustache and beard. He wears what appears to be a smoking jacket that may be a replacement. Full-bearded dolls are very hard to find. *From the collection of Gail and Ray Carey. Photograph courtesy of Gail Carey.* Insufficient examples to establish value.

5″ tall male dollhouse dolls featured mutton chop side whiskers. The doll on the left is all original. His outfit included a long black felt coat with tails in the back, a white shirt and a cummerbund around his waist. Doll on the right has been redressed. *From the collection of Gail and Ray Carey. Photograph courtesy of Gail Carey.* $150/each.

Two male dollhouse dolls, each 6.75" tall. Both dolls had molded hair parted in the middle and mustaches. The doll on the right wears his original clothing while the doll on the left is dressed in his original shirt and a replaced grey suit. It is unusual to find a bisque doll with dark hair, because many coats of tint would have been required to create the desired tone. Often, as with the doll on the right, glaze was used to create darker colors giving the doll a china head look. *From the collection of Gail and Ray Carey. Photograph courtesy of Gail Carey.* Doll on left, $200+. Doll on right $250+.

Uniformed soldiers were popular subjects of German doll makers. A 7" tall clean-shaven soldier wears an original uniform and removable hat. *From the collection of Ann Meehan. Photograph courtesy of Ann Meehan.* $1,500.

Soldier dolls were made of different materials and wore the uniforms of many armies. Pictured from left, a 7.5" impeccably dressed, beribboned bisque soldier with "postured" hands in high leather boots ($750); a 7" helmeted bisque soldier, also in leather boots ($1695); a 5.25" bisque soldier, without elaborate uniform, was beautifully molded with moustache and full beard, but his body was oddly scaled to his head and arms ($175); a 6.75" china head soldier with moustache and goatee added to a female head to differentiate it as a male, dressed in the uniform of a Union soldier ($750). The 9" rare soldier on the right not only had full graying beard, but was molded with age lines ($2800). He was dressed with all his medals and signs of rank, including a saber. Soldier dolls were also produced with molded hats on their bisque heads. *From the collection of Ann Meehan. From the collection of Lucy's Dollhouse.*

Black, stereotypical "Mammy" doll 7.25" tall. This large size African Heritage woman had a bisque shoulder head, lower arms and legs, and a cloth body. Most of the shoes on the black dolls were not defined. *From the collection of Ann Meehan. Photograph courtesy of Ann Meehan.* $1,500.

For several decades Hertwig and Co. produced a number of dolls that can be used in dollhouses. Pictured are 8" and 5.5" tall shoulder head bisque dolls shown in the Hertwig 1914 catalog. The smaller model was #354, listed in eight sizes. She had a brown sawdust-filled body with her hands, blue shoes, and socks of molded bisque. The doll had blue molded hair bows, molded blonde hair, painted features, and a molded ruffle around her shoulders. The larger white bisque bonnet head doll was model #208, made in thirteen sizes. She had a white molded bonnet trimmed in pink flowers and a blue band. Her hair was molded as were her features. Her lower arms and legs were white bisque with glazed brown boots. The dolls are pictured with Star living room 1:10 scale furniture. *From the collection of Dian Zillner. Photo courtesy of Suzanne Silverthorne.* Smaller doll, $75-100. Larger doll, $150+.

Red jacketed black footman 6" tall. This doll had soles on his feet to represent shoes. *From the collection of Ann Meehan. Photograph courtesy of Ann Meehan.* ($950).

6.5" tall Hertwig doll with a one-piece head and upper body made of molded bisque. The doll is from a set of four different boy and girl character dolls featured in the 1914 Hertwig 50th Anniversary catalog. The girls were dressed in plain brown skirts with cheaply made aprons. This doll has been redressed. She had a molded braided hairstyle, painted features, and a molded vest and blouse front. Her hands, originally attached to tan muslin arms, were bisque as were her yellow shoes and molded stockings. She is pictured with a marked German bisque baby doll 2.75" tall with jointed arms and stationary legs. The baby is in its original wood baby walker from the period. He had molded hair and painted features. These sets were still being sold as late as 1929. The dolls are pictured with a Gottschalk breakfront dating from 1910 and a chair made in Japan. *From the collection of Dian Zillner. Photo courtesy of Suzanne Silverthorne.* Hertwig doll, $150+. Baby in walker, $40.

All-Bisque Children

In addition to these types of popular dollhouse dolls, all-bisque dolls were often used for dollhouse children. Babies, toddlers, and both boys and girls were available in all sizes. Although most of these dolls had molded hair, the more expensive dolls can be found with glass eyes and wigs. The German firm of Hertwig & Co. probably designed the largest number of small dolls for dollhouses. The firm produced both all-bisque dolls and interesting models of dolls with bisque shoulder heads, lower arms and legs and cloth bodies. Because the 1914 Hertwig catalog is reproduced in Florence Theriault's *Hertwig & Co. Archives 1890-1937*, these dolls can now easily be identified.

An extended Hertwig family originally pictured on the cover of the 1914 Hertwig 50th Anniversary catalog. Dolls had a one-piece, waist up torso. Lower torso, arms, and legs were made of muslin. Shoes, molded to the lower bisque legs, were painted blue or yellow. These dolls are modern day dolls cast from original Hertwig molds, painted as the originals, with fancier dress. They were sold by the Mary Merritt Museum. $450/set.

4.75" pair of dolls pictured in the Hertwig & Company 1914 50th anniversary catalog. Both dolls had bisque shoulder heads decorated with molded ruffles and bisque arms and feet also decorated with molded ruffles. Their shoes were painted blue. The sawdust stuffed bodies were red. The doll on the left had a wig and the doll on the right had molded hair. They were sold by the firm undressed. They are the perfect size for dollhouse children in larger dollhouses from the period. *From the collection of Dian Zillner. Photo courtesy of Suzanne Silverthorne.* $75+ each.

In addition to small cloth-bodied dolls, all-bisque dolls in small sizes were also often used as dollhouse children in antique dollhouses. Pictured are 4.5" and 5.5" all-bisque little boy dolls made in Germany. The smaller boy on the right was marked "2 ½" on his back. He had molded curly hair, painted features, and was wire jointed at the shoulders and hips. He wore one strap blue painted shoes and stockings shirred into little squares. He has been redressed and is c. 1900-1910. Since he was made in a "chunky" style, he would need to live in a larger dollhouse to be appropriate in size. The larger doll on the left was made by Hertwig & Co. and was pictured in their 1914 catalog. He wears molded clothing including a hat, sweater, and over-the-shoes leggings. His hair was also molded and his features painted. He was jointed with wire at the shoulders and hips. *From the collection of Dian Zillner. Photo courtesy of Suzanne Silverthorne.* Doll on left, $100+. Doll on right, 5.5" $150+.

3.75" tall pair of all-bisque dolls made in Germany. They had glass eyes, closed mouths, matching mohair wigs, and black shoes. Both dolls were jointed at the shoulders and hips. They wore matching sweaters, caps, and leggings. The little girl carried a doll while her brother held a red metal ship. *From the collection of Gail and Ray Carey. Photograph courtesy of Gail Carey.* $300-400 pair.

Armand Marseille fine-tuned the concept of mass production, exporting dolls from Germany all over the world. Despite the quantity of dolls produced, the quality was quite high, as seen in the pictured all-bisque, glass-eyed boy and girl. The children, with the same head mold but different hair lengths, were dressed as twins. The little girl's hat is a newer addition. *From the collection of Penny Hadfield of A Quiet Place Dolls.* $250-270/each.

Kling 3.5" all-bisque glass-eyed doll with braided wig. She was jointed at the shoulders and hips. Her lower legs had patterned stockings and low-heeled strap shoes. She was dressed in a crocheted outfit typical of the period, and the usual hallmark of Carl Horn. *From the collection of Penny Hadfield of A Quiet Place Dolls.* $285.

5.25" and 5.75" all-bisque Kestner dolls made from molds #620 and #130 respectively. Both dolls had sleepy glass eyes, original wigs, and closed mouths. The smaller doll had a swivel neck. Their stockings were shirred, and they wore two strap shoes decorated with painted bows on their toes. Both dolls were loop strung, jointed at the shoulders and hips, and have been redressed. *From the collection of Dian Zillner. Photo courtesy of Suzanne Silverthorne.* Larger doll, $250-$300. Smaller, $350-$400.

All-bisque glass-eyed dolls, ranging in size from 3.5" to 4", were dressed in traditional Swiss costumes. It is not known whether they were of German or Swiss origin, but would have been similar to dolls sold by Franz Carl Weber in his Swiss toy shop. *From the collection of Penny Hadfield of A Quiet Place Dolls*. $330-350/each.

Although most collectors use a number of small, all-bisque dolls as children in their dollhouses, a limited number of regular doll house children dolls were also produced. These dolls were made with bisque shoulder heads, molded hair, painted features, bisque lower arms and legs and cloth bodies and upper limbs. The pictured dolls represent several different hair styles in three sizes. The smallest doll (center) measured 4" tall. His painted molded hair came down on his forehead between his eyes. He has probably been redressed. The 4.75" little girl doll (right), dressed in white, may have been a larger model of the little boy but her hair did not dip down on her forehead. Both the boy and girl had white shirred stockings and black heeled boots. She has also been redressed. Bangs across the forehead highlighted the hair of the 5" girl (left). This redressed little girl had black heeled shoes with two straps. Her white shirred stockings had a red line at the top. *From the collection of Dian Zillner. Photo courtesy of Suzanne Silverthorne*. $135-165/each.

This unmarked 4" tall all-bisque German child doll c. 1900-1915 also fits nicely in a dollhouse. She had molded short hair, and depending on costume could also be used as a boy. Doll had painted features and was jointed at the shoulders and hips. She had one strap blue painted shoes, and shirred white stockings. The doll has been redressed. She is pictured with 1:12 scale furniture thought to have been made by the Moritz Gottschalk firm c. 1913. *From the collection of Dian Zillner. Photo courtesy of Suzanne Silverthorne*. $75.

All-bisque German babies were made in all sizes and can be found to match the scale of any dollhouse, large or small. Pictured is a 2.25" tall all-bisque German baby doll with molded hair and painted features. He was jointed at the shoulders and hips. Most of these tiny dolls, sold for many years, were displayed in filigree metal buggies or used in dollhouses. *From the collection of Dian Zillner. Photo courtesy of Suzanne Silverthorne.* $75.

Doll Reform

The German doll reform movement started with exhibits and contests in cities across Germany. Much of the credit for change is given to Marion Kaulitz who first opened her studio in 1908, collaborating with twelve members of the Art Workers Guild. German toy retailers scorned Kaulitz when she first exhibited her dolls dressed like peasants from Munich's environs. A sampling of the dolls was sent to the United States in 1909, and their acceptance was overwhelming. Resulting orders swamped her small studio and the home workers Kaulitz had recruited to help her. Her success gave encouragement to many others.

The dolls of Käthe Kruse were likewise a major departure from the stylized dolls of the former century. The company had its beginning when an *avant-garde* young woman named Katharina Simon, born in 1883, moved to Berlin to become a stage performer. Instead, she met and married a Berlin sculptor named Max Kruse. Soon after their first daughter was born, Max encouraged his wife to make the child a doll. He felt that the commercial dolls then available were not soft enough to resemble real children. By 1905, Käthe was making her dolls commercially. Her style of doll making evolved from her first attempt, transforming a towel into sand filled cloth dolls that looked like real children. First selling to neighbors and friends, her dolls were shown in a German exhibition around 1909. This exposure resulted in an order from FAO Schwarz in New York City for 150 dolls. Although Kruse tried to get commercial help to fill the order, she was not satisfied with the results. During the rest of her years of doll making, she supervised the production of each doll. In an article in *Toys and Novelties* in March 1913, Kruse described her perfect doll: "It must be unbreakable, a character doll closely resembling a real child and it must be a real play doll."

Although nearly all Kruse dolls were made in larger sizes, the company, based in Bad Kosen, did experiment with smaller dolls in 1916 when they began production of dollhouse dolls. These dolls were produced only about ten years as they were costly and time consuming.

The Käthe Kruse firm continued to produce their larger dolls through World War I, the Depression years, and World War II. When facing nationalization by the East German government, the firm moved to Donauwörth, Bavaria, where dolls continued to be made. In 1953, Kruse passed control of the company to her daughter and son-in-law. She died in 1968. Majority owners of the company today are Andrea and Steve Christenson.

The French doll industry adopted the reform movement as well, partially in its efforts to create dolls that were distinct from their German competition. Rather than follow the German movement to molded realism, the French adopted fabric with facial detail added by careful hand sewing. Costuming was less elaborate and oriental color palettes were adopted. Regional peasant dolls were introduced, and a home craft industry re-emerged.

The Edwardian Era essentially ended with the beginning of WWI in 1914. German toy makers were shut off from their lucrative markets in England, France, and the United States. At war's end, many changes and challenges would be faced.

Käthe Kruse, as part of the Doll Reform movement, experimented with realistic dollhouse dolls. The dolls in 1:10 scale included various adult family members, 7.5", and children 3.75" in height. Max Kruse, her husband, helped with the modeling of the heads made with a liquid papier-mache material. The dolls had molded hair and painted features. Men with molded beards and mustaches followed the look of bisque dollhouse dolls then being produced. According to Lynn Murray's Doll News article, "Kathe Kruse Dollhouse Dolls," the dolls were constructed with simple wire armature wrapped in wool to shape the body, resulting in a completely mobile and flexible doll. *From the collection of Nancy Smith.* $3500/pr.

Section Two

Conflicts, Peace, and the Great Depression

1915-1945

The thirty-year period between 1915 and 1945 was tumultuous - politically, socially, and economically. Almost fifty years of European peace ended with the beginning of World War I in August 1914. The war imposed hardships on citizens of many countries as goods were rationed towards the war's end. Men were conscripted into military service, leaving a shortage of skilled industrial laborers. German manufactured goods were banned from import to the United States and other Allied countries, opening the door for supply of goods from countries like Japan. German dominance in toy making was broken as other manufacturers developed technologies and methods to compete.

When the war ended in 1918, the Central Powers were punished by the Allied powers. Three Empires were broken up: German, Austro-Hungarian, and Ottoman, ending the aristocratic rule of a number of traditional ruling families. Germany was saddled with huge reparations payments, which slowed its industrial redevelopment and helped bankrupt its economy. England and France were faced with huge debts taken out to support their war efforts. Taxes were raised in all countries to help pay for the loans, many of which were held by United States banks. Industrial capacity increased in the former Allied countries, particularly in the United States, generally left untouched by the war.

The rise of Socialism coincided with the fall of the aristocratic classes. The Russian Revolution had occurred in 1917, glorifying the place of the laborer in society. Less revolutionary class realignment occurred in England, the United States, France, and Germany. The idea of a hereditary privileged class faded and was replaced by economic class definition, which allowed for upward movement based upon achievement.

As war-weary Europeans, referred to as the "Lost Generation," struggled with depressed economies, Americans entered the Roaring 20s. Women had won the right to vote, the economy boomed across all economic levels, unemployment was low, and demand for consumer goods was at an all time high. Fashions were much less restrictive, as seen in the clothes and hairstyles of the Flappers.

American toy and doll makers began to develop new materials to replace the traditional media used by the struggling German toy industry. Japan continued its heavy imports of toys to the United States, for the most part copying German designs and materials, but without the same level of quality.

The continued decline of Europe's economies spread to the United States in October 1929. The world entered the Great Depression, a period that lasted until countries started rearming before the start of WWII. Unemployment in the United States rose to 25% by 1933. The Depression hit cities and urban areas particularly hard, although farm prices dropped 40-60%. Consumer spending was minimal, especially for non-essential items like toys.

Commercial dollhouses made in America became common during the period. Companies like Tootsietoy, Frier Steel, Schoenhut, Tynietoy, Keystone, and Rich found their place next to German companies like Gottschalk and Christian Hacker. Miniature furniture and accessories were produced to help fill the houses. The commercial dollhouses and miniatures were not as fancy, but far more affordable than display houses of previous generations. Perhaps, most importantly, they became toys to be played with. Inhabitants changed as well. Dolls were dressed in modern clothes. Extended families became more common as grandparent dolls sometimes replaced butlers, chauffeurs, and maids. New materials were introduced that hinted at things to come.

In the United States the Great Depression was finally easing by the start of the 1940s. The middle class of the industrialized nations had survived financial calamity, in part, by limiting extravagant spending. Children had been taught to treat their toys with respect - they weren't about to be replaced if broken! Young people saved their allowances or earnings from odd jobs so they could occasionally buy playthings. Toys that encouraged imagination and play value were the norm in a pre-TV society. By 1940, however, most of the rest of the world was at war and its production was geared for military goods. Likewise, key raw materials were being shifted away from consumer goods. While United States toy makers were able to meet domestic demand with limited offerings, toys for export were not being produced by countries rich in toy making history: Germany, Great Britain, France, and Japan. In late 1941, when the United States entered the war, non-essential consumer production was substantially curtailed. Metal was allocated to military goods. Over time, plastic, glass, leather, rubber, and cloth became limited commodities. Toys that were made were produced from paper, cardboard, fabric scraps, scrap plastic, and some inferior woods. People were exhorted to "make do with what they had" and to accept substitutes for their accustomed goods.

Chapter 3

The Roaring Twenties

The period from the end of World War I through late 1928 was known by many names: the Golden Twenties, the Années Folles (Crazy Years), the Lost Generation, the Jazz Age and, most recognizable, the Roaring Twenties. The century started with the optimism that the "war to end all wars" had just occurred and that the League of Nations would act to ensure ongoing peace that would bring unprecedented worldwide prosperity. This optimism proved naïve by the beginning of next decade.

America had built its industrial base as a war material supplier to the Allies, and turned its capacity loose to produce consumer goods. Additional restrictive tariffs were instituted to protect American producers. European countries did not begin to see economic recovery until the mid-20s. Technology drove America's prosperity. Henry Ford's Model-T was the single biggest influence on the economy. Jobs in the automotive industry were available. Roads needed to be built. Electricity and indoor plumbing was installed in most homes, as were telephones. Sewers, power plants, and telephone exchanges needed to be built. Similar if not as dramatic change occurred in Europe and Japan. Women began to enter the workforce in large numbers, although often in low paid clerical positions. The net result was an increase in disposable income at all social levels.

Artistically, many of the changes seen before the war accelerated. Art Deco, initially a French decorating and architectural style, spread across Europe and North America. Jazz became the universal music style of the young and its influence was spread by the development of radio broadcasting. The Charleston, tango, Bunny Hug, and the Shimmy provided entertainment. Movies spread popular style throughout the world.

Fashions changed as well. It was the time of the "Flapper," a phrase coined in Great Britain to mean an impetuous young girl. It came to describe a freer woman, recently given the vote, who challenged long established rigid mores. Hemlines rose to just below the knee, arms were bared, and dresses had a loose, straight, and boyish look. Hair was worn in short bobs, often with hair bands or close fitting Cloches. Bead strings and Art Deco pins, rings, and brooches were popular. Men's dress reflected this younger, more modern look. Cuts of suits and leisure clothes were sleek and slimming. Faces were clean shaven and hair was worn close to the head, often greased back with pomades.

The Doll Industry

All of this great cultural change could be seen in the toy and doll industry. Perhaps the single biggest change was the challenge to German toy dominance. The war had closed the market to German made goods. In 1920 German toy makers were only producing on a three-day-a-week schedule. The cost of the coal used to fire the kilns was at all time highs. Freight rates had risen 800% since prewar levels, so shipments to non-domestic markets were prohibitive. The United States Toy Manufacturers Association sponsored clubs like "The American Made Toy Brigade," encouraging children to "Buy American."

The quintessential "Flapper" wore hemlines just below the knee, arms were bared, and her dress had a loose, straight, and boyish look. Hair was worn in a short bob, and bead strings were typical adornments. This 6.5" tinted bisque was made with desirable bent arms and a well-styled wig. *From the collection of Lucy's Dollhouse.* $300.

Larger 6" doll featuring the old "bun" hairstyle continued to be popular into the 1920s. They were often updated with the choice of dress. This example was updated with a stylish felt hat and shorter dress that appears to be original. She is pictured in a Tynietoy dollhouse bedroom furnished with Tynietoy wood furniture from the 1920s. A 2.5" all-bisque baby doll with painted hair and eyes sits on the floor next to a vintage baby scale. The baby has jointed arms only. It is molded in a sitting position. *From the collection of Gail and Ray Carey. Photograph courtesy of Gail Carey.* Woman, $125-150. Baby, $25-35.

Japanese doll makers filled the void left by the restrictions on wartime German imports. While bisque dolls were of inferior materials, detail, and finish, they sold at such low prices that they were available to children of all economic levels.

Changes in fashion meant that German bisque dollhouse dolls, at last, were manufactured with new styles of hair and clothing. Gone were long dresses and men's formal wear. The men became clean shaven without beards and mutton chops. Women sported bobs, not elaborate hair-do's. Kämmer & Reinhardt continued to advertise some of the older type "character dolls" through 1927, limited to a female maid and a male chef with a mustache. Women wore the short Flapper styles. Male dolls were dressed in suits with spats or wore uniforms of chauffeurs, soldiers, aviators, and other professions. Children, smaller dolls, and an increasing number of adults were made of all-bisque.

Male dolls were updated as well. They became clean shaven without sideburns. 1920s German men were also produced in 6" sizes. They had bisque heads, molded hair, painted features, lower bisque arms and legs, and cloth bodies and upper limbs. The doll on the left wears his original jacket, vest, shirt, and tie but his knickers have been replaced. He is still wearing his original knickers under his new replacements. The doll on the right has been redressed. *From the collection of Gail and Ray Carey. Photograph courtesy of Gail Carey.* Partly original,$150-200. Redressed, $150-175.

The new 1920s hairstyle for women was used on a variety of different sized dolls. The smaller doll measured 5.25" and is all original. The larger doll was 6.5" and has been redressed. Both dolls had newer style high-heeled shoes. Jan Foulke, writing in *Kestner King of Dollmakers*, states that the German Kestner firm featured 5" dollhouse lady dolls similar to ones pictured here in their 1930 catalog. It is not known what numbers (if any) were used on the shoulder plates of the Kestner dolls. *From the collection of Dian Zillner. Photo courtesy of Suzanne Silverthorne*. $100/each.

Men of the Roaring Twenties dressed for bedtime lounging, as was this 6.25" tall all original, boxed German dollhouse doll. He carried a tag reading, "Made in Germany." He has a bisque head with molded hair, painted features, lower bisque arms and legs, and a cloth body and upper limbs. His original box is marked "Nr. 39 (or G) 6/3 Pyjama." *From the collection of Gail and Ray Carey. Photograph courtesy of Gail Carey.* $250+.

Updated men dolls were dressed in various professional uniforms. A similar 6.25" tall doll which also carried a "Made in Germany" tag was dressed as a doctor. All of his clothing is original. *From the collection of Gail and Ray Carey. Photograph courtesy of Gail Carey.* $200-225.

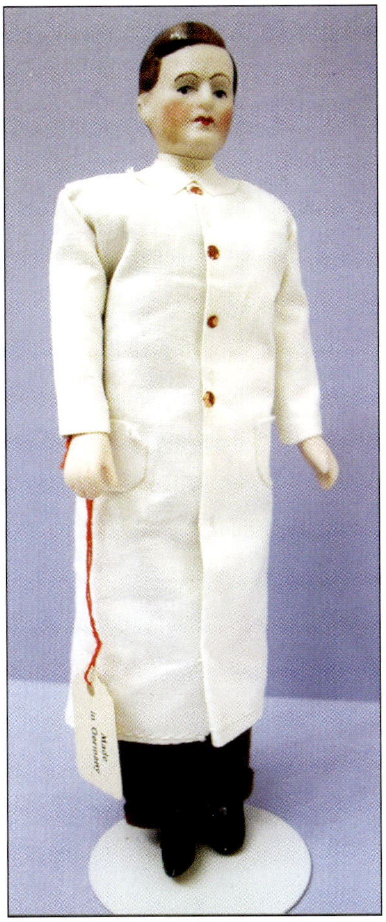

Other more expensive 1920s dollhouse dolls included applied wigs instead of molded hair. Pictured on the right is a 5.5" tall doll with a fancy mohair wig styled in braids around her head. She wears her original underwear, dress, and apron. She had a bisque head with painted features, full bisque arms and lower legs, and a cloth body and upper legs. The doll on the left was 5.5" tall and was also made with the same type body including the full bisque arms. She had a very unusual molded hairstyle with bangs and short hair. Her features were painted. She has probably been redressed in a stylish coat of the era. A cabinet made by the German Gottschalk firm is pictured with the dolls. *From the collection of Dian Zillner. Photo courtesy of Suzanne Silverthorne.* Doll on right, $200+. Doll on left, molded hair $150+.

Maids were also produced in the 1920s using the old hair style, which included a bun in the back. They ranged in size from 5.25" to 5.5" tall. Both maids are all original and appear to be the same dolls still being sold in the FAO Schwarz Christmas catalog in 1930. The doll in the pink outfit still has her original dipper tied to her arm. Both dolls have bisque heads, lower arms and legs, and cloth bodies, upper arms, and legs. The stove was made in England by Taylor and Barrett for A. Barton & Co. *From the collection of Dian Zillner. Photo courtesy of Suzanne Silverthorne.* $100+/each.

Maid dolls with molded caps were also sold in a number of sizes. Pictured in the back are 3.75" and 5.25" maids of the same design. The larger doll's clothing appears to be original. *From the collection of Gail and Ray Carey. Photograph courtesy of Gail Carey.* Large doll, $150-200. Small doll, $75-100.

Family dolls of the period are particularly appealing. Through the decade, FAO Schwarz sold multi-member families of various sizes. The sets pictured in their catalogs included either 5, 6, or 9 dolls. The smallest set included mother, father, boy, small girl, and older girl dolls. The nine doll set added a grandmother, grandfather, butler, and a nursemaid. The larger sets of six and nine FAO Schwarz dollhouse dolls could be purchased in two different sizes. The smallest dolls included adults 5.25" tall and the larger adult dolls measured 5.75" tall. The set of six dolls in the smaller sizes sold for $4.75 while the 5.75" size dolls sold for $5.75. The set of nine dolls in the 5.25" size (adults) was priced at $7.50 while the 5.75" size sold for $8.75. The dolls were less than $1.00 each. The set of five dolls came only in a 5.25" size (adults). They cost $4.00. The catalogs appear to show children fitted with wigs, while other dolls have molded hair. The child dolls' measurements were not given but it is likely that they ranged from 3"- 4" tall, depending on the size of adults in sets they accompany.

In addition to family sets with molded hair, other firms offered family sets of dolls with molded hats. These sets of all-bisque dollhouse dolls included either a mother, father, and two children, or the family plus a maid. At least two different types of molded hat family sets were manufactured. One family included both the father and son wearing molded caps with bills, while the mother and daughter wore molded 1920s cloche hats. Father was dressed in knickers. The four dolls came in a boxed set that included tiny balloons in the children's hands. In the other set of dolls, father wore a molded fedora, and the mother and daughter wore modern molded hats with brims. The maid wore a molded white piece around her head. These dolls ranged in size from 2.5" to 4" tall.

Many other dollhouse bisque dolls were available through department stores or toy stores without catalogs. Chicago's Marshall Field's carried a set of family dolls in the late 1920s. These dolls were grouped in sets of five, six, or nine dolls. The smallest set included a mother, father, maid, boy, and girl. The largest set featured a mother, father, grandmother, grandfather, butler, maid, nursemaid, a boy, and a girl. Adults measured 5" and children were 3" in height.

This late 1920s set of German family dolls included a father and mother each 5", and a boy and girl each measuring 3." The boy and girl were identical dolls with only their clothing giving them their gender. Dolls had molded hair, painted features, and wear their original clothing. Mother's hair was styled in the new short hairstyle and both children had bangs. Children were made of all-bisque while adults had bisque heads, lower arms and legs, and cloth sawdust-filled bodies and upper arms and legs. FAO Schwarz was still selling these types of family dolls as late as 1930. *From the collection of Dian Zillner. Photo courtesy of Suzanne Silverthorne.* Children, $50+/each, Adult,$100/each.

A 1920s dollhouse family included a 5.25" father, 5" mother, a 3" boy, and a different 3.125" girl. This girl had no bangs. Her hairstyle came to a point in the middle of her forehead and formed a Valentine type frame around her face. The children both had the same molded shoes and socks. Despite the new trends, the mother wore the older hair style with a bun in the back that had been used on dollhouse dolls for decades. Her stylish hat covered the bun. All of the dolls include molded hair, painted faces, and painted shoes. Children are all-bisque and parents have sawdust stuffed cloth bodies and upper arms and legs with lower bisque limbs. The four dolls wear their original clothing. All of the 1920s ladies wore high heel shoes without straps. *From the collection of Dian Zillner. Photo courtesy of Suzanne Silverthorne.* Children, $50/each. Adults/$100 each.

Dolls were sometimes molded wearing the latest fashions in hats. The pictured dolls ranged in size from 2.25" to 4" tall. They include a man wearing a molded fedora, a mother and daughter wearing molded cloche hats, and a maid wearing her molded headband. Dolls with molded hats are particularly collectible. *From the collection of Patty Cooper. Photo courtesy of Patty Cooper.* Child, $50. Adults, $100/each.

Other small dolls from the period can also be used as dollhouse residents. The all-bisque German dolls ranging in size from 3.5"– 5" provided children for dollhouses made in larger sizes. These dolls were still being produced in the 1920s with painted or glass eyes, molded hair, or with wigs. Some unusual dolls were molded with hats and others with molded clothing.

Some bisque head dolls of the period were produced with *papier mâché* or a type of composition bodies. Those with a slim body design were particularly popular in the 1920s.

Smaller bisque dollhouse dolls were also made in Germany during the 1920s. 4" German all-bisque dolls make perfect dollhouse children for larger 6"-7" parent dolls. These appear to have been nicely redressed. Both dolls had mohair wigs, painted features, and were jointed at the shoulders and hips. *From the collection of Gail and Ray Carey. Photograph courtesy of Gail Carey.* $75 -100/each.

German bisque dolls c. 1920s. The pink-tinted boy was 4.25" with molded hair, painted features, molded socks, and painted flat shoes. He was wire jointed at the shoulders and hips. He has been redressed. The 4.25" little girl had molded hair with a molded pink hair bow, painted features, molded shirred stockings, and painted shoes with molded heels. She was wire jointed at the shoulders and hips. Both have been redressed. They are pictured with a wood dollhouse piano also dating from the 1920s. *From the collection of Dian Zillner. Photo courtesy of Suzanne Silverthorne.* $75-100/each.

Low-priced children of the late 1920s and early 1930s appeared with molded clothing and hats. Pictured on the right is a 4.5" all-bisque little girl. Her molded hair was decorated with two hair bows. She wore a molded bathing suit or sunsuit. The doll was wire-jointed at the shoulders and hips. A 5" all-bisque doll marked "3/0" appears to be a German product. She wore a molded cloche hat typical of the 1920s, had eyes looking to the side, and a watermelon shaped mouth. She was jointed at the shoulders and hips and wore black painted one-strap shoes and shirred stockings. She has been redressed. *From the collection of Dian Zillner. Photo courtesy of Suzanne Silverthorne.* Doll on right, $50-75. Doll on left, $125+.

7" Armand Marseille doll c. early 1920s with a bisque sockethead marked "Germany/390/A 13/0.M." She had sleep eyes, open mouth with teeth, and a composition body jointed at the shoulders and hips. Her blue shoes were molded with heels. The dress and wig are replacements. She is pictured with over-scaled dollhouse bedroom furniture produced by the Florence V. Cannon Co., Inc. of Camden, New Jersey, in 1921. *From the collection of Dian Zillner. Photo courtesy of Suzanne Silverthorne.* Doll, $150+.

As competition became more intense and the Depression made less money available for playthings, new materials were introduced to lower the cost of dolls. While these 5.5" tall German made little girl dolls had bisque heads with painted eyes, closed mouths, and mohair wigs, their bodies were crudely made in five pieces from rough composition. Their "thin bodies" made them a popular choice to accompany normally proportioned adult dollhouse dolls. They wear their original clothing and are pictured with large scaled iron Arcade living room furniture. *From the collection of Dian Zillner. Photo courtesy of Suzanne Silverthorne.* $50+/each.

Tynietoy - The First American Dollhouse Dolls

The first American made dolls specifically made for dollhouses appeared toward the end of the decade as residents of the Tynietoy dollhouses being sold by Marion I. Perkins and Amey Vernon in their Toy Furniture Shop in Providence, Rhode Island. The shop opened in 1920 to showcase fine miniatures made by Ms. Perkins. The houses and furniture were expensive for the time and aimed more as adult display houses than playthings for children. Two different styles of dolls were offered: cloth over wire armature, as well as peg-wooden. Linda Edwards in her April 2005 *Antique Doll Collector* article "Tynietoy and the Toy Furniture Shop" ventures that Marion designed the wood dolls first to replace German bisque dolls being sold in their shop. The cloth dolls followed, and the two overlapped for some period of time. Ms. Edwards believes that Tynietoy ceased production of the wood dolls before the cloth dolls. To confuse matters, however, a recent in-depth study by Judith Armitstead, "Tynietoy's Elusive Cloth Dollhouse Dolls," appearing in the April 2008 edition of *Antique Doll Collector*, points out that the 1200 series catalog numbering of cloth dolls suggests that they pre-date the 1900 series peg-wooden dolls. Judging by the number of wood dolls found today, it would suggest that they were made for a longer period of time than cloth dolls.

Heads of cloth dolls were flesh-colored stockinette with hand-painted details. Judith Armitstead points out that some dolls have been found with stitched facial details. Wire armatures inside the cotton stuffed, stockinette bodies allowed them to be bent into various positions. All of the dolls were sold fully clothed. Composition shoes were molded to the wire frames. Women wore mohair wigs, but men's hair was generally painted. Some children had embroidered hair. At least one Tynietoy catalog lists the cloth dolls as "Marion Winter" dolls although other catalogs do not mention a designer. An early catalog lists: "Father 5.5" - $2.50, Mother 5.5" - $2.50, Maid 5.5" - $2.50, Cook 5.5" - $2.50, Nurse 5.5" - $2.50, Boy 4" - $2.00, Girl 4" - $2.00, Baby 1.75" - $1.00, Colored Mammie with twins - $4.50, Young Hunter - $4.50."

The first truly American commercially made dollhouse dolls were produced by Tynietoy of Providence, Rhode Island, in the 1920s. At 1:12 scale , they fit well with Tynietoy's beautiful homes and furniture. It is believed that their first "hand made" dolls were cloth, designed and/or made by Marion Winter. The 6" #1202 father and #1203 5.5" mother had stockinette bodies covering cotton-padded wire armatures. Women dolls were wigged, but the hair of men was painted. The women were particularly well-dressed, obviously appealing to Tynietoy's high-society clientele. *From the collection of Lettie Schwarz*. $700/each.

While the Tynietoy cloth family members were all quite well dressed, they had household retinue to care for their homes and children. Pictured at far left is the #1204 Maid. Seated, holding a #1209 baby, is the #1206 nurse. The household staff also included a cook and an African American "Mammie." The dolls stand in front of the facade of a magnificent fully furnished Tynietoy house on display at the Toy and Miniature Museum of Kansas City. *From the collection of the Toy and Miniature Museum of Kansas City. Photo courtesy of the Toy and Miniature Museum of Kansas City.* Adults, $700/each.Children, $500/each. Baby, $400/each.

One of the most intriguing of the Tynietoy cloth dolls is the #1211 Young Hunter, pictured on the left dressed in jodhpurs, short boots, and a red riding coat. Missing from his outfit is a riding hat and crop. The majority of the #1202 fathers are found with black suits, although, as pictured on the right, brown suits were also made. The Young Hunter sold for $4.50, but the rest of the adult dolls sold for $2.50. *From the collection of the Toy and Miniature Museum of Kansas City. Photo courtesy of the Toy and Miniature Museum of Kansas City.* Young Hunter, $800, if complete. Father, $700.

The #1206 5.5" nurse comforts a #1209 baby just before naptime. Nicely detailed facial features were painted on the stockinette heads. *From the collection of the Toy and Miniature Museum of Kansas City. Photo courtesy of the Toy and Miniature Museum of Kansas City.* Nurse, $700. Baby, $400.

Tynietoy's cloth line cataloged a #1207 4" boy, #1209 1.75" baby and #1208 4" girl originally costing $1 or $2 each, depending on size. The girl had a mohair wig and the boy's hair was embroidered thread. Pictured children vary in size, typical of cloth dolls: Girl, 3.5"; Boy, 2.5"; baby, 1.75". *From the collection of Lettie Schwarz.* Boy and girl, $500/each. Baby $400.

Tynietoy's wooden Peggity Dolls were evocative of the peg-wooden dolls of Grödner Tal. In fact, their catalog reads, "The Peggity Dolls are our original reproductions of the old wooden pegged dolls. They are 5.5" high; are jointed and hand-painted. They stand, sit, move their arms and legs." Some of these dolls were marked "Peggity" on the back of the left thigh in blue and "Doll" on the right thigh; others had the word "Peggity" added with ink on the right thigh, and some were unmarked. Each had a distinctively carved shoe, fit on the tapered bottom of the leg.

The fashions worn by Tynietoy dolls fit well in the firm's beautiful and highly sought after dollhouses, all designed to imitate styles found in New England's towns and villages. Tynietoy furniture was made and hand-decorated by local artisans in early 19th century style, and the doll's clothing complements the period and decor very well. Each doll was hand made and the Toy Furniture Shop did not have a supply on hand. Catherine Dorris Callicott explained in the book *In Praise of Dollhouses* that her own collection of Peggity Dolls did not include a father doll, despite the fact that it had been back-ordered for some time.

By 1933, Vista Toy Company of New York City, a maker of its own line of dollhouses, was advertising itself as the "exclusive

Marion Perkins advertised her "Peggity Dolls" as reproductions of the old wooden pegged dolls. At 5.5" both the men and women were well sized for Tynietoy's carefully decorated wood houses. Men sold for $1.75 and women, $1.00. *From the collection of Lettie Schwarz*. $500/each.

Tynietoy peg-wooden dolls were often marked by a wood-burned signature, as was the doll on the left. The redressed doll on the right was inscribed with ink. Some dolls were unmarked. The feet of the Peggity dolls were distinctively wedged shaped, with a hole drilled to accept a tapered leg. *From the collection of Lucy's Dollhouse.* Redressed doll, $350. Doll in original costume, $500.

Miss and Mrs. Peggity were dressed in a variety of fabrics and styles. Cataloged as #1900 and #1901 the 5.5" dolls were advertised as wearing "quaint floral designs," a theme found on hand-painted "upholstered" Tynietoy furniture. Although both dolls had a marking, the doll on the left is in a modern dress and her facial features differ somewhat from the older doll on the right with her hand sewn single color dress. Dolls were made over a number of years, and were decorated by a number of different artists. *From the collection of Lucy's Dollhouse.* Redressed doll, $350. Doll in original costume, $500.

sales representative" of Tynietoy. It is not known whether they carried dolls, or only Tynietoy's furniture. Ms. Vernon died in 1940 and Ms. Perkins turned over management to others in 1942, before her death in 1947. Tynietoy continued in existence until 1953, but over the last decade it appears that it did little but sell off existing inventory. The dolls are highly desirable today, not only as residents of Tynietoy's fine houses, but also for their historical significance as America's first commercially produced dollhouse dolls.

Although bisque dollhouse families were sold by department stores and by FAO Schwarz into the early 1930s, the age of the bisque head and all-bisque dolls was nearing its end. Composition as a doll material began replacing bisque, even for dollhouse dolls, by the late 1920s. Collectors still treasure the bisque head dollhouse dolls, perhaps for the reminders they bring of a by-gone age of large dollhouses populated with chauffeurs, maids, butlers, and finely dressed adults and children. They forget that only children who lived in similar real life houses could afford such toys. Most children made do with very little in the way of playthings. New materials introduced over the next 20 years would finally make dollhouses available to everyone.

Grandmother Peggity often wore a magenta silk dress with long train. Fine lace was used to decorate her dress and cap. She was cataloged as #1903 and sold for $1.25. *From the collection of Lettie Schwarz. $500.*

Nora the #1904 maid in her starched black uniform shared household duties with a kerchiefed, stereotypical African American "mammy." Tynietoy did not catalog a peg-wooden mammy, although they did offer a cloth "Mammie." Construction of the doll matches that of other Peggity Dolls. They sold for $1.25 each. *From the collection of Lettie Schwarz.* $600/each.

Chapter 4

The Depression Years

The boom of the Roaring 20s started to peak, then falter by 1928 in Europe. The 1929 stock market crash in the United States speeded up the process, spreading the economic slump across the world. A major factor of the collapse was the rampant consumerism of the previous decade. Mass consumption had been fueled by mass production. People took on debt to pay for their new homes, autos, furniture, and radios. Businesses had looked to banks to finance the growth to meet consumer demand. Cities and towns took on debt to build the infrastructure needed to support the changing urban landscape. In Europe the war reparations imposed on Germany raised that country's taxes and forced the German government to borrow from the United States, thus limiting German post-war recovery.

When the stock market crashed, it wiped out the savings of many individuals who had invested in the bubble and lessened the confidence of others who were not as affected. People no longer had the cash to pay off their debts, much less to buy new products. Without consumer spending, businesses didn't have the revenue to repay their debts, and many closed. Farm prices dropped, partially a result of retaliatory tariffs imposed by countries in response to the doubling of import duties by the United States in 1930. Additionally, the Midwest suffered from a years-long drought that cut production. Banks that had extended themselves, granting credit both to industrialists and farmers, faced unprecedented defaults in repayments and a number of large banks failed. As a result, people withdrew money from smaller banks causing further failures. United States unemployment jumped to 25% by 1933. Similar downward spirals, many linked to the loss of the boom in the United States consumer market, occurred across the world.

There was great social and labor unrest in all countries throughout the decade. People looked to place blame. They put their faith in demagogues who promised relief from the sins of the past and a way out of current misery. The rise to power of Hitler in Germany, Mussolini in Italy, Franco in Spain, and the militarists in Japan pushed the world towards another war. The spending undertaken by these countries, as they armed in preparation to achieve the greatness promised by their leaders, brought economic recovery by the end of the decade, but it did not bring a return of consumer production. Industry was aimed at building armaments.

The 1930s saw a return of social conservatism. Speakeasies closed and the "naughty nightlife" of the 1920s lost its glitter when Prohibition was repealed. Dress lines dropped nearer the ankle. "Feminine" shapes were preferred over "boyish." Cloche hats were replaced by berets, pillboxes, and turbans, showing longer wavier hair. For many women working outside the home, and for those who stayed home doing chores previously left to the hired help, "practical" clothes were required. New synthetic, easy care fabrics were introduced, as was the zipper, all facilitating an inexpensive, ready-made, less formal style. Movies were a form of recreation and escape from the realities of the depression and film helped to set fashion standards for young and old. The Empire waist was a popular formal style decorated with bows and fabric flowers. Shirley Temple set the fashion style for little girls with short ruffled dresses and "Shirley Temple curls."

Men's suits were often double breasted or had wide lapels, if single breasted. Padding gave a square, large shouldered look. Blazers were common, and lightweight "Palm Beach" suits made from poplin or seersucker were worn during the summer months. Boys wore knickers, vests, and soft caps, often looking like the *Little Rascals*, and hoping for the day they could finally wear long pants.

The Depression Years were a time that people "made do" and had a keen sense of price and value. They recycled and repaired rather than purchased new. For the most part people did with less. Extravagances were few and far between, and children learned the value of money when faced with choices between toys and food. New materials were introduced that lessened the cost of new goods, and simpler, less elaborate items were now the norm. Old sources of supply closed as global conflict began. Japanese and German goods were boycotted or banned. Mass catalog retailers like Sears and Montgomery Wards, competed with 5 & 10¢ stores like S.S. Kresge, W.T. Grant, and F.W. Woolworth for lower priced goods and more efficient systems of distribution and sale. It was a time of significant change for all industries and markets, and especially for toys and dolls. The traditional fine-bisque dolls of earlier decades quickly disappeared from the market early in the 1930s to be replaced by more affordable dolls made from new materials.

Painted-over Bisque

Porcelain dolls that began to appear in the 1930s differed in two major ways from the earlier fine-bisque and parian-like dolls. The differences were clearly aimed at lowering the cost of the doll. In making "traditional" bisque dolls, finely ground materials gave extremely smooth surfaces to dolls once they were fired. During the early part of the 20th century, less finely processed materials began to be used, resulting in dolls with rougher more porous looking surfaces, sometimes referred to as sugar-, salt-, or stone bisque. Bisque dolls of the 1930s were made of this coarse material. Additionally, the color found on traditional bisque needed to be carefully applied, often in multiple layers successively fired onto the greenware. Newer dolls had painted details that were not set by firing. Painting was an easier skill that required less trained labor; it could provide vivid colors without the need for successive layers; it did not need firing, especially important when coal was scarce and expensive. The use of unfired paint gave the dolls their name, "painted-over bisque."

Dolls were clothed in simply made outfits or were sold nude (sometimes with crepe paper clothing), allowing an economy-minded owner, or her mother, to make an outfit from scraps. Many dolls were jointed at the shoulders and hips, with the balance being "frozen." They were made in large quantities in Germany and Japan. Dolls were produced to represent father, mother, children, babies, and maids in a variety of sizes ranging from 1" to 6".

As the Depression deepened in the early 1930s, manufacturers looked for cheaper materials and methods to produce toys. Coarse white bisque became a material of choice. Rather than colored glazes, paint was used to provide the bright colored details of the dolls. Painters were less skilled artists than glazers and paint saved having to heat coal burning furnaces for successive glaze firings. The three dolls on the right are painted-over bisque dolls all marked "Germany." The young children measured 2.625", the older boy in his "Little Rascals" type suit and hat measured 4". Their skin was painted as well as their facial details and shoes. The girl on the left is a mid to late 1920s 3.75" doll, of somewhat higher quality pink tinted bisque and more carefully highlighted, painted features. Boy, $25. Young children, $20. Girl, $35.

Pair of painted-over bisque Hertwig baby dolls. The Baby on the right is pictured in the 1933 Montgomery Ward catalog ad. Both marked "Germany" on their backs, they were rubber band jointed at their shoulders and hips. Their molded hair and painted features differed. The larger doll was 3.5" tall and the smaller one, 2.75". They are sitting in iron potty chairs produced by the Kilgore Manufacturing Co. in the 1930s. *From the collection of Dian Zillner. Photo courtesy of Suzanne Silverthorne.* $20-35/each.

6" tall painted-bisque doll made in Germany c. mid 1930s by Hertwig & Co. similar to one of the dolls in the 1933 ad. She was marked "Germany" on her back in incised letters. The doll had molded short hair, painted features and was jointed at the shoulders and hips. She has been redressed as a girl but could also be used as a boy. Furniture was produced by the Wisconsin Toy Co. of Milwaukee, Wisconsin, c. early 1930s. *From the collection of Dian Zillner. Photo courtesy of Suzanne Silverthorne.* Redressed doll, $30.

The German firm, Hertwig & Co., well attuned to changes in the market, was a major producer of these dolls. Theriault's book, *Hertwig and Co. Archives 1890-1937,* pictures many of these dolls. A number were marked on the back with a simple outline of a house with an "H" inside. Painted all-bisque dolls pictured in Theriault's book range in size from 3.5" to 7.5" tall. Dolls had molded hair, paint features, and shoes, and were dressed in regular children's clothing. A few dolls were dressed to represent occupations including chefs, monks, nurses, and men in various uniforms. The firm also offered an assortment of painted-over bisque baby dolls ranging in size from 2.25" to 5" tall. They all had painted features, molded hair, and were jointed at the shoulders and hips. Babies originally came with pacifiers.

Advertisement in the Montgomery Ward Christmas catalog in 1933 pictured painted-over bisque dolls made by the German Hertwig Co. The larger dolls pictured on the right were 6.25" tall and the baby was 5" tall. The set sold for 29 cents. *Photo courtesy of Dian Zillner and Suzanne Silverthorne.*

Painted-over bisque unmarked set of family dolls. The man and woman were 4"; the boy, 2.5"; the baby, 1.25" high. They were all jointed at their shoulders and hips and wear their original clothing. A maid with the same hairstyle as the mother came with this set of dolls. They may also be Hertwig products but the clothing covers any markings. *From the collection of Dian Zillner. Photo courtesy of Suzanne Silverthorne.* $125/set, including maid.

More unusual are the two 6" tall dolls pictured by Theriault in an original Hertwig sample box with glass eyes and openings on the top of their heads to allow the insertion of a wig. They were jointed at the shoulders and hips and were undressed.

In addition to dollhouse dolls, painted-over bisque nationality dolls were popular offerings in seasonal catalogs in the United States. These dolls were later sold after WWII, as well. A November 1949 issue of *House & Garden* offered the dolls for $3.50 a pair. Possibly the dolls were made by Hertwig, in business until 1953. The dolls at one time were sold in pairs attached by string to orange cardboard boxes. The box bottom had paper lace adhered to the edges. Sometimes the bottom of the box was stamped with the country the doll represented. Some boxes were also stamped "Germany." Some dolls were incised with Germany on one leg; some have Germany imprinted on the bottom of one shoe, and some were marked Germany on the back of the head. Female dolls were 3.75" and male dolls, 3.875". Dolls had cloth clothing of felt, cotton, and rayon. Hairstyles were molded and then sometimes painted to represent a nationality. Facial features and shoes were painted. Some had a shiny finish and others were dull. They were jointed at the arms and legs with elastic cord. Some held accessories like books and flowers.

Manufacturers sometimes used the different sized child-like dolls to create a family. Pictured is a four member family sold as a boxed set with the name "Biedermeier" stamped on its side. The dolls were dressed in the middle class styles of the mid-19th century typical of the Biedermeier period. The parents were 3.5"; the girl and boy, 3". They are ink stamped "Germany" on the leg, and probably date from the early 1930s. Family, $225 MIB.

Small 3.75" painted-over bisque dolls dressed in national costumes were popular subjects both before and after World War II. They were generally sold either boxed as pairs or singly. Boxes were marked Germany. One company, Hertwig offered 42 different nationality dolls, or "Trachten-Puppen," in its 1937 catalog. Pictured Front row: North Irish boy; French royal couple; Scots girl. Middle row: Early American boy; Welsh girl; Early American girl. Back row: Bulgarian. $40/each MIB.

A pair of beautifully detailed 2.5" nationality dolls made by Kestner. The dolls with their exaggerated faces and shaded, painted hair were produced from a darker grained tinted clay. Dolls such as these are usually found in South America, suggesting that they were made exclusively for that market. *From the collection of Penny Hadfield of A Quiet Place Dolls.* $300/each.

Painted-over bisque dolls continued to be sold immediately after World War II. Pictured in a 1950 *House and Garden* is an array of family, baby, and profession dolls assumed to be made by Hertwig.

Painted-over bisque nationality dolls were made in a number of sizes. The late 1920s carefully shadow painted pair on the far right and left of the first row were 3.875". The boy was marked "Made in Germany" on one leg, whereas the girl's clothing was tagged "Made in Germany." She also had markings incised on her back under her clothing. The Polish couple in the middle of the first row was 3.75". The boy's arm was ink-stamped "Made in Germany." They were probably made in the late 1930s or immediately postwar. The 3.125" dolls in the back row were marked "Germany" on their legs and on their necks. Their painted features were of good quality, indicating early 1930s production. Tall early dolls, $60/each. Small dolls, $50/each. Later dolls, $40 each MIB.

Painted-over bisque dolls were dressed in professional costumes, some with desirable molded hats. They ranged in size from 3 to 3.25." $50/each.

5" tall bride and groom in their original clothing. Their hair was molded in up-to-date hairstyles. They wear their original clothing. They were jointed at the shoulders and hips, and attached with rubber bands. They may originally have been used on a wedding cake. *From the collection of Dian Zillner. Photo courtesy of Suzanne Silverthorne.* $75-100/set.

3.25" bride and groom appear to be late 1930s vintage. The groom's hat was molded. They too appear to have been cake toppers. $30/each.

Japanese producers closely followed the trends, exporting small-bisque dolls made in the "white bisque" style, without skin-toned paint. Many of these dolls were "frozen" without moving parts and painted molded clothing, while others, with shoulder and hip joints, were clothed. Most of these dolls had molded hair and painted features. Dolls were made in families with pets, as cartoon characters, cowboys and cowgirls, Native Americans, and ethnic dolls of African and Oriental heritage. In order to keep the cost as low as possible, molds were made using the German originals and paint was not as carefully applied. In fact, some dolls can be found only painted on the front. Lower end dolls were often sold on penny-candy counters at 5¢ to 25¢ each, so every element of cost needed to be considered.

6" white bisque doll marked "Made in Japan" c. 1930s. She had molded hair, painted features, and was wire jointed at the shoulders and hips. She has been redressed. Her china dog was also made in Japan. She sits in a "Grand Rapids" wood rocking chair. *From the collection of Dian Zillner. Photo courtesy of Suzanne Silverthorne.* Doll, $40-50.

Boxed set of dolls made in Japan called the "Perfection Doll House Family." Most of the dolls are made of white bisque although the maid appears to have painted-over skin. Children were 3.5"; parents and maid, 4.5." Each was stamped "Japan" on the legs and some clothing had labels marked "Japan." The dog came as part of the set. $150/set MIB.

Japanese painted-bisque dolls, often called Penny Toys, were found in a number of styles and sizes on the counters of Depression era variety and candy stores. They ranged in price from 1 to 10¢ each and in size from 3" to 3.75". Cowboys and cowgirls with fully molded costumes were popular subjects. "Boopsie" dolls copied popular trends. African American dolls, stereotypically made as "Pick-a-ninnies" were common. The baby on the far right was a copy of Grace Storey Putnam's "Bye-Lo Baby." $10-25/each.

Japanese manufacturers copied their German counterparts producing 3.75" nationality dolls. Their molded features and painting were not as precisely done as similar German dolls, but their costumes had certain charm. Top row: Mexican, Black Forest, Scots. Bottom row: Russian, "Peasants," Irish. $120/set MIB.

Wedding sets were popular novelties used as wedding shower decorations and cake toppers. Japanese made figures ranging from 3" to 4.5". Molded details included hair ribbons, eye glasses, and top hats. $10-15/each.

Set of five 4.75" "Quintettes" painted-over bisque dolls c. 1930s. The dolls were produced in Japan to take advantage of the popularity of the Dionne Quintuplets, born in Canada. Dolls had molded hair and painted features and were rubber band joined at the shoulders and hips. *From the collection of Dian Zillner. Photo courtesy of Suzanne Silverthorne.* $125-150/set MIB.

Wood and the Julie Ann Dolls

Families faced many changes during the Depression. Even if a family owned a farm that was still capable of growing a cash crop, chances were that the prices they received for their output would not be enough to sustain the farm and pay mortgages. Families turned to other skills to supplement their income and stave off foreclosure. A wonderful example of this ingenuity brought us the Julie Ann Dolls of Shreveport, Louisiana. The history of the Julie Ann dolls is well documented by the noted Louisiana collector, dealer, and doll appraiser, Cynthia Orgeron, in a *Doll News* article (Summer, 1998). It is based upon correspondence and discussions with a then surviving family member.

In 1930 the widowed matriarch of a large family with long time land holdings in Shreveport, Hattie Robards Mayer, owned a cotton plantation on Shreve Island, just south of the city. Her oldest daughter, Julia Mayer Cline, and her family lived with her, as did her youngest son, Charles. Nearby, her son Randolph lived with his wife, Ruth Annon and their family. Around 1932, Julia, apparently searching for a way to help her mother, collaborated with Margaret Annon, the sister of her sister-in-law Ruth, to design a doll that could be cut from thin wood, then painted and dressed. Margaret, a talented artist who made architectural models for her father's clients, was paid a small royalty for each doll sold. Apparently, it was Julia, however, who ran the fledgling business from the second floor sun porch of the plantation house. Two of her nephews, sons of Randolph, cut the dolls in a converted chicken coop on the property, and were paid pennies by the piece. Five or six friends of Julia did the sewing, and college art students painted faces and other details.

Dolls' boxes, marked " 'Julie Ann' Made on the Shreve Island Plantation," are sometimes found with paper stick-on-labels printed with the names of local gift shops. Somewhat intriguing is Cynthia's theory that the dolls might have been sold as souvenirs at the Post Exchange on nearby Barksdale Air Force Base, and possibly at other PXs. Much of her correspondence with other Julie Ann collectors points to this common source, and explains why dolls are found in diverse locales across the United States.

Apparently, Julie Ann helped save the plantation. It remained in family hands until after Hattie's death in 1949, when it began to be sold in plots to real estate developers. Today there is little to suggest that the plantation or Shreve Island existed, except through the little Southern Belle, Julie Ann.

Julie Ann Dolls were produced in Shreveport, Louisiana, as part of a family business of the Mayer family to raise income during the Depression. Dolls were 3.75" in height, 1.75" wide and .1875" thick. They might have blonde or dark hair and some had a small satin ribbon bow glued to the hair. An Afro-American doll was produced with holes drilled in the head so that yarn could be inserted in the stereotype "Pick-a-ninny" style. Originally the dolls were hand cut from wood. Each doll had painted underclothes and came with one or more interchangeable dresses, some long in the "plantation style," others shorter and modern. *Dolls courtesy of Cynthia Orgeron*. $25-35/each.

Dolls were originally packaged in small yellow boxes with cut-out tops displaying them. The box was marked " 'Julie Ann' Made on Shreve Island Plantation, Shreveport, Louisiana." There is some mystery connected with another variation of the doll. A *Julie Ann* doll, packaged in a similarly imprinted white box, with the same dimensions and decorations, was produced in a dense bakelite-like plastic, suggesting post-war production. Randolph's son, Paul Mayer, Cynthia Orgeron's contact with the family, had no knowledge of the origins of the plastic doll, nor of any rights that the family might have granted for the doll to be made by others. $35-40/each MIB.

Celluloid

As bisque began to fade as a medium of choice for dolls, a number of previously known materials began to be used to produce miniature dolls in quantity. Celluloid was known for a long time. An American, John Wesley Hyatt, invented the first synthetic plastic, cellulose nitrate, in 1868. Hyatt improved on the formula of an Englishman, Alexander Parkes, mixing cellulose, nitric acid, camphor, and cotton seeds to form a moldable paste that became tough yet slightly elastic when cooled. He found that dyes and pigments could be added to the material to make the object almost any color desired. Hyatt was looking for a replacement for ivory that could be used to make billiard balls, piano keys, combs, knife handles, and jewelry. Hyatt's material, trade named Celluloid, was soon in demand to make a wide range of products, generally replacing a more expensive or scarce natural material.

Cellulose nitrate had a drawback when it came to making toys, however. It was highly flammable. The development of synthetic plastic materials continued slowly over the next few decades, with some improvement in flammability. Tennessee Eastman Company developed a less flammable material in 1911, cellulose acetate. A major breakthrough occurred in 1932 when Tennessee Eastman developed a variation of cellulose acetate, Tenite, which could be formed by any of the three principal technologies for molding objects: injection, compression, and extrusion. It was the development of these molding technologies, replacing the traditional blow molding used by the early producers, which would later help make mass production of safe celluloid toys possible.

Celluloid filled the need for low-cost, easily produced material. Perhaps the best known German producer was Rheinische Gummi, later named Schildkrötwerke, Schildkröt being the German word for a turtle, the firm's trademark. This wistful German costumed doll measured 4.75". She was marked with the turtle in a diamond together with "12½ Germany" on her back. $25.

In 1895 Lenel Bensinger Co., in Mannheim, Germany, recorded the turtle as the first symbol for a celluloid doll. By 1899, Rheinische Gummi and the Celluloid Fabrik Co. made celluloid dolls from a less flammable mixture they had developed, and used a turtle within a diamond as their trademark. Rheinische

Gummi eventually became Schildkrötwerke, Schildkröt being the German word for "turtle". Rheinische Gummi, in addition to making celluloid dolls, exported doll parts to the United States in abundance. In 1903, celluloid dolls could resemble wax dolls as the result of a new bisque overlay. Dolls were produced in Europe, Japan, and the United States. Famous companies who made dolls of celluloid included Germany's Minerva, the maker of metal head dolls, Kammer & Reinhardt, Kestner, and Celba, Horsman in the United States, as well as Petitcollin and Societe Industrielle de Celluloid in France. The Societe first advertised celluloid dolls in 1909, and, in addition to larger dolls, made small, jointed Jeanne D'Arc dolls, hallmarked "SIC" inside of a diamond. Petitcollin had commercial success with its Petit Collin doll in 1924, and between 1930 and 1957 was one of the most successful French doll makers, specializing in souvenir dolls made from celluloid. Poland was known for lovely celluloid heads. Evidently, many of the German celluloid heads were sent to Italy to be decorated by Italian girls.

The German firm of Buschow & Beck, best known for metal head dolls, also produced celluloid dolls, marking them under their "Minerva" tradename until they ceased operation in 1950. The 8.5" girl was marked "MINERVA/ Germany/8 ½" along with Minerva's helmet trademark. *From the collection of Swantje Köhler. Photo courtesy of Swantje Köhler.* $45-55.

Manufacturers in many nations made celluloid dolls. The two 3.25" costumed dolls pictured left and center were made by Petitcollin in France. Petitcollin had commercial success with its Petit Collin doll in 1924, and between 1930 and 1957 was one of the most successful French doll makers, specializing in souvenir dolls made from celluloid. The doll on the right is the previously described German Schildkröt. The simply dressed dolls in the rear, measuring 3.625" were marked Japan. $5-25/each.

Initially, dolls emerged with cloth bodies and only limbs and heads of celluloid. By 1908, a totally celluloid doll was available. At first the dolls were not jointed. Celluloid had its good and bad characteristics: it was lightweight and easy to clean, but was easily crushed and broken, and colors were known to fade. There were also different grades of celluloid. Fine quality celluloid was said to resemble ivory while the cheaper grade produced an overly pink doll with a rough exterior finish.

In 1913 the first celluloid Kewpie Doll, based on Rosie O'Neill's comic strip character, was made. J.D. Kestner in Germany made quality celluloid Kewpies to replace their bisque versions. The Japanese firm founded by Moto and Tomokichi Sekiguchi, bearing their name, made their own version of Kewpie dolls, named "Cupid" as well as a Betty Boop carnival prize knock-off known as "Boopsie." United States firms made inexpensive Kewpies as well. The Kewpie helped to make celluloid a favored material for small doll production. The doll kept its popularity throughout the 1930s, and one of the small dolls was included with other icons in the time capsule buried at New York's 1939 World's Fair. Dollhouse dolls were also made of celluloid. Dolls usually represented either children or babies and ranged in size from 3" to 6" tall, appropriate for dollhouse use.

Japanese manufacturers often copied the Kewpie look for their dolls. The bridesmaid in her crepe paper dress was marked with the Chrysanthemum mark. The bride, groom, minister, and attendant each measured 3.75". $10/each.

American producers embraced the technology. The Viscoloid Company founded in 1901 in Leominster, Massachusetts, became one of the largest producers of celluloid holiday novelties and dolls. Recognizing the dominance of the Germans in the field, Viscoloid hired a German designer, Paul Kramme, to assist them. They were so successful that they were purchased by E. I. du Pont de Nemours and Company in the mid 20s and continued to turn out large quantities of dolls throughout the 1930s. Another Massachusetts firm, Irwin Corporation, claimed to have the biggest celluloid toy factory in the United States by 1940. Companies such as Parsons-Jackson Company of Ohio produced celluloid babies. The danger of flammability, however, caused United States manufacturers to reduce their celluloid toy production in the late 1930s. The new stronger plastics developed during and after the war prompted United States manufacturers to abandon the material. German, French, and Japanese producers continued to make small celluloid dolls until the late 1950s, however.

5.5" little girl and 5" little boy are celluloid dolls made c. 1930s. Both had molded hair and painted features. The girl was marked with a star on her back. She was jointed at shoulder and hips, while the boy was jointed only at the shoulders. He was marked "Made in USA." on his back. They are pictured with "Grand Rapids" furniture. Both have been redressed. *From the collection of Dian Zillner. Photo courtesy of Suzanne Silverthorne.* $25-35/each.

Major United States manufacturers such as Viscoloid Company and Irwin Corporation challenged German and Japanese manufacturers with domestically made products. The stylishly dressed 4.5" Viscoloid girl on the left was, in fact, a toothbrush holder. The boy on the right, marked "Irwin," was made as a baby's rattle. The Irwin baby, seated on a Jaydon toilet, found its way into many plastic dollhouse furniture settings. $10-20/each.

Composition and The Effanbee Company

Composition is a term applied to dolls made from a mixture of sawdust and glue with added resins, starches, and clays, sealed with shellac, varnish, or lacquer. Composition could be pressed into molds taking the shapes common to all other media. It was heavier and sturdier than *papier mâché*, and often used to make doll bodies after the 1870s. It wasn't until around 1910 that heads made from composition were introduced. While it was used in Germany and France, it became very popular with American manufacturers who did not have porcelain skills. It was a readily available substitute for German bisque that was unobtainable during WWI and immediately thereafter. Japanese manufacturers adopted the medium in the late 1920s-30s. The medium reached its peak in the 1930s and 1940s, but was quickly replaced by plastics in the post WWII period. Composition was brittle and could break if dropped. It absorbed water, causing surface crazing, bubbling, and some disintegration, making it less than desirable for a doll that might take an occasional bath or need a good cleaning. While many composition dolls are in the mid-sized 14-18" range, there are some wonderful examples of miniature dolls that merit discussion.

In 1910 Bernard Fleischaker and Hugo Baum, taking the first letter of their last names, founded the Effanbee Company in New Jersey. By 1912 they had made the decision to focus their company on the production of dolls that could compete with German doll makers. Over the next century, Effanbee created a vast array of dolls, made from composition to vinyl, and its name is still in existence today.

6" composition Wee Patsy dolls were produced by the Effanbee Company beginning in 1932. The dolls had molded hair, painted features, and were jointed at the shoulders and hips. Clothing differentiated the dolls by gender. Their changes of clothing are pictured on the clothes tree and on the bed. All of the clothing is original. *From the collection of Dian Zillner. Photo courtesy of Suzanne Silverthorne.* Dolls in "played with condition" with two sets of original clothing, $275+/pr.

First introduced in 1928, Effanbee's composition "Patsy" became one of their most famous dolls. Bernard Lipfert, a German immigrant sculptor and toy maker, designed the doll. Well proportioned, she was created in the likeness of a real child. With puckered lips and bobbed hair, she was stylish and quite lovable. F&B was one of the first companies to recognize the importance of a doll's wardrobe, and her numerous outfits and accessories made her all the more popular. Even in 1942, when key materials were rationed, F&B offered a doll's sewing set for their *Wee Patsy* doll. The set included enough precut fabric and trim to make a slip, bathrobe, dress, and coat, ensuring that Patsy would remain well dressed. The sewing kit, including a doll, appeared in the Montgomery Wards *Christmas Book* and cost $1.10. *Patsy* was such a hit that Effanbee reinvented her over and over. There were as many as 11 versions of the original *Patsy*, smaller and larger, all using the same adorable face and all claiming some form of the name Patsy - *Patsy Ann, Patsykins, Patsyette* and *Wee Patsy*. Effanbee introduced other very successful dolls such as *Skippy*, *Grumpy, Bubbles,* and *Dy-Dee*. The list goes on indefinitely, making the company one of the most prolific in the commercial doll field.

Wee Patsy was the smallest doll in Effanbee's series of *Patsy* dolls and was first marketed in 1930. Made from a composition material like the other members of her extended family, the doll is approximately 5.75" tall and jointed at the arms and hips. Her hair, eyes, mouth, socks, and shoes were painted. On her back she was marked "EFFANBEE WEE-PAT." She was dressed either as a boy or a girl. She became the primary inhabitant of a very famous dollhouse castle, even though she was not originally created with royalty in mind.

Colleen Moore, the famous silent screen actress of the 1920s, was a miniaturist at heart. As a young girl, then known as Kathleen Morrison, she had dreamed of a fairy castle in the clouds, and her dreams came true in 1928 when she commissioned Horace Jackson, a famous Hollywood set designer, to draw up plans for an elaborate miniature castle. The childhood fantasy of Colleen Moore became a reality. Over a seven year period, with the guidance of her friend, noted interior designer Harold Grieve, the enthusiastic support of her father, Charles Morrison, and efforts of over 700 artisans and craftsmen who used nothing but the finest jewels and materials in its creation, the castle became a reality. When the palace was finished, Colleen Moore traveled with it to many cities across the United States raising money for children's charities.

Effenbee packaged its Wee Patsy as the "Fairy Princess" selling it in a box imprinted with a stylized copy of a Colleen Moore castle. It also came packaged in a suitcase box of varying sizes containing castle information and additional clothes. This famous Patsy was not "wee" any longer, but was forever remembered as the Fairy Princess doll, and, maybe in Colleen Moore's mind, as the little girl who had always dreamed of a castle in the sky.

Madame Alexander Company created a new group of "Wee Patsy's" in 1995 after it purchased Effanbee. Although this doll is vinyl, it is painted to resemble the original composition doll. When the Robert Tonner Doll Company acquired Effanbee in 2002 from Madame Alexander, they also issued a vinyl 5" Wee Patsy. This doll has a painted face, rooted hair, and removable shoes and socks.

The Fairy Princess Colleen Moore dollhouse doll produced by the Effanbee Company during the mid 1930s. The 6" composition doll was really a special version of the company's Wee Patsy doll manufactured to tie in with the publicity generated by the national tour of the Colleen Moore dollhouse. *From the collection of Dian Zillner. Photo courtesy of Suzanne Silverthorne.* $375 MIB.

Although Colleen Moore wrote that inhabitants had never been designed or made for her Castle, if a child were lucky enough to see the fairy castle in one of the touring cities in 1935, he or she could also purchase a doll called "Fairy Princess, The Colleen Moore Dollhouse Doll." She wore a metal pin designating her official title. This doll was F&B's Wee Patsy. The Colleen Moore Fairy Castle, containing more than 20,000 miniature antiques, including early gifts from her father, is now permanently housed at the Museum of Science and Industry in Chicago. $275 w/pin.

Perhaps the first United States made composition dolls actually marketed as dollhouse dolls, were produced by Effanbee. In the late 1930s Effanbee introduced a five-member family made from wood pulp composition. The dolls proved fragile, and probably difficult to make. In the winter of 1940, Effanbee reintroduced three members of the family made from the supposedly unbreakable cellulose acetate. Universal Plastics Corporation molded them for the F&B Doll Company. A father and mother were later added, but production ceased in 1941. Dolls were made for the Canadian and United States markets. They are clearly marked on their backs: "F AN B, made in USA"; or "F AN B, made in Canada." Effanbee dollhouse dolls were sold in better department stores and toy shops in boxes marked "Effanbee Durable Dolls," and proudly proclaiming "quality made them famous."

When Hugo Baum died in 1940, Bernard Fleischaker moved to the West Coast and started Fleischaker Novelties, leaving the F & B Company to the original founders' sons. As the company converted its production to adopt the new methods and materials required for postwar competitiveness, it began to experience financial troubles, leading to its 1947 sale to Noma Electric, best known for its Christmas tree lights and decorations. Eventually, the ownership of F&B was regained by Hugo Baum, Jr. and others from the original company and remained stable until the early 1970s. While the company has changed hands a number of times since, its subsequent owners, Stanley and Irene Wahlberg, The Madame Alexander Company, and the Robert Tonner Doll Co. have each tried to preserve the magic name: "Effanbee Dolls – Finest and Best."

In the late 1930s Effanbee introduced a five-member composition family. Dolls were sold clothed in simple outfits. Dolls' arms and legs were attached with elastic string, and there was some slight hand-painted detail. Dolls were sold clothed in simple outfits. The composition family measured: father and mother, 4.125"; brother and sister, 3.5"; baby 2.125". The composition proved fragile and dolls in very good condition are hard to find. Pictured dolls exhibit typical "crazing". $150/each in very good condition.

In 1940 Effanbee produced the children in plastic. Interestingly, as of November 1940, the mother and father dolls had not been molded, making them harder to find today. This family, with facial features of the mother and daughter apparently copied from an unnamed F&B doll introduced in 1926, was made only in 1940-1941. Non-poisonous, vegetable coloring paints were applied by hand to the molded hair and facial features of these dolls. Boy and girl dolls had painted socks in addition to their shoes. The plastic F&B father and mother dolls were approximately 4.5" tall; brother and sister, 3.75"; baby, 2.25". $125/each.

Composition Dolls of Canzler & Hoffman

The German company, Canzler & Hoffmann, had its beginnings in 1906. The company was named after its two founders. The firm sold a variety of dolls and doll products, including doll clothing. Later, the firm obtained porcelain doll heads from Schoenau & Hoffmeister and marketed assembled dolls. One of their small baby dolls was an all-bisque model, wire jointed at the shoulders and hips. It had painted features, molded hair and on its back, and was marked "1125/3 1/0/Germany/CAHO/DRG." The abbreviation "CAHO" trademark was finally registered in the 1920s. The firm applied for a variety of German patents over the years including a doll body in 1923, a mama doll in 1925, and a doll with a leather body, celluloid head and arms in 1927.

The company was advertising miniature dolls in 1927 but it wasn't until 1928-29 that dollhouse dolls were included in their advertising. By 1930, dollhouse dolls were being made with composition heads, flat metal hands, long narrow metal feet, wrapped flexible limbs, molded hair (some of the little girls featured applied wigs), and painted features. Eventually, the firm offered families of dolls as well as individual models. Boys, girls, mothers, fathers, and grandparent dolls were all available. A chilling German schoolroom room box was produced in the late 1930s to early 1940s. Decorated with military themed wallpaper, it included a teacher wearing a "Brownshirt" SA uniform and armband, and six students dressed in the brown uniforms of the Hitler Youth, some with high boots.

Production was suspended during World War II. After the war, dolls were made with the materials available to the company. It is likely that leftover doll parts made before the war were also used to produce the dolls. According to German researcher and author Swantje Köhler-Verlag, dolls with plastic-wrapped limbs were made at this time.

After Hoffmann's death in the 1950s, the company trademark was changed to Caco using the first two letters of Canzler's last name and the first two letters of the German town Coburg, where the factory was then located.

Dolls continued to have composition type heads with metal hands and feet for many years, but these body parts were molded more distinctively with separate thumbs and different types of shoes. Molded hairstyles also changed over the years to reflect the changing times. By the early 1960s, lady dolls were wearing high-heeled shoes as pictured in FAO Schwarz' Christmas catalog of 1961.

Two Caho women dolls made during early years of production. The firm advertised dollhouse dolls by the 1928-29 season. Each doll had a composition head with molded hair and features. Dolls such as the one on the right were packaged in a box marked as shown in the inset with the original Caho trademark. The wrapping on her flexible limbs was a thread like material. Her hands and feet were metal and feet were large, giving her stability. *Trademark from the collection of Countess Edith v. Zedtwitz. Trademark photo courtesy of Count Alexander v. Zedtwitz.* Unboxed, $75/each. $100/each.

Early grandmother and grandfather dolls wearing their original clothing. Both have composition type heads, molded hair, and features that include visible wrinkles. Metal hands on the first version dolls were nearly flat with no separation between the fingers and thumb. *From the collection of Countess Edith v. Zedtwitz. Original photo courtesy of Count Alexander v. Zedtwitz.* $75/each.

Early 1930s Caho family members were flexible with wire limbs wrapped with flesh-colored cotton tape. Dolls also had heads made of a composition type material with metal hands and feet. In the 1930s both the fathers' and the mothers' metal shoes were made with no heels and came up to their ankles. Both the boy and girl dolls wore one strap "Mary Jane" shoes. Hands were still flat metal. The man measured 5.5"; the woman, 5"; children, 3.25". $250/family of four.

Caco dolls were made with a wire armature, padded with layers of excelsior, and then wrapped either with flesh-colored thread in earliest models or flesh-colored tape on 1930s and later. Heads were made of composition and were attached by wire to the armature. Wire was molded into the hands and feet and then wrapped on the frame.

Caho/Caco modified hair styles and shapes of faces, hands, and feet over the years. At left is a 1930s mother with flat hands. The mother holding the baby has a more upswept hairstyle, but still has flat hands. The 4.5" doll with a yet different upswept hairstyle, dressed in a red suit, was featured immediately after the war in an advertisement carrying the Caho trademark. She wore large brown oxfords and brown stockings. Her limbs were wrapped in a plastic type material. Hands were somewhat cupped and thumbs now separated from the rest of the fingers. The mother on the right is from the early 1960s. Her head was remolded and she wore cast metal high-heeled shoes. Her costume was less formal and up-to-date. *Dolls from the collections of Patty Cooper, Lois Freeman and Dian Zillner. Original photos courtesy of Suzanne Silverthorne and Lois Freeman.* $35-75/each depending on age.

Four different styles of Caho/Caco little girl dolls. All of them had composition type heads with molded hair and painted features and metal hands and feet. The first two oldest dolls wear painted Mary Jane shoes used in the 1930s. The tallest doll measures 3.75". The 3.25 doll in the red plaid dress was made in the late 1930s. The third doll, measuring a little over 3" in the black and white dress, probably dates shortly after WWII. She has a different molded hairstyle, cupped metal hands that continue above the wrists, and metal feet that include painted socks. Instead of being wrapped in cotton tape, her limbs were wrapped in plastic tape. She had red dots on the top of her feet. The fourth doll, with yet another molded short hairstyle measured 3.25" tall. She was a later doll made after the trademark changed to Caco in the early 1950s. This style little girl was still being sold in 1959. *From the collection of Patty Cooper. Photo courtesy of Suzanne Silverthorne.* $30-60/ each depending on age.

Male dolls dating from the 1930s to 1950s underwent similar change. The first doll on left was 5.25" and dates from the 1930s. The second and third dolls are approximately 5.5" tall. The doll in the sweater, likely from the late 1930s, had a different head, but the same smaller feet and closed hands used on the first doll. The third doll has bigger feet, cupped hands and wears bulky felt clothing with cuffed pants c. 1950s. The final doll wore more tailored clothing as pictured in a Mark Farmer catalog for 1961-62. He was 5.75" tall. All dolls had composition heads, metal hands and feet, and limbs wrapped with cotton tape. Each of the heads was made from a different mold. *From the collection of Patty Cooper. Photo courtesy of Suzanne Silverthorne.* $35-75/ each depending on age.

Four different styles of Caho/Caco boy dolls. The first three dolls had composition type heads, molded hair, painted features, and metal hands and feet. The oldest 3.25" doll from the 1930s wore painted "Mary Jane" shoes. His limbs were wrapped in cotton cloth. The boy doll dressed in the green felt short pants was 3.5" and made immediately postwar. His limbs were wrapped with plastic tape. His feet included painted red spots on the tops. The boy dressed in pajamas was a mate to the little girl doll dressed in pink pajamas pictured earlier and includes the same type hands and feet dating from the 1950s. The boy in the red sweater was slightly taller than 3.5" and had metal feet, plastic hands, and a plastic head. He dates from the 1960s or later. A boy wearing this same outfit was pictured in the 1961 FAO Schwarz Christmas catalog. *From the collection of Patty Cooper. Photo courtesy of Suzanne Silverthorne.* $30-60/ each depending on age.

In addition to family dolls, Caco dolls were also dressed as professionals. A nurse and doctor set of dolls was produced mid to late 1960s. The nurse and doctor had new hairdos and plastic hands, plastic heads, and metal feet. The maid, with flat soled metal feet and composition head, was pictured in a 1959 FAO Schwarz Christmas catalog. An unusual chef and golfer were also produced as Caco dolls. Both dolls had composition heads, and cupped metal hands and feet. The chef was 6" tall not including his hat. *From the collection of Gail and Ray Carey. Photograph courtesy of Gail Carey.* $40-80/each depending on age.

Caco obviously aimed at the United States market with dolls in "regional" American clothing. A 3.75" cowgirl. $50.

Caco made a smaller scale line of character dolls. The 3" chimney sweep, with Caco hang-tag, had a plastic head with molded hat. Feet were metal, as were hands molded in a different stubby style. It is not known if family dolls were made in this scale. $50.

In addition to being sold individually throughout the 1950s and 60s, FAO Schwarz and others marketed Caco dolls as family dolls to be used in dollhouses. Two different sizes of these dolls were being produced by the late 1950s. Smaller dolls were 1:18 scale while the larger dolls were 1:12 scale. The firm also sold a modern schoolroom set during this time period that included a Caco teacher and four pupils, four student desks, a teacher desk and chair, and a blackboard priced at $6.95.

As the years passed, materials used to produce the Caco dolls began to change. First, plastic hands replaced metal hands of earlier years, and then plastic heads were added to the dolls. Later even the metal feet were discontinued and replaced with plastic. It is this model that is still sold today.

Larger scale children were also dressed in peasant dress through the years. Pictured are 1950s 3.5" boy and girl, sold as a set. They had composition heads, cupped metal hands, and metal feet without dots. Limbs were wrapped with cloth tape. Girls were wigged with pigtails. The seated little girl, slightly over 3" tall is newer, but she, too, had the composition head with metal hands and feet. She carried a Shackman tag with "Caco Flexible" on the back. She also had a braided wig. She sits in a rocking chair that was made to accompany a peasant dollhouse sold by FAO Schwarz in the late 1950s and early 1960s. *From the collection of Dian Zillner. Photo courtesy of Suzanne Silverthorne.* $25.

Caco was importing to the United States immediately after the war. In this *House and Garden* ad published during the 1948 and 1949 Christmas seasons, the pictured family was the variety with plastic tape, typical of the period.

Sometimes on larger scale 3.25" dolls, c. late 1940s/early1950s, wigs were simply glued onto the heads of little boy dolls. They were tape-wrapped with cupped metal hands and "red dot" feet. $25/each.

Set of 1:12 scale Caco family dolls similar to those pictured in the 1961-62 Mark Farmer catalog. The father was 5.75"; mother, 5.25"; son; 3.25"; daughter, 3.5". The dolls were priced from $1.00 to $1.95 each. All of the dolls pictured with the box were wearing their original clothing. They had composition type heads, metal hands and feet, and cotton tape-wrapped limbs. Mother and daughter were wigged. The mother wore cast metal high heel shoes. *From the collection of Dian Zillner. Photo courtesy of Suzanne Silverthorne.* $75-100/set MIB.

In addition to the 1:12 scale dolls, 1:18 scale Caco dolls were also produced. This set included a 4" man and woman, and 2.25" boy and girl. Dolls were made with plastic heads, but metal hands and feet. They were bendable and had limbs wrapped in cotton tape. They were pictured in the Shackman 1973 catalog. Notice the woman's flat shoes. *From the collection of Dian Zillner. Photo courtesy of Suzanne Silverthorne.* $75-100/set MIB.

Dolls were also offered in peasant dress as early as the 1959 and 1961 FAO Schwarz Christmas catalogs. The dolls, in 1:18 scale, were from 2.25" to 4" tall. While these dolls are dressed somewhat differently, they are the same sizes as those pictured in the ad, but are probably from the late 1970s or early 1980s. In this later set dolls had plastic heads, hands, and feet with limbs wrapped in cotton cloth. *From the collection of Dian Zillner. Photo courtesy of Suzanne Silverthorne.* $50+/set.

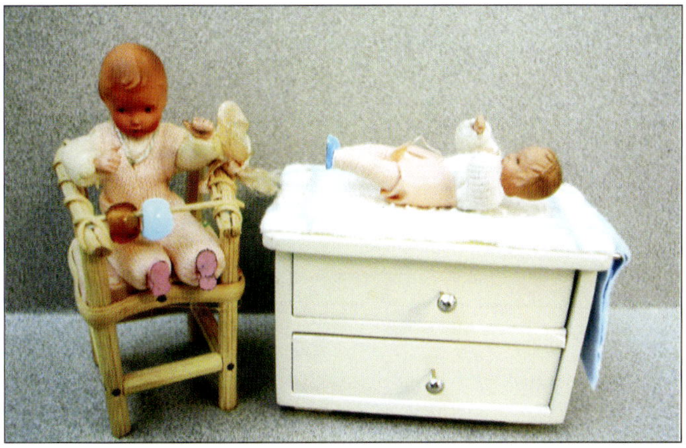

Caco baby dolls were sold in a variety of styles in the 1970s. Many of them came with a special accessory such as a basket, cradle, or stroller. The Shackman catalog in 1973 offered several of these items. The pictured small baby was 2.25" tall. It came with the two-drawer chest. The baby had a plastic head but its hands and feet were metal. The larger baby, sitting in a high chair, is nearly 3". He had metal hands and feet but the doll was also produced with a plastic head, hands, and feet. *From the collection of Gail and Ray Carey. Photograph courtesy of Gail Carey.* $20-25/set.

By the 1980s, Caco, as well as other doll makers, tried different ways to reduce the cost of their dolls so they could compete with low-priced dolls made principally in Hong Kong. Unfortunately, quality lessened, as well. This family had an orange-hued foam tape covering their wire frames. Heads, hands, and feet were all-plastic. The father stood 4.5": mother 4"; baby, 2". $15/each.

Set of three Caco dolls from the 1990s. The man measured 5.25" tall; woman, 5"; boy, 3". They had plastic heads, hands, and feet. The woman still wore high heels, although her clothing was much more casual. The original German Caco box is also shown. *From the collection of Dian Zillner. Photo courtesy of Suzanne Silverthorne.* $25 each.

Grandparents from Caco's 2008 offering see their grandson off to school, still carrying a backpack similar to postwar school children dolls. Made in 1:15 scale, Grandfather stands 5.5"; grandmother, 5"; boy 3.5". They each have plastic heads, hands, and shoes. $20-35/each.

A late 1960s vintage Caco school set in an FAO Schwarz schoolroom. The two dolls in front of the classroom are earlier versions. The girl with backpack is immediately postwar from the Caho era. The taller girl carrying a book bag over her shoulder is from the late 1930s. 1960s dolls all had plastic heads and hands, but metal feet. Teacher stands 5.5"; children 3.5". Schoolroom set, $200. Older dolls $35-60 depending on age.

Rubber Dolls

Rubber and gutta percha had been used to make doll components, without much success since about 1825. Natural rubber and gutta percha are natural latex saps gathered from certain trees, generally found in the tropics. The two materials are similar but have different properties. Natural rubber will return to its original shape, if stretched. Gutta percha is pliable but will not return to its shape if stretched. It is moldable, however, and objects could be made by pouring the heated material into molds. Neither material holds up well over time. When exposed to air, objects will darken, harden, and lose their pliability, crack, craze, and crumble. When Charles Goodyear developed the vulcanization process in 1839, he appeared to solve some of the problems associated with natural latex. By adding sulphur and then heating the latex, Goodyear made a stronger, more pliable material that stood up better to heat and exposure to the air. Unfortunately it did not entirely solve the problems of drying and cracking. Many doll makers attempted to improve upon the material and found some use for it in heads, bodies, and skin coatings. It never rivaled other materials for making dolls, however, and it fell into disuse until the late1930s when the search for bisque substitutes intensified.

One firm, Fred K. Braitling Company of Bridgeport, Connecticut, made a remarkable effort to produce a line of rubber dollhouse dolls. The Braitling family had a long history in the doll business tracing back to its patriarch, Charles F. Braitling. Charles, born in Paris around 1840, emigrated to the United States and settled in New Haven, Connecticut. He worked in leather as a carriage trimmer and superintendent of a carriage factory in Bridgeport, Connecticut. While on a return trip to Paris, Charles became interested in fine French bisque dolls and apparently saw a market in the United States for fine dolls and toys. Returning to New Haven in 1868 he opened a toy store, one of only three in the country.

A lot of his adult clientele favored china head dolls, but Charles wasn't happy with their sawdust bodies or the manner in which they were sewn. He decided to manufacture his own doll body, using his wife Anna, as a model. He created a doll body of fine quality muslin, hand-cut in his shop. He then expanded his line to include a full kid doll body and sold both types in his store, in at least 20 sizes from 8 to 28". Bodies were ink-stamped on their backs with the Braitling name. Charles had another sideline that he had started in 1869, the crafting of doll shoes. He felt that his kid doll body deserved kid shoes and began to create them. Customers would often ask for shoes for their dolls as well. The sideline was so successful, that Charles sold his toy shop, and by 1891 incorporated a new company focused on tiny footwear, C.F. Braitling & Sons, located in a small factory on Cedar St. in Bridgeport. His hunch proved correct, not only did French and German porcelain dolls need shoes, but the new American made composition dolls needed fashionable footwear as well.

In 1897, Fred K. Braitling, Charles' son took over the reins, eventually renaming the company after himself. According to Miriam Formanek-Brunell in her book *Made To Play House: Dolls & the Commercialization of American Girlhood, 1830-1930* (pg. 55), Fred Braitling "launched his career at age 12, sweeping the floors of his father's doll shoe factory. First pushing a broom and then paper, Fred rose steadily in the hierarchy as sons of entrepreneurs often did." His two-story factory was located at 104 Silliman Avenue in Bridgeport, Connecticut, where machines were capable of producing 300 pairs of shoes an hour. The production of doll bodies was discontinued in 1916 when imported German doll heads became unavailable. At the time, Fred was making over 30 different styles of shoes in all colors and styles to replicate the shoe fashions of the overall female population. Sandals and stockings were made for all of Ideal's Shirley Temple dolls. Also produced were doll stockings, wigs, and other accessories. In prosperous times, his factory could employ 30-50 people. America was known for its finely crafted doll shoes, and New England was the center of this activity. Fred built his business rapidly. He retired in 1934 and turned the company over to his brother, Ted. Fred Braitling died in 1935.

Ted, twenty one years younger than his brother, had also started in his father's business as a teenager, and was apparently comfortable at running it. He became a frequent advertiser in Playthings magazine. In a March 1938 *Playthings* magazine ad for the New York Toy Fair, Fred K. Braitling, Inc., was advertising doll shoes, doll stockings, doll wigs, and dollhouse dolls. He exhibited at the Toy Fairs until 1943, when toy production in the United States virtually ceased.

The True family included "Grand-daddy" and Grandmother, each with a distinctly molded head sculpted to show their age lines. Grandmother's bun hair style, was slightly old fashioned for the time. Here, the True Nurse assists them. Both her shoes and stockings are painted white. Although rubber tends to become brittle, discolor, and crack over time, the pictured nurse is in excellent condition, making her a rare find. Nurse, $125 in excellent condition. Grandparents, $75/each in average condition.

"The True Family, Real People Dolls" were introduced by Fred K Braitling, Inc., in 1938. Made in 1" scale, father was 6"; mother, 5.5"; boy, 4.5"; girl 4". The dolls were dressed in clothes appropriate to the period. Males had felt suits with a "dickey" resembling a starched dress shirt. Felt ties were glued under the collar. Shoes were black metal. Female dolls wore clothing of many styles. Seams on clothes were machine sewn, with collars glued. One-inch scale females wore white or black shoes with a small heel. Some female dolls had painted legs to resemble stockings. All dolls had molded painted hair and hand-painted facial features. Here, Mother and "Daddy" True converse with the suited doll wearing an up to date hat. Family members, $75/each in average condition.

Danny True attends school with the primly dressed school teacher. The teacher was not just the mother doll dressed in a black dress. She had a different molded head with a severe hairstyle. Her stockings were painted on with a medium brown paint, typical of the silk stockings of the 1930s. Teacher $75 in average condition. Danny, $75 in average condition.

Linda, the True's African American maid, and Amos, their waiter, serve cocktails to the True's guests. The man's tuxedo had black satin lapels and pant leg stripes. The woman in the silk dress was catalogued both with and without a cloche hat. Amos was sold carrying a serving tray, as was the French maid, Suzette (not pictured). Linda wore a miniature crocheted lace cap. $100/each in average condition.

Braitling offered a wide variety of dolls, costumed in the most up-to-date style. His 1939 catalog shows twenty-four different variations of the "True" family. The catalog drawings illustrate the different hair styles on the women, indicating that the heads were separately molded and added to the bodies before the final rubber coating was applied.

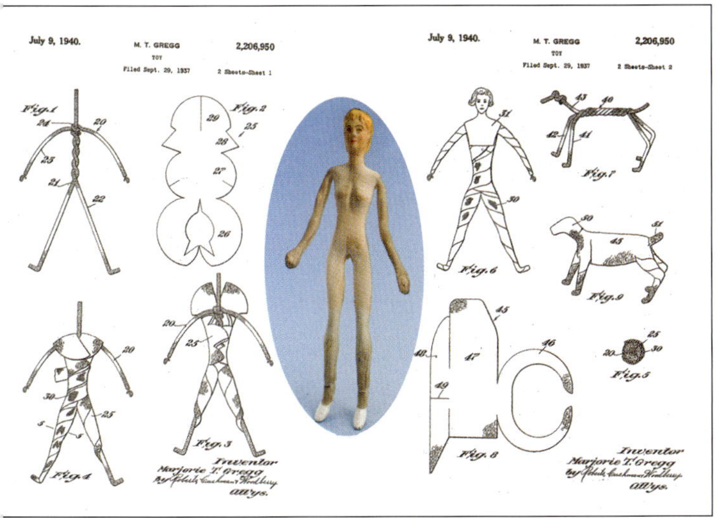

The dolls were the brainchild of Marjorie True Gregg. She applied for her first patents in 1936 and 1937. Ms. Gregg's labor-intensive design started with a twisted, fiber-coated, wire frame. A cloth "blank" was then placed around the frame to create further bulk and shape, but carefully cut to enable bending of the joints. Fabric tape was then wrapped and glued around the body. A molded head and shoulder plate combination was added. The whole assembly was then placed into a two-part mold and coated with rubber. Starting in 1939, a molded metal foot and ankle was attached to the frame after the rubber coating, apparently replacing a molded rubber foot, to aid the doll in standing. The metal frames were subcontracted as was modeling of the doll heads.

It is believed that at some point 3/4" scale dolls were added to Braitling's line called "TinyKins." Males were 4.5", females 4" and sitting baby was 1.5". These dolls had the same look, clothing, and features as the 1" scale line. Dolls were sold in a plastic bag with a 1.5" x 3.25" paper label reading: "TinyKins; Doll House Doll; ¾" Scale." $85/each in excellent condition.

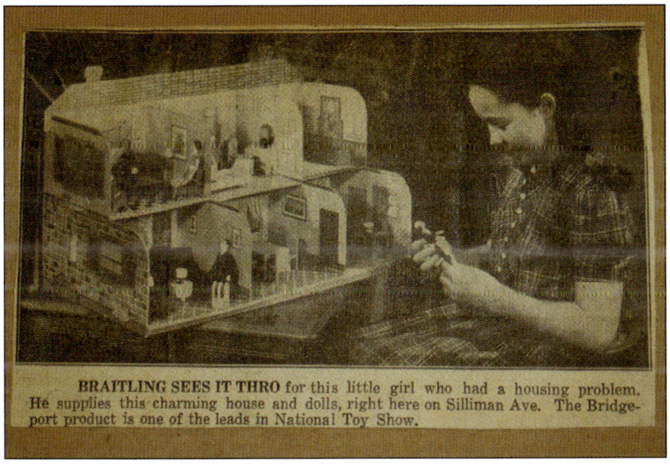
BRAITLING SEES IT THRO for this little girl who had a housing problem. He supplies this charming house and dolls, right here on Silliman Ave. The Bridgeport product is one of the leads in National Toy Show.

Braitling often advertised his dolls residing in a cardboard Strombecker dollhouse as seen in this March 1941 *Connecticut Sunday Herald* ad relating his success at the 1941 Toy Show.

Ted Braitling helped convince dealers to carry his line of "Real People" dolls by creating a complete beach scene featuring his inventory that was installed in his New York City, Toy Building showroom. The display idea was featured in a 1941 *Playthings* press release.

One of his biggest contributions to the company was the 1938 introduction of a new line of rubber dollhouse dolls, "True Family Real People Dolls." The idea for "real people dolls" was that of Marjorie True Gregg of South Tamworth, New Hampshire. In a letter quoted by Janet Johl, in *Fascinating Story of Dolls* (at page 198), Ms. Gregg wrote: "I hope both as toys that children may play with, and as material for artistic creative work my own dolls will someday be important." Gregg wanted the dolls to be fully flexible, sanitary and washable. Apparently, a licensing arrangement was made with Ted Braitling, and the "The True Family, Real People Dolls" were introduced in 1938 selling for about $1 apiece. With over two dozen varieties, they were also sold in various combinations as boxed sets. It is believed that at some point 1:18 scale dolls were added to the line.

In 1938 Braitling also offered over-stuffed, fabric-covered furniture to accompany the doll line and to be used in the cardboard and fiberboard dollhouses of the time. Cardboard frames were covered with cotton upholstery and draped with a patterned percale fabric to create chairs and ottomans. In 1941 a line of pink, overstuffed bedroom furniture was added to the offering.

Braitling continued to tinker with the dolls. A 1939 *Playthings* ad stated that the "True Family" had been greatly improved and the line expanded for the coming season: "Dolls are now made with life-like molded hands and arms, molded in one piece with the head and shoulders, but still retaining flexibility." According to a December *Bridgeport Sunday Post* article in 1939, the dolls did very well for the Christmas season. The dolls were requested by the New York Stock Exchange to illustrate a point in a roundtable discussion. A jeweler in Los Angeles ordered a bride, groom, and minister for his window display. Braitling also announced that he was considering entering a new market, offering the dolls for use in store display dioramas.

The war ended the production of the dolls and doll shoes, as rubber was no longer available for consumer use and leather was severely rationed. By 1943 the company had stopped advertising in Playthings, although a small ad appeared in *Toys & Novelties* magazine in 1944-45, but the business was no longer listed as operating in the 1946 Bridgeport directory. Obviously facing a switch to the new materials of the postwar, and needing to redevelop a workforce skilled in the sewing of miniatures, Mr. Braitling was either unwilling or unable to reopen after the war. Ted Braitling died in 1954 at the age of 63.

Braitling was not the only company to experiment with rubber dollhouse dolls. Dolls known as "Minikins" appeared in the late 1930s to 1940 time period. The figures were rubber, molded in one piece over a wire frame, but do not appear to utilize the True patents. Dolls were made for dollhouse play in two scales. Despite the fact that the dolls are more commonly found than those by Braitling, only one reference to the dolls or their doll makers has been found. The 1940 Boston City Directory lists, "The Small World, Frederick & Beatrice J. Ryan, 34 Greenleaf, Roxbury, Massachusetts."

The Minikins and True Family Dolls, in the end, suffered from the same defects as the rubber dolls of a century earlier. Despite their wire cores that initially aided flexibility, they became brittle and broke as they were exposed to play and the air. The new postwar materials overcame all the defects and added new features.

The larger Minikins family consisted of a 6" father; 5.5", mother; 4" boy and girl. Fingers were lined to give the appearance of separation. Dolls had painted facial features and hair of varied color. Father's shoes were painted black, and mother had painted black pumps. Children, including boys, had painted black Mary Janes. Their cloth clothing was machine sewn. Dolls were not hallmarked. $65/each in excellent condition.

The large scale Minikins children had a variety of costumes and painted detail. Rubber dolls of this type have dried and become brittle over time. Finding examples in excellent condition without crazing is very difficult. $65/each in excellent condition.

Minikins made a 1:18 scale family as well. Smaller figures from father to daughter were 4.5", 4.25", 3.25" and 3.125". The maid doll has been found with a tag taped to the inside of her skirt reading, "Minikins – trade mark miniature mannequins; handmade by The Small World, Boston, MA, Frederick Bld. ©1939, patent pending." FAO Schwarz offered both scales of the five-piece Minikins family in its 1941 and 1942 catalogs. $65/each in excellent condition.

Minikin dolls had some level of popularity, as a family appeared in the December 9, 1940, issue of *Life* as residents of a colonial mansion dollhouse. It was featured as gift ideas for parents emerging from the Depression.

Other manufacturers experimented with rubber. The hairstyles and faces on this family were reminiscent of German painted-bisque dolls. The adults stand 5.25", the girl was 3.5". They were advertised as having composition heads and flexible rubber bodies. They have hardened and cracked with age. A 5-piece family, as pictured, was offered by FAO Schwarz in 1939 for $3.50. The family with maid & cook sold for $4.50. *From the collection of Patty Cooper. Photo courtesy of Patty Cooper.* $85/ each in excellent condition.

Not every rubber doll had a wire interior frame. Some were hollow-molded somewhat like educational dolls of later times. The pictured family of four is 1:12 in height, although they are "chubby" additions to a dollhouse. The 3.75" girl was marked "Repsie" on the bottom of her skirt. The 6" father, 5.375" mother, and 4.25" boy were unmarked. $40/ each in excellent condition.

Chapter 5

When Materials Were Scarce and Creativity Counted

Starting in 1937 with the Japanese invasion of China, the world moved toward a global war. The increasing hostilities had significant effect on the worldwide toy industry as well as on the full range of United States civilian goods production. America became the military supplier to the non-Axis nations before it actually entered the hostilities in 1941. This industrial production led to economic recovery by putting people back to work and giving families money to spend on non-essential goods that had been unaffordable during the Depression. At the same time the impending global war created scarcities of these same goods.

Three primary factors affected civilian production: availability of materials, availability of production capacity, and availability of skilled labor. By April 1941 the war in Asia was making certain materials scarce. Rubber, silk, cork, kapok stuffing, and certain lacquers all were sourced in the Far East. Large chain retailers like Woolworth's and Grant's joined in boycotting Japanese finished goods. Plywood and most metals were being used for aircraft and arms manufacturing. Urea, formaldehyde, and other chemicals used to produce plastics were also used to produce explosives. Even if materials like wood were available in the United States, the ability to find ships to transport them from one coast to another was limited.

In September 1941 it was reported in the industry magazine *Playthings* that aluminum was not available for civilian use. Rationing of many materials was being suggested, as was the need to begin material substitution. Rayon and cotton replaced silk, and later wool. It was recognized that substitutions using plastic would be a short lived strategy, because plastic and the chemicals that produced it would soon be needed for the war effort. Wood and paper were seen as the best long range alternates for toys. Controls were being instituted to regulate price gouging. Industries could apply for exceptions to rationing controls based upon three factors, the most relevant to toys being civilian morale.

After America entered the war, factors affecting the toy industry deteriorated. All materials faced increasing control, while, at the same time, factories were being shifted from consumer to military manufacturing. At first toy factories were not considered for conversion, but as the war progressed all available capacity was being converted. Even if toy factories were not converted, labor was being directed either to critical war production or to the military.

Controls became tighter with continuing regulation of the toy industry by the War Production Board. Metals, rubber, and many plastics became "prohibited materials" in November 1942. In a February 1943 address, Donald Heaney of the Department of Commerce reported, "American-made toys will still retain their power of captivating the imagination of children. For this, parents must thank our toy manufacturers and dealers who, in the face of severe shortages of materials, have successfully maintained the traditionally high educational and recreational standards of American toys."

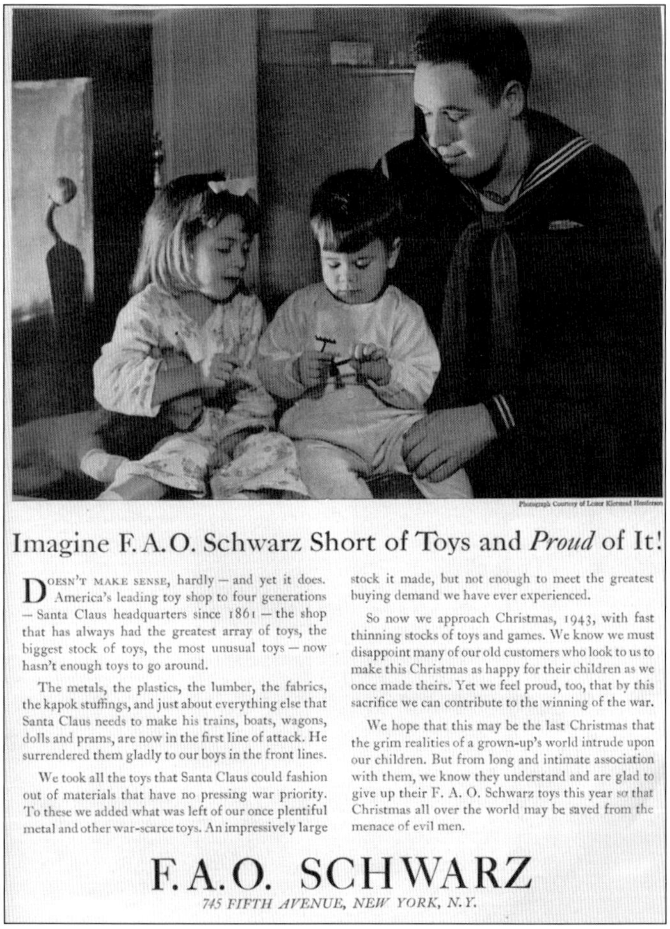

As this December 1943 *House Beautiful* ad proudly announced, some distributors and retailers like FAO Schwarz and Kimport Dolls held stockpiled prewar inventory, but supplies began to run scarce. The large retailers like Sears and Wards continued to carry a limited offering of toys from a variety of sources. Department stores and toy specialty shops, short on help, had shifted from clerks helping customers from behind counters to "cafeteria style" self service, a precursor of modern retailing.

Those dolls and miniatures that were produced were generally constructed of wood, paper, cardboard, or clay. Artisans, either retired or working part time in their homes and selling their products by mail-order, made many of the toys. Those toy manufacturers still able to produce depended on men exempt from military service and men and women working second jobs.

The President of the Toy Manufacturers Association optimistically reported in *Playthings* in early 1944, "American toy manufacturers' traditional ingenuity is being maintained, as evidenced by the toys which are being produced. Buyers are finding a wide variety of toys from which to select." By 1945, however, the annual Toy Fair had been cancelled as the War Mobilization Director asked for a curtailment of all trade shows and conventions. If hostilities had extended much longer, it is clear that home-made toys would be all that was available to entertain American children.

Hand-made Cloth Dolls and Edith Flack Ackley

Cloth dolls have been made since ancient times, but making rag dolls at home became a very popular hobby during World War II. Some women made dolls for their own pleasure or for their young children. Others made dolls to sell for profit, while still others made them to be sent overseas to brighten childrens' holidays in war-torn areas, like the United Kingdom. Many individuals, some working as parts of cottage industries, thrived with this media. Fabrics like silk and wool were scarce, so simpler choices prevailed. An expensive sewing machine was not required.

One well-known artist deserving special mention is Edith Flack Ackley. Born in Greenport, New York, in 1887, she shared artistic talents along with her parents and siblings. One outlet for her handiwork was the rag dolls she made for her sisters. When her husband died during the Depression, Edith honed her design and sewing skills and began making dolls for sale. Her doll making was a source of income to support herself and her daughter. Working from Ackley Studios on MacDougal Street in Manhattan, she and other family members displayed their work.

In addition to making and selling dolls, she started to assemble doll materials in kit form that were sold through the magazine *Women's Home Companion*. In 1938, she published a book, "Dolls To Make For Fun and Profit". Her thinking was that if she could make a livelihood for herself, so could others. The book offered doll making instructions and patterns as well as insight into how other women might likewise profit in this industry. Many women read and used her books as well as her magazine patterns to create unique hand-made dolls.

One chapter in her book was devoted to making dollhouse dolls. Patterns existed for a father, mother, child, and baby. The patterns, as cut but unassembled, ranged in size from an 8" father to a 5" baby. A 5" pattern, when made up, would produce a doll that was approximately 3". Edith instructed that her patterns could be adjusted to create even smaller dolls. She suggested sewing the dolls by hand and using white muslin for their bodies. Fine wool with some luster was recommended for the hair. She gave needlework facial patterns but suggested experimentation using different mediums, like watercolors.

Authentic Ackley dolls were stitched entirely by hand. Edith used Japanese silk crepe for the doll body. When she couldn't get this material during World War II, she switched to cotton crepe. Known for very fine handwork, faces were hand embroidered with dolls sharing similar characteristics. They had rectangular eyes, spaced far apart. She used one thread and a single stitch for their eyebrows and each nostril. Doll shoes were leather. Her dolls were sold in the New York City shop of the infamous spy, Velvelee Dickinson. Later she made smaller 4 " dolls, which were sold through the New York City Women's Exchange. Many of her smaller dolls were packaged with a watercolor painted by her daughter, Telka. Christmas cards picturing her dolls were offered in a catalogue of the doll distributor Mark Farmer. She actively made dolls for decades after the war until arthritis slowed her down in later years. Edith died in November 1970 at the age of 83.

Many patterns and how-to books could be found at the time. Some books were designed for teaching the craft to young children and others were "how-to" manuals for adults. The major pattern companies like McCall's, Simplicity, and Butterick issued patterns for dolls and clothes in the 1940s. This McCall's pattern was copyrighted in 1942.

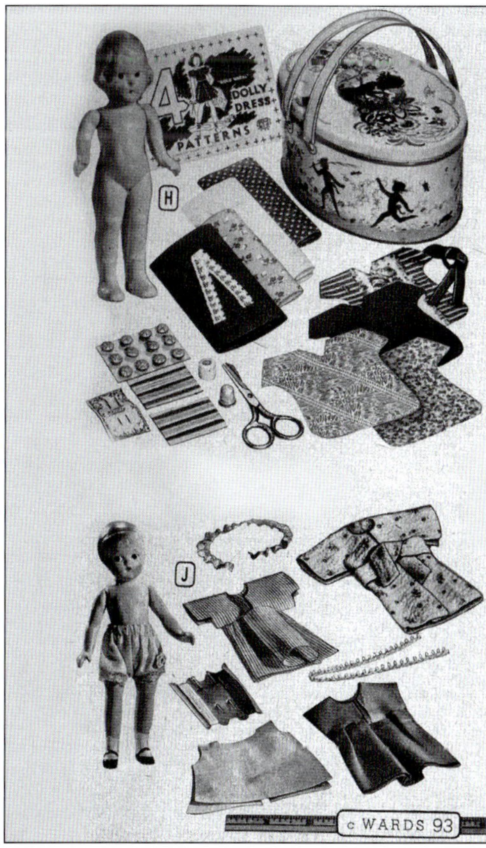

As pictured in the 1942 Montgomery Ward's catalog, companies like Effanbee offered sewing kits, complete with precut materials, so individuals could make clothing that would spruce up a prewar *Wee Patsy*. Not pictured is the *Junior WAACS Sewing Set* complete with khaki material offered by New York Toy & Game Mfg. Co.

Edith Flack Ackley's hand-made cloth dolls inspired many doll makers. Generally, Edith's dolls were not hallmarked, making it difficult to determine whether the dolls were made by her or by someone closely following her patterns. This 8" original Ackley doll, however, was a 1960 gift by Ms. Ackley to its original owners. It illustrates the pattern outlined in her book, and has well detailed embroidered features typical of her originals. *From the collection of the Museum of the City of New York. Photo provided by the Museum of the City of New York.* Insufficient examples to establish a market value.

Handmade toys were still popular right after the war as peacetime production began to ramp up. Edith Flack Ackley's dolls were a recommended Christmas gift by *House and Garden* magazine in 1946, just as the American toy industry began its recovery.

Edith Flack Ackley's dolls and books have not been forgotten, and dolls are still being created today using her timeless patterns. She served as the inspiration for a whole generation of postwar doll makers, crafting in fabric. Today, Sue Sizemore of Vancouver, Washington, makes fine cloth dolls such as this 4.875" girl in many sizes following the Ackley designs. $45.

Alice Shield's miniature dolls, generally 5.5" tall, were made of muslin and stuffed with cotton. She embroidered their faces. Eyebrows consisted of a single slanted stitch, as opposed to an arc. Two small stitches comprised the nose. Their closed mouths had full stitched lips. Cheeks, however, were painted. Dolls had yarn hair and many have been observed as redheads. Dolls wore cloth clothing with stitching, ribbons, and lace for trim. Their shoes were made from old leather gloves. Alice made a lot of nationality dolls and was meticulous about the authenticity of their clothing. $100-110/pair.

By the 1960s, distribution companies like QT Novelty carried dolls that resembled Ackley's designs. This 4.5" pantalooned daughter doll with painted facial features was offered at $1. $10-12.

June B. Jenkins' 3.625" stockinette doll with painted features and pipe cleaner limbs. $50.

Well known doll makers drew their inspiration from Mrs. Ackley. They often refined the patterns, making cloth dolls more in scale for dollhouses. A good example was Alice T. Shields. She was born in New York in 1885, but raised her family in Agawam, Massachusetts. Painting and doll making provided an outlet for her creativity. Her grandson remembers a large grouping of her dolls sitting on a shelf above the piano in her home. Her granddaughter remembers a large dollhouse built by her father and brother that came alive with a family of dolls made by her grandmother. Alice Shields died in 1973.

June B. Jenkins started making dolls in the late 1940s, crediting Edith Flack Ackley as her inspiration. Janet Johl told June's story in her 1952 book, *Your Dolls And Mine*. Ms. Jenkins used different media to create her 150+ doll variations. They were made in many sizes. She used cloth over *papier mâché*, or women's stockings over padding for doll faces with either painted or embroidered features. Bodies were stuffed cotton with pipe cleaner limbs. She also made clay dolls. After polling state libraries to determine the woman "most representative of Connecticut history," she designed a 12" clay Harriet Beecher Stowe doll, known as the Connecticut State Doll.

Instead of embroidery, whimsical and very detailed faces were often painted on cloth dolls of this period. The tiny patterns of the fabrics used to costume these cloth covered wire armature dolls were well sized to their 1:12 scale. The Toy and Miniature Museum of Kansas City displays them on hand decorated Tynietoy furniture. Their maker is unknown. *From the collection of the Toy and Miniature Museum of Kansas City. Photo courtesy of the Toy and Miniature Museum of Kansas City.* $50-65/each.

Therapeutic Dolls and Joan Beringer Pripps

Joan Beringer was a noted painter and doll maker, born in 1912 in Wauwautosa, Wisconsin. She studied portrait painting, but soon branched out into the making of elaborately costumed character and historic dolls. An article featuring her dolls in the *Roto* section of the Milwaukee Journal in the early 1940s caught the eye of Dr. Helen Sargent of the Northwestern University psychology department, who was searching for small dolls that could be bent into any shape and used by a child to act out real life or perceived events. Costume dolls were far too elaborate for the purpose. Faced with wartime shortages in materials, Joan worked with Dr. Sargent in 1944 to design a series of dolls with felt clothing and felt covered pipe cleaners. Faces were hand-painted, and yarn was used to make realistic hairstyles. The dolls were so effective that additional sets were made for the psychology department at Ohio State University and for two private clinics.

Wire armature cloth dolls provided good play value. They could be made in good proportion and scale to fit miniature furniture of the time period. Yarn and/or thread were often used for hair, although mohair and theatrical hair could be shaped to form more elaborate hairstyles. *From the collection of the Toy and Miniature Museum of Kansas City. Photo courtesy of the Toy and Miniature Museum of Kansas City.* $50-65/each

Joan Beringer was called upon to make families of miniature dolls, not to inhabit "normal" dollhouses, but to assist child psychologists, an obvious exception to wartime toy making controls. Her family of dolls provided a vehicle by which "problem children" could act out their feelings while being observed by trained professionals. A psychologist could often interpret a child's hidden feelings by the interrelationships and activities a child established for the dolls. This use of dolls was often seen in the postwar era, forming a real market niche. No examples are available for valuation.

Joan Beringer married Norman Pripps in 1948. She commandeered a small cabin he had built on Little Muskie Lake as part of a real estate development plan. The cabin became her "Little Studio in the Woods", where she continued her doll making and landscape, wildlife, and portrait painting until her death in 2005 at age 92. While she made dolls in three sizes, she is best known for her series of 12-14" cloth head dolls and, later, another version of these larger dolls with beautifully painted ceramic heads. Considered an expert in costuming, the dolls were dressed to show the history of costumes and to illustrate various themes: famous women of Wisconsin, White House Women, queens, peasants of other countries, and dancers. Mrs. Pripps used her finely dressed dolls in lectures she gave throughout Wisconsin and Illinois.

Joan Beringer made at least three variations of costume dolls after her marriage, including 4.5" nationality dolls. The figures, mounted on a wooden block signed on the underside, were constructed of cloth-covered wire frames and cloth heads with painted faces. $20-30.

Clay Dolls and Paint-Pals

In 1941, assuming that young children wanted to "play pretend" and act out the events of the world around them, the Detroit Toy Company began manufacturing 5" tall uniformed figures, molded in plaster-like clay. These unpainted *Paint-Pal* statues, a soldier, sailor, nurse, marine, and aviator, were available for mail-order from Detroit, Michigan.

The *Paint-Pal* boxes pictured fully painted and detailed, uniformed servicemen and a nurse. The statues could be purchased singly for 50 cents, a double box with a sailor and nurse for 75 cents, or a soldier, sailor, and marine for $1. Interestingly, a 1941 *Playthings* ad said they were made of "non-critical" ceramics. The dolls were pre-cast with all uniform details on a base enabling them to stand. A full sheet of instructions was included in each box. Directions told how to mix colors and showed pictures of each uniformed doll to be used as a guide. If you didn't create the desired effect, you could wash off the paint, let the doll dry and begin again. On the reverse side of the directions, the company included the uniform insignia of the Army, Navy, and Marine Corp as well as the "Pledge Allegiance to the Flag." Insignia could be cut out and pasted on the figures to decorate the miniature hero. Detroit Toy Company did mention that more dolls would be forthcoming, but no evidence exists that the line was ever expanded.

Although Paint-Pals were not suggested for use with dollhouses, at 5", they are a perfect size for typical 1:12 scale dwellings of the time period. They could, however, be used to re-enact homecomings and farewells. $5 per doll or $30 for set of three.

Composite Dolls and Playwood Plastics "Meet the Family" Dolls

Another example of the use of molded dolls made from available materials was the figures made by Playwood Plastics Co., Inc. The company, incorporated in 1941, was a subsidiary of the Transogram Company. Transogram, founded in 1915, made a variety of games and toys. In the late 1930s Transogram produced a series of toy soldier accessories, adding soldiers for Christmas 1940. In 1942 Transogram was introduced to an inventor who had developed a mixture that was not dependent upon war-controlled ingredients. In need of toys that could fill the market demand, Transogram used Playwood Plastics as the vehicle to exploit the proprietary composition of wood flour, unbleached white flour, 20-Mule Team Borax, and water. Playwood was able to obtain enough scrap metal to make molds and began producing toy soldiers with the look of prewar lead soldiers. Their selling office was the Toy Building in New York City at 200 Fifth Avenue; their factory was on Floyd Street in Brooklyn. The company was very successful during World War II, employing 125 people.

Immediately after the end of the war, Playwood tried to utilize their special mixture to meet the need for dollhouse figures, producing families sold in sets packaged in colorful cardboard boxes. They were supposedly unbreakable. The dolls continued to be sold in the late 1940s, probably grabbed up to live in the vast number of metal and fiberboard dollhouses gracing store shelves and catalogs. The dolls and soldiers soon lost favor, however, as figures of newer materials became available.

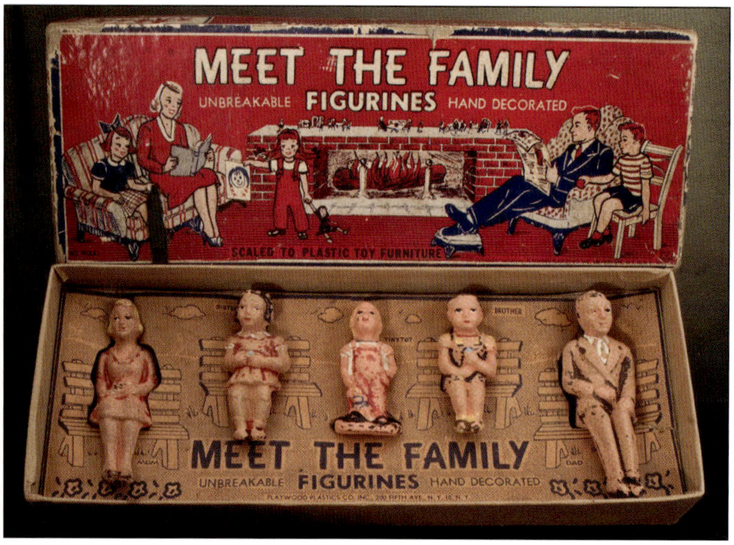

Playwood's "Meet the Family" boxed sets advertised dolls would fit 1:12 scale plastic furniture, although they are somewhat "bulky" for that purpose. The figures made were: grandfather, grandmother, father, mother, older sister, younger brother, and younger sister. These dolls were all molded in a sitting position and were between 2.75" and 4" high. Playwood also created two toddlers, a boy and a girl, and a tiny tot, all on bases. These three dolls stood upright and were 2.625" to 3.75" high. The dolls were often marked "Made in USA with 2 "P's" in a circle. A boxed set of five figures sold for 98¢ just after the War. $35 per boxed set of 5.

The dolls had hand-painted facial features and clothing. Some were holding objects, like grandma with her knitting and tiny tot dragging a doll. The figures found today may be flaking and peeling due to drying of the base material. $5 per doll.

Stockpiled Plastic Dolls by Q.T. Novelty and B. Shackman

Q.T. Novelty Company and B. Shackman & Co. were toy distributors located in New York City who sold imported and United States made toys, dolls, and dollhouse items. Their goods were sold to retailers at the annual toy show in New York City or to consumers through direct mail-order. A 1960s Q.T. Novelty catalog states that they had been specialists in imported dollhouse accessories and furniture for 67 years.

In a March 1942 issue of *Toys & Novelties* magazine Shackman first offered a line of American made costumed 3.25" bending dollhouse dolls. Montgomery Wards offered three of these dolls in their 1942 Christmas catalog for 59¢-75¢, calling them Celluloid, obviously made from stockpiled or scrap plastic. The dolls resembled painted-over bisque nationality dolls made in Germany and Japan in the 1930s.

In March 1946, six months after the end of the war, Q.T. Novelty announced that they were now making the dolls with plastic heads, arms, and legs, and could offer them in limited quantities. While it is not clear who actually made the dolls, in a 1947 trade magazine, QT advertised that they were expanding the line that had been so popular the year before. Calling them new and improved dolls, the ad mentioned a family, including a 4.75" mother and father, 3.5" boy and girl, as well as a baby, nurse, and maid. The dolls were offered at wholesale prices between $7.20 and $9.00 a dozen, suggesting a retail price of $1.20 to $1.50 each.

Small dolls made from stockpiled plastic were first offered to retailers in the March 1942 issue of *Toys and Novelties* magazine.

After the war QT Novelty packaged similar 3.5" plastic dolls in a brown cardboard box. The box top had a label identifying them as "Bending Dollhouse Dolls." Early and later dolls were generally painted in a satin sheen flesh-colored paint over white plastic, although one variety of the postwar dolls was finished with a shiny paint. The hair on the pictured postwar dolls was painted, unlike earlier dolls. $25 MIB.

Dolls were advertised as hand-painted and hand-dressed with pipe cleaner frames. Their clothing was primarily felt, but cotton, lace, netting, and fur was also used. Figures were dressed to represent basic family, character, and nationality dolls. Prewar dolls had only lower legs made of plastic with a cloth wrapping covering the pipe cleaners of the upper legs. Shoes had a slight heel. They had pipe cleaner arms and plastic heads. Legs of later dolls extended up to the hips, where they were attached to the torso. Their shoes were generally flats, although heels could be found. Plastic arms were added, attached at the shoulders. All dolls had molded eyes and lips, highlighted with paint.

It is not known how long these dolls remained on the market. By 1948, Q.T. Novelty was featuring another line, Flagg Dolls, in its advertisements for the annual New York Toy Fair.

Many dolls wore hats or tams. Some dolls were holding objects such as these tailgating college students on the way to a football game holding pennants and schoolbooks. $15.

A 3.5" war years nurse on left with pipe cleaner arms. The maid on the right is postwar with plastic arms, although her shoes have heels, as found in war year's dolls. Variations in the dolls could be the result of the fact that they were first made in 1942 and then re-introduced again after the war in 1946 drawing upon available inventory. $15.

Paper Dolls and the Lowe Paper Dollhouse

Paper dolls, two-dimensional figures with paper clothes that could be easily attached and reattached, were seen in Europe in the 18th and 19th centuries. It is possible that they were used as paper mannequins to illustrate hair and clothing trends.

Dolls were sometimes dressed in national costumes not unlike prewar and postwar bisque dolls from Germany and Japan. This Spanish couple had the flat shoes, painted hair and plastic arms of the postwar variety. $15.

In 1942 or 1943, a Lowe paper doll and dollhouse set with dolls, clothes, storybooks, cardboard dollhouse, and furniture was exclusively offered by Sears. Lowe used the designs of ten dolls from their previously published #1028 book *Playhouse Paper Dolls.* The dolls were produced for Sears on slightly heavier cardboard stock. Their clothing, with different color combinations, was on a better grade of paper. According to Mary Young, author and paper doll expert, the artists who created the paper dolls and their clothes were Doris and Marion Henderson. Doris drew dolls and collaborated with Marion on clothes and product layout. The sisters also illustrated children's books. The cutouts were approximately 6" tall and they had various outfits to choose from. The cardboard dollhouse when extended to include the second floor measured 19 inches. $150 MIP uncut.

Paper dolls were not produced prolifically in the United States until the 20th century, although *Godey's Lady's Book* published their one and only paper doll in 1859. After the turn of the century, *McCall's, Good Housekeeping,* and *Ladies Home Journal* began to consistently include a paper doll page in their monthly issues. Advertising companies also produced paper dolls to create visibility for their products. Specialty paper doll publishers included Merrill, Lowe, Whitman, and Saalfield. Popularity of paper dolls soared in the 1930s and 40s and they reached a peak in their production history. Here was a doll, costing five or ten cents at retail, that could still be afforded by most families during the Depression and could be produced under wartime rationing. These specialty publishers expanded their wonderful books of paper dolls to sometimes include a dollhouse, furniture, and accessories. After the war paper dolls returned to their own status, no longer needed as dollhouse dolls. They still provided a great deal of fun and education at a reasonable cost.

Wooden Head Dolls and the Dolls of Elvy Kalep Miller

Many artists and homemakers had for years used small simple wooden balls or buttons to create dollhouse dolls. Even with wartime rationing, individuals were able to continue the craft. Features were hand-painted. Hair was either painted or made from yarn or flocking. Bodies of the dolls could be made of many different materials, but early in the war, were often made from wire or pipe cleaners, until even scrap metal became scarce. Clothing was often made from scrap material or crepe paper.

Elvy Kalep was an aviatrix, children's book author, illustrator and a creator of small dolls. Originally born in Estonia in the early 1900s, she was sent to safety in Russia during WWI. When the Communist Revolution started in 1917 she escaped across Siberia to Shanghai. After returning home at the end of the war she studied both art and aviation. She later emigrated to the United States and there combined her two interests. In 1936 United Airlines commissioned her to write and illustrate a book to help children understand more about airplanes and flying, and, in fact, calm their fears about air travel. The resulting *Air Babies* was quite whimsical and well received being mentioned in a 1938 *Time* magazine article. In 1941, as part of the nationwide promotion of the 1941 movie *Parachute Battalion*, Elvy Kalep drew upon one of the characters from her book, Patsy Parachute, and issued two wooden head dolls, now called Patty and Pat Parachute. Ms. Kalep brought out a series of 12 dolls known as the "Bendy Dolls", with wood heads, brightly painted faces, scrap fabric clothing, and bendable, perhaps fabric or paper covered pipe cleaner bodies. The Bendy Dolls are now quite scarce, although her Parachute dolls are occasionally seen.

Advertised in an early 1940s *Playthings* magazine as "roguish little dolls of 1000 and 1 poses", Elvy Kalep's Bendy set included a sailor, cowboy, and fashionably dressed young lady and retailed for 75¢ each. No dolls have been found in order to establish value.

Elvy Kalep's Patty and Pat-Parachute dolls, about 5" tall, had hand-painted faces, khaki cloth costumes, and attached parachutes. An RAF version in light blue coveralls was made for the United Kingdom market. $65 per doll with parachute.

Cardboard Dolls and Katie Berl's Mini Dolls

As the war progressed, the ingenuity and creativeness of artists and toy makers was being challenged. As one material after another became restricted, the toy makers had to turn to the simplest of media, like cardboard. The results were not meant to be long lasting, but simply to meet children's desires for toys to play with. One delightful example was the *Mini Doll* line, designed by Katie Berl and first introduced by Grand Products in 1943. Dolls were formed by simple and inexpensive construction methods. The entire body was cut from thick multi-layered cardboard painted a flesh color. Small strands of wire attached the arms and legs at the shoulders and hips, making the doll somewhat flexible. Padded flesh-colored fabric was glued to a wooden disk to serve as a head. Faces were then hand-painted, as were the popsicle-stick shaped cardboard shoes that enabled all but the baby to stand.

Katie Berl's dolls had yarn hair and fabric clothes cut from a variety of material such as burlap, felt, cotton, and organza. Pictured are brother, sister, maid, aunt, and uncle. *Dolls from the collection of Patty Cooper. Photo courtesy of Patty Cooper.* $35/each.

Mini-Dolls are news on the market as they fill a long-felt need of little people for doll house dolls. Dolls range in size from 3 to 5 inches, are attractively costumed and come in a large variety of styles. Made of fibreboard, they have movable arms and legs and can adapt themselves to numerous positions. Boxed separately, in sets and family groups; Mini-Dolls may be retailed for 75c each, and in sets for $3, $4 and $5.

Mini-Dolls

The Mini Doll line, designed by Katie Berl was first advertised in a March 1943 *Playthings* magazine. Berl designed the dolls in the likenesses of everyday people including families and household help, dressed both as city and country folks. The line included international dolls as well as a wedding set. The cost was typically expensive for wartime commercial toys, selling individually for 75 cents and in boxed sets ranging from $2.95 to $5. Montgomery Ward offered four sets in its 1944 Christmas catalog selling for $1.79 per two-doll set. $35.

Advertised by *Playthings* magazine as fiberboard dolls specifically designed for dollhouses, *Mini Dolls* ranged in size from 2.5" for a baby to 4" for an adult. $35/each.

All Wooden Dolls - Jaymar & the Woodettes

The name Marx is well known to any toy collector. Usually, people are thinking about the Louis Marx Co. that dominated mass-produced toys in the postwar years. Less famous, perhaps was the Jaymar Specialty Co., a joint enterprise of Jacob and Rose Marx, Louis Marx' father and sister. The company was founded in the late 1920s with some financial support from Louis. While Louis focused on tin and plastic toys, Jaymar was left to exploit the market for wood, paper, and cloth toys. With the restrictions on materials imposed as a result of the war, most toy makers shifted their production to military goods, or ceased production altogether. Jaymar, however, was able to continue its production throughout the war making jigsaw puzzles, wooden doll accessories, and a unique line of small character dolls. Jaymar continued its existence as a family-run business until 1990, when it ceased operation.

Jaymar character dolls most often represented copyrighted comic strip characters like those from the *Popeye, Moon Mullins, Joe Palooka*, and *Andy Gump* strips. Fairytale figures like Little Red Riding Hood and Humpty Dumpty were also represented in the line, as were policemen, sailors, Native Americans, a Chinese man, and clowns.

Dolls were constructed of various wood parts formed on a lathe. The small wooden pieces were strung together and a small metal grommet was attached to the end of the elastic strings protruding from the feet, hands, and heads to hold all the parts together securely. Many of the parts were interchangeable among the dolls, but each doll had its own unique combination. If the doll was of a copyrighted character, it usually carried its identifying name and copyright owner stenciled on its body or foot. Most of the dolls also carry the stamped legend, "Made in the USA" on the bottom of their foot. Dolls were produced in a variety of sizes, 3.75" to 7.5" tall. Some characters were made in multiple sizes.

Jaymar's character dolls were often copied by other manufacturers, as was the common practice of the day. The simpler, unmarked and less detailed copies rarely have metal grommets, although a grommet could have been removed from a Jaymar doll if a child added a knot to the end of a stretched piece of elastic.

Toys that were introduced during the war not only had to be made from non-controlled materials, but were also designed to minimize the need for labor in their production, assembly, and decoration. Children became the "labor force", decorating and assembling their own toys. A wonderful example of wartime toys was the *Woodette* line of dolls first introduced at the New York Toy Fair in February 1943.

A well known Chicago artist and children's book illustrator, Mary Alice Stoddard, originally designed the dolls. Mary Alice, born in Illinois in 1912, related in a September 1943 *Chicago Tribune* interview, that she could trace the inspiration for the dolls as far back as first grade when she drew a doll on the blackboard. She couldn't understand how her classmates could later alter it, being the "perfect" doll in her eyes. Following the background in part instilled by her artist mother, she continued to draw and study art and design throughout her life, including a period in Philadelphia where she worked as a fashion designer.

The clothing and facial features of Jaymar's dolls were all painted on clear wood, and little embellishments like Popeye's pipe, Moon Mullin's cigar, and Andy Gump's nose were small wood pieces inserted in their heads. It was rare for felt to be added, although Humpty Dumpty had a cloth collar, as did the Jester. Pictured dolls are 4-4.5". $45-150 depending on character and size.

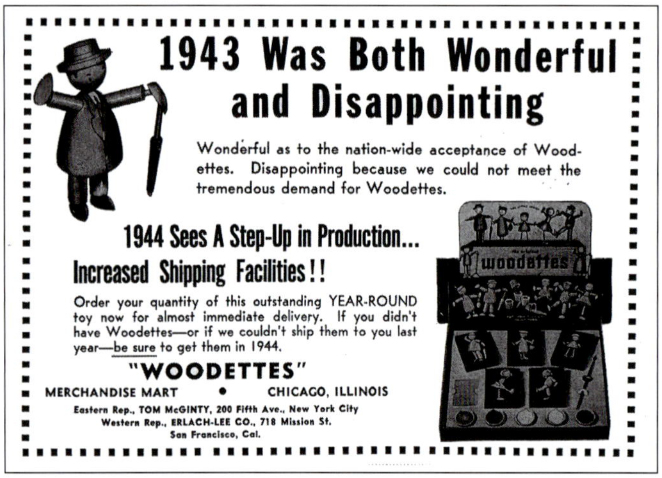

A 1944 Playthings ad reflected wartime shortage even for dolls that needed to be assembled and painted by toy-hungry children.

In 1944 *Version 2*, the *Woodette Village* was introduced to complement the *Little Family*. A small 6.5"x3.5"x 2.25"cardboard building housed each doll in this five-piece set. There was Officer Kelly in a police station; Farmer Jones in a farmhouse; Mr. Green in a grocery; Johnny Little in a schoolhouse and Hilda, the maid, in a house. $50 per unpainted, unassembled set.

A family of five dollhouse dolls 3–3.75", *The Little Family*, was the first Woodette set, or "version" introduced. Each doll was named: Mother, Father, Suzie, Sally, and Tom. $40/ unpainted, unassembled set.

Apparently, Stoddard's illustrations were not yet capable of supporting her, so she took a series of jobs, including a job drawing designs in a woodworker's shop in Oak Park, Illinois. While there, she conceived the idea of having wooden parts for small four inch dolls turned on a lathe. The shop obliged her and made up a set. At first, she was unable to interest a toy maker in her prototypes, so they languished on a windowsill in her home.

It took the keen eye of a friend a few years later to realize that the almost forgotten dolls might have a market in the material-constrained war economy. The friend excitedly contacted a toy manufacturer to gauge his interest. The manufacturer turned to his business manager, Mildred Marshall, who saw potential in the dolls.

Woodette doll sets were clearly the product of a very talented and giving artist. Although her preferred medium was watercolor, Mary Alice Stoddard became a prolific illustrator of children's books but used her watercolor techniques and palettes. The artist found the time to also use her aesthetic abilities to support children's causes. In 1948 she transformed a drab, institutional, and somewhat scary children's clinic at the Northwestern University Hospital with a huge mural. One entire room was devoted to a farm scene, introducing city children to a more tranquil setting. Other segments of the main room used her familiar characters of circus and zoo animals, children's classics, and fairytales. She resumed her book illustrations after marrying E. Philip Reid in 1950, but never returned to doll designing. She continued her active participation as an artist and supporter of the arts until her death in 2001.

In 1946, after the end of the war, a set of six 4.75" Woodette fairytale characters was introduced in a box labeled *Version 4, Woodette Library*. The set clearly drew upon Mary Alice's children's book illustrations. Instead of a house, a colorful backdrop was included for each character: Little Jack Horner, Robin Hood, Jack and the Beanstalk, Mary and her lamb, and a pre-assembled and ready to paint Alice in Wonderland. These figures were slightly taller than dolls in the original sets. Previously in 1945 a clown and performing animal circus set had been introduced as *Version 3*. $50 per unpainted unassembled set.

It is not clear who was the actual manufacturer of the dolls. The "home office" of *Woodettes* is listed as Chicago's Merchandise Mart, with the trademark registered to the Dupligraph Company. A later line of non-doll toys carried the *Woodette* name, but the name seemed to be owned by a company known as Print-o-Matic, perhaps a successor to Dupligraph. The name was later used on toys made by a tool and die company, Winzeler Gear of Harwood Heights, Illinois.

Constructed of hard white birch, the doll bodies were assembled in parts and placed in individual cardboard boxes nestled in a larger box with directions, sandpaper, watercolor paints, and a brush. The purchaser was instructed to sand the individual pieces, paint them, if desired, using the color guide on the box, and assemble by using glue to hold the pegged pieces in their allotted holes. Sometimes the holes were not properly sized, and some adjustment was needed to make sure that the assembled dolls were balanced and able to stand. Small accessories, like mother's purse, the feather in her cap, gentleman's umbrella, or Alice in Wonderland's magic mushroom, added life to the sets and a sense of whimsy to the creator. With the availability of ready-made plastic toys after the War, no new *Woodette* dolls were introduced after 1946.

Clothespin Dolls

Many of the clothespin dolls of this period were made by individuals for their families, but at least one group, patients at a VA hospital in Texas, made a 4" cowboy and cowgirl pair, well carved, dressed and decorated that were offered by the doll merchandiser, Kimport, as Yippee and Yippette. Offered in the 1944 Kimport catalog at 75¢ each, these dolls represent good examples of the use of folk-craft to overcome wartime rationing. $50 per set.

Dolls made from wooden clothespins have long been natural folk-art. The ready-made heads and torsos could be decorated in hundreds of ways, simple to quite elaborate. They could be made to be kings and queens, Robin Hood, a nurse, lawyer, farmer, maid, mother, or father. From a dollhouse scale perspective, dolls made from clothespins, whether decorated with fabric, or simply painted, fit in a 1:18" scale house quite nicely. During the war, clothespins were used to create "substitutes" for the missing commercially produced dolls made from controlled materials.

One doll maker, Cecil W. Perry of Wheaton, Illinois, specialized in clothespin dolls before the war and adapted her craft to meet wartime themes. Her use of small doll-sized clothespins resulted in finished figures about 2.5" tall. She changed her prewar crepe paper costumes of angels, choirboys, bridal parties, and storybook characters to uniforms of soldiers, sailors, nurses, and party girls. The dolls were well received as they were sent in care packages to servicemen around the globe. After the war Cecil Perry continued her craft, making *Miniature Marvel Dolls* with elaborate and detailed costumes that she often traded with other miniature doll makers. Cecil Perry died in 1961.

Wilma Eubank Pulliam of Hannibal, Missouri, gained a name for herself in the 1930s as a maker of 6" composition dolls based originally on Mark Twain's characters. Her offerings included historical figures such as Buffalo Bill Cody, Andrew Jackson, and Betsy Ross, as well Gibson Girls and fashionably dressed Gay Nineties society folks. By the 1940s, her media was expanded to include clothespin dolls, again centering on Mark Twain's characters.

As can be seen from the previous examples, the ingenuity of wartime doll makers addressed not only the scarcity of materials, but also the scarcity of a skilled workforce. While the dolls were certainly not elaborate, they had playful and endearing charm. The craft continues through succeeding generations and handcrafted dolls are still welcome additions to a dollhouse.

A 2.5" Cecil Perry wartime clothespin "Party Girl" with woven yarn hair, lace and a feather fan, is scaled nicely to fit with a Marx Newlywed tin roombox. $50.

During the early 50s, charging $2, $2.50, or $3 a doll, Cecil Perry advertised her creations for sale in a publication called "The Toy Trader."

During the war, sets were sold encouraging little doll makers to assemble their own dolls from the included materials, wooden clothespins and colorfully printed paper costumes. The set on the right contains patterns and paper to clothe the dolls in Russian costumes. Clothespin crafts were popular throughout the next few decades as evidenced by the 1974 instruction manual featuring a Marx tin dollhouse filled with an extended clothespin family and domestic help on its cover.

While these 4" clothespin dolls appear to be made by Wilma Pulliam, the cardboard stands are round and unmarked. Bernard Ravca made similar dolls from clothespins mounted on round stands. $25/each.

Wilma Eubank Pulliam's clothespin dolls often drew upon the tales of her fellow resident of Hannibal, Missouri, Mark Twain. The 4" Tom Sawyer, Huck Finn, Aunt Polly, and prim Becky Thatcher were all hand-painted with their eyes cast mischievously to the right. The fabric of their clothes was well chosen to match their characters. The dolls were found on a cardboard base marked "Eubank Dolls, Hannibal, Missouri." $25/each.

Immediately postwar Native American dolls and cowgirl made from clothespins stand 3.25"-3.5" tall. Dressed in leather, linen and felt, the seller ascribed them to Bernard Ravca, although no evidence has been found to substantiate the identification. $25.

Section Three
The Baby Boomer Era
1946 - 1960

The Baby Boomer era is generally defined to be the post-WWII period between 1946 and, depending on the sociologist, 1957 or 1960. The era, however, was a natural evolution from the events, social milieu, and economy of a world at war, and it is interesting to look at the War years together with the Baby Boomer era as one connected period.

When WWII ended in 1945, consumers had a huge pent up demand for goods, which had been scarce during the War and unaffordable during the Depression. The United States peacetime economy boomed as American industry became the supplier to the rest of the war-ravaged world. Employment surged, as did disposable family income. The restraints to consumption that were rooted in the Depression and World War II were removed. The American toy industry, utilizing materials and mass production techniques developed during the War, answered the demands of the Baby Boomers and their parents. Retail distribution channels added chain merchandisers. Low-cost toys were made available through 5&10¢ stores like S.S. Kresge, F.W. Woolworth, and W.T. Grant and through the catalogs of Sears & Roebuck, Montgomery Ward, and J.C. Penney. Higher quality toys, including miniatures and dolls, continued to be made following more traditional methods. Many were sold through independent toy sellers and high-end department stores found in major urban areas.

As Europe recovered, toys were some of the first goods produced for domestic consumption and for export to the booming United States market. At first toys were made by hand from scrap materials and suffered by comparison to their American made counterparts. The term "made-in-Japan" was often used not to describe the country of origin, but rather to describe the quality of the toy (or other consumer good). Without established distribution relationships and outlets, toys produced in Germany and Japan were often initially made to be sold to United States military personnel stationed in occupied countries, and were intended to be brought home as souvenirs.

Women were urged to stay at home and practice "homemaker's arts" so that their husbands, re-entering civilian life, could find employment in the booming postwar economy. Miniatures were advertised, somewhat stereotypically, to appeal to little girls emulating their mothers. Dollhouses, their furnishings, and inhabitants, however, had now become toys to be played with, no longer set on a shelf to be admired. Furnishings had opening drawers and moving parts, and dolls could be posed for chores and play in their miniature environments. The new materials withstood heavy play, but weren't quite as unbreakable as packaging and advertising trumpeted. Toys were now replaceable, however, with pricing set to appeal to the masses rather than to the wealthy few.

The 1950s saw less emphasis on quality and detail, lower pricing, and mass distribution as toy giants such as Louis Marx & Co. dominated, driving many of the small, classic toy makers and artisans from the market. Late in the period, foreign manufacturers established sales distribution and began to reappear in the United States, some copying the mass production concepts being used in America, while others reverted back to higher quality, hand-detailed dolls and miniature accessories.

The Baby Boomers experienced rapid evolution of their toys and playtime. Children enjoyed incredible choice and availability. The next chapters will detail some of that choice, following the shortages and ingenuity of the War Years through the abundance of the succeeding two decades.

Chapter 6

The Miracle of Plastics and the Plastics Pioneers

The word "plastic" has a much broader meaning than we generally think of it today. The term simply means "able to be shaped, molded, or modeled" or "capable of adapting to external conditions during development." It has come to be used today to describe a material that is made from organic chemical compounds, synthetically produced, that can be molded, cast, extruded, drawn, or shaped into endless designs.

Plastic materials can be been found in nature. Amber, tortoise shell, and animal horn was, from ancient times, subjected to heat and pressure and molded into objects that were used and admired by men and women. Some researchers credit Leonardo Da Vinci as the inventor of man-made natural plastics, developing mixtures of animal or vegetable glues, organic fibers, and colors that, when hardened, took on the shape of objects that it had been layered on.

As discussed previously, the first synthetic plastic, cellulose nitrate, was invented in 1868 and subsequent improvements, cellulose acetate being the best known, were made to reduce its flammability over the next few decades. Eventually cellulose acetate was made to be moldable. It was the development of molding technologies coupled with the further development of plastic materials like vinyl, acrylic, cellulose acetate butyrate, polystyrene that would later help make mass production of plastic toys possible.

During World War II, plastic was first used in consumer goods as a substitute for war-restricted materials, but was soon seen as a restricted strategic material itself. Plastic was a logical material to be used for a toy. It could be molded into shape, was easily cleaned, was strong and difficult to break, and did not shatter into sharp pieces. Toys made principally of cellulose acetate were available just before the war and during the early war years. This plastic had drawbacks, however. Most notably it warped and its color faded.

The next generation of plastics, polystyrenes, developed by Dow Chemical Co. in 1937 and refined by military contractors during the war, began to replace cellulose acetate and cellulose acetate butyrate after the war. Not only was it more cost-effective to use, but it did not warp, had bright shiny colors, and could even be produced in a clear variety to resemble glass. Companies like Monsanto and Dow continued to develop "impact resistant" polystyrenes that were well suited for toys. There were active efforts by all-plastic manufacturers to advertise the materials themselves, encouraging parents to buy hard plastic toys that were "better" than their wood and metal predecessors. In its advertising, Celanese trumpeted *Lumarith* toys as having "extra play life, extra play safety, with economy." Monsanto's ads encouraged children to buy toys made from *Lustrex* because there would be "no worry about peeling or chipping – their brilliant colors aren't just painted on – they're solid clear through." Dow claimed that toys made from *Styron* were "5 times tougher – for more realism."

As toy pricing became more competitive, many of the toy manufactures searched for lower price materials or materials that could be produced more efficiently. The rubber-like vinyl acetate was an early substitute. Polyethylene, first developed in 1943, was far more flexible, lighter, and cost-effective in a manufacturing process than either polystyrene or vinyl acetate. Polypropylene gave superior flexibility and manufacturing efficiency. These "soft plastics" did not have the same sharpness of detail, bright shiny color, or dimensional stability of the earlier "hard plastics" and toys made from this "rubbery material" are generally not as highly valued today.

Modern engineered plastics have come a long way since the post-war era and commercially produced mass market dolls are made from combinations of vinyls and polyvinyls that require little compromise to produce colorful, damage-resistant, detailed toys with tremendous play value. As early as June 1951, A.M. Katz, Chairman of Ideal Plastics Corp. wrote in a *Playthings* article that plastic was "no longer a substitute for other materials: it stands on its own feet." Parents today no longer needed to be "encouraged" to purchase plastic toys, their children preferred them. The Baby Boomer Era was the real beginning for this movement to low-cost, readily available, quality dolls, toys, and miniatures and companies like Renwal, Ideal, Plasco, and Acme were among some of the first toy manufacturers of this era who recognized opportunity in plastic. Of course, it is impossible to tell the story of plastic toys in general, without acknowledging Louis Marx, *Time* magazine's "King of Toys", and Islyn Thomas, dubbed the "Prince of Plastics" by Bill Hanlon in his *Plastic Toys Dimestore Dreams of the '40s & '50s*. Both men made indelible contributions to every phase of the postwar toy industry: design, material, production, marketing. These pioneers not only helped to develop plastic as an acceptable material for toys, but they exploited plastics as they refined their concepts of mass production and mass marketing, forever changing the toy industry. No longer would Germany enjoy a low-cost advantage in making toys. It would never recover its domination of the industry that it had enjoyed for almost 100 years. It would be replaced by the United States, Japan, Hong Kong, and now China.

Renwal Manufacturing Company

Renwal, one of the best-recognized post World War II toy manufacturers, epitomized the plastic revolution. Originally founded as Renwal Manufacturing Company in 1939 by Irving Lawner, the company was soon purchased by two employees, Irving Rosenbloom and Edward Horney. During the war, Renwal naturally moved its focus from kitchen novelties to military components. As the end of the war neared, Mr. Rosenbloom began to plan for a transition to a postwar economy as a manufacturer with a focus on toys. He planned to utilize mass production methods and the "wonder" material, polystyrene plastic. By the end of 1945, the company began to offer a line of toy military airplanes and a line of dollhouse furniture. Almost all pieces were hallmarked with the Renwal name and bear an item number, making them easy to identify. The fortunes of the company soared during the rest of the decade as they broadened their line and distribution to include major retail dimestores and catalogue giants. In order to meet the demand, Renwal relocated its manufacturing from Brooklyn to Mineola, New York, in 1950. With higher quality toys that were more costly to produce, Renwal began to falter as it faced increasing competition. By 1956, they ceased production of dollhouse furniture and dolls and Rosenbloom and Horney delegated operations of the company to their senior managers. Renwal shifted its focus first to die-cast metal vehicles and later to plastic model kits. Renwal's dollhouse furniture molds changed hands many times over the next two decades, with a number of companies producing copies of the originals. In 1961 the Sear's Christmas catalogue offered an undecorated family of 5. It is known that the Empire Company in North Carolina was offering dollhouse furniture under the tradename "Little Miss Carolina". It is not known whether the Empire Company produced the dolls and furniture themselves or whether they were produced by Renwal and simply marketed by Empire.

In 1949 Renwal introduced a four-member family, produced in 1:18 scale to complement the company's line of hard plastic dollhouse furniture. These items were introduced to a post-World War II market clamoring for consumer goods. Appealing to the mass market, they were often sold in Five & Dime or variety stores. In its 1952 catalog, Renwal encourages dealers to purchase these dolls:

"They stand, they sit, they kneel" was the advertising slogan used by Renwal to highlight the play value of its family of dolls: father, mother, brother, and sister. The dolls were sold in the pictured individual cardboard boxes and in larger sets, as well. $50/each.

Over time, Renwal dolls were made in different colors including a light purple and pale pink dress for Mom, green and pink for the sister, and bright green for the brother. Depending on who was doing the painting, you might see different touches, like the boy with a painted handkerchief. Still later, these dolls were sold entirely in one solid color such as turquoise, yellow, pink, and blue with no added paint details.

Easy to identify, each doll was embossed on the back with the name Renwal together with a number: Father, #44; Mother, #43; Brother, #42; Sister, #41. In height, the father measures 4.25"; mother 4.125"; brother 3.75"; sister 3.625". The dolls were jointed at the arms, hips, and knees and held together with metal rivets. Later, Renwal redesigned the figures so that arms and legs simply snapped onto the body. The dolls were molded in one solid color and in addition to the dolls' facial features, the flesh color of the skin on arms, legs, and face was hand-painted. Common attire for the father was a blue or brown suit, white shirt, and colored tie. Mother generally wore a simple rose red or light blue dress with painted white collar together with black painted heels. Brother was dressed in a shirt and slacks of blue or brown with a colored tie and brown shoes, and sister was most often found in a yellow dress with molded socks and painted shoes. Red hair bows held her pigtails in place. $30/each.

If you don't have the doll family you are missing sales! From communities where they are not now sold we get letters from mothers asking where these dolls can be purchased. Some of these requests are for replacements; some result from their being seen in schools and institutions. Many kindergarten teachers use them or ask us where they can be bought. Show them on your toy counters!

Although generally sold individually, in 1950, a family, together with a larger scaled No. 8 baby, was packaged in a sturdy cardboard box decorated with a circus motif and labeled "Renwal's Doll Family." To attract potential buyers, the dolls were placed in the now very rare Renwal clear Lucite counter top display house. In 1954, the No. 233 Doll Family Painting set was introduced featuring a family of undecorated dolls and a No. 8 baby with a paint brush and 6 water color paints that could be used to decorate the dolls to a child's liking. The 1954 catalogue also advertised a set of undecorated dolls including two babies in a rectangular box with cellophane windows. In 1955 family dolls were included in some of Renwal's highly prized boxed sets, the No. 247 Cook 'n Serve and the No. 249 Busy Little Mother set.

In 1951, Renwal extended its basic family to include "profession" dolls: Doctors, nurses, veterinarians, mechanics. Accessories were added or subtracted over time, but the standard figure always served as the base for the dolls with no change in molded detail. Renwal made dollhouse babies to complete their plastic dollhouse family of four. Marked as "No. 8", the baby, however, was not in proportion to the family.

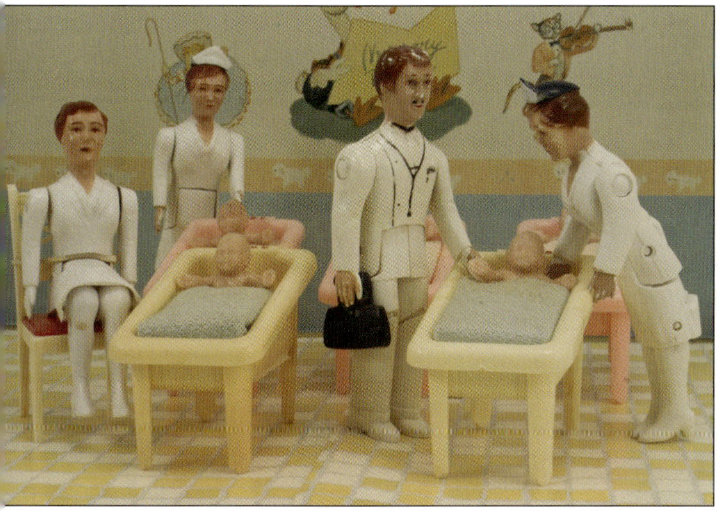

Renwal's nurse with a hat was the #43 mother doll molded in white plastic with painted hair, face, and hands. A doctor with a painted mustache and stethoscope carrying a black doctor's bag was the #44 father in white plastic. The "profession" dolls were changed slightly over time. The nurse without a hat looked after newborn babies in the No. 214 Hospital Nursery set. In 1954, Renwal introduced its #214 "Hospital Nursery Set." The set included furniture, blankets, bottles, diapers, a nurse, and seven "new" babies. These vinyl dolls were molded in a sitting position with open arms and measured 1.25". They were a perfect fit in Renwal's small nursery crib. The vinyl babies were identical to dolls made by the Thomas Manufacturing Company. Renwal had begun to make some "boys toys" from vinyl, but was not known for producing dollhouse products from this soft rubbery material, so it is possible that either the dolls were outsourced or molds were purchased or copied from Thomas. Dolls were also offered in packages of eight in 1957 and 1958. Nurse with hat, $65, without hat, $40. Doctor with bag, $80.

Renwal's mechanic was simply a #42 blue brother doll painted to depict him wearing overalls, although his molded necktie was still visible. The mechanic without a hat, and with metal riveted arms, is sometimes referred to as the gardener, being offered in 1949 as such by W.T.Grant. A blue plastic hardhat was added to the mechanic in the later non-riveted version. The policeman was the #44 father, molded in solid blue. A blue plastic policeman's hat was added to his costume. His hands and face were painted, as was his policeman's badge. Policeman, $125. Mechanic w/hat, $100. Mechanic w/o hat $80.

The doctor in Renwal's No 272 Animal Hospital set shaved his mustache and appeared as a veterinarian without his stethoscope or bag caring for a selection of molded dogs and cats. Veterinarian, $50.

At 2.25" Renwal's babies were more of a 1:9 scale. The baby, marked as "No. 8", was sold separately and was included in many of Renwal's boxed furniture sets, from 1948 through 1955, and is very easy to find today. They were so popular that it is not unusual to find them dressed in hand crocheted outfits or even creatively dressed and strung to be used as window shade pulls. Baby was jointed at the arms and hips. Babies generally had hand-painted facial features; some examples had painted hair and either a hand-painted or spray-painted diaper. $10/each.

The #8 Renwal baby had painted facial features and sometimes wore a two-piece outfit. Eyes on these babies were usually painted looking sideways. In 1947, Renwal offered their #1200 School House Set. This set had a teacher's desk and chair and 6 colored student desks. The students happened to be #8 babies. These hand-painted little scholars had blue, red, or yellow pants, a colored shirt with various decorations including collars, bow ties, and buttons. The presence of their painted black shoes indicated that the baby came with this very popular School House Set, making them more desirable to collectors. Baby w/shoes, $25. Baby w/o shoes, $10.

Ideal Toy & Novelty Co.

The Ideal Toy & Novelty Co. was founded in 1907 by Morris Michtom and his wife, Rose. In 1903 Michtom, the owner of a small toy and novelty store in Brooklyn, attached the label "Teddy's Bear" to hand-made stuffed plush animals, after receiving written permission to do so from President Teddy Roosevelt. Roosevelt, always with an eye to favorable publicity, had refused to shoot a small bear cub captured during a hunting trip in 1902. The accompanying press saw to it that Teddy's sportsmanlike gesture was well publicized and the Michtoms benefited from the press coverage. The bear was so well received that the Michtoms ultimately moved their store to larger quarters and established Ideal as what would soon become a premier toy company.

Under the brilliant leadership of the founders' son, Benjamin, Ideal found real success in selling "celebrity dolls" during the Depression Years. Following on the heels of the fabulously popular Shirley Temple doll in 1934, Michtom introduced dolls resembling Judy Garland, Deanna Durbin, Charlie McCarthy, and Fanny Brice. In 1937 Ideal introduced "Betsy Wetsy". The success of this "feeding/wetting" doll gave the company added financial strength, allowing it to invest in early plastics injection-molding machines, used during the War years to fulfill military contracts for such top-secret projects as the "proximity fuse". In fact, Ideal attributed military involvement for failing to deliver plastic toys as the War ended. During the War, Ideal's plastics manufacturing capability was further strengthened by the arrival of the legendary plastics engineer, Islyn Thomas, General Manager of Ideal's newly formed plastics division. Thomas helped Ideal obtain scarce quantities of surplus raw materials that were used, even during the War, to make some quantities of commercial goods and toys, such as the first plastic toy tea sets.

By the end of World War II, Ideal was positioned to become one the largest of the postwar American toy and doll manufacturers. Its Chairman, A.M. Katz, fully dedicated his strategy to building and refining the company's plastics capabilities. In 1947 Ideal introduced a line of beautifully detailed 1:18 scale dollhouse furniture from brightly colored hard plastic. The toys generally are marked with the Ideal trademark and one or more mold numbers. Early boxed sets included room box walls that could be set up and used in place of a full dollhouse. The 1:18 scale furniture was produced until 1952 at which time Ideal, showing a new direction, changed its name to the Ideal Toy Corporation.

As companions to their impressive line of 1:18 scale hard plastic dollhouse furniture, Ideal Toy and Novelty Co. created a dollhouse family of four. Ideal correctly claimed they were "perfectly proportioned to scale for dollhouse furniture." They were catalogued only in 1949 and are very hard to find today. They were sold in 5&10¢ and variety stores that displayed Ideal dollhouse furniture. No evidence has been found that the dolls were ever packaged separately in their own box or container. An extended family was never produced. If one is lucky enough to find this family today, they will discover that they have not become brittle and still remain reasonably flexible. Often, however, fingers and even noses are missing, apparently as a result of the failure of the plastic to fill the mold. Ideal marketed 4 babies that were sold either separately at around 10¢, or inside a boxed set of dollhouse furniture selling for around $1.30.

By 1964, Ideal was firmly under the control of its visionary President, Lionel Weintraub. The company not only focused on dolls like *Saucy Walker, Kissy* and *Thumbellina*, but it expanded its offerings to include games. Ideal reentered the dollhouse market when it introduced a line of dollhouse furniture in 1:18 scale. The *Petite Princess Fantasy Furniture*, with real cloth upholstery, had glass and metal details and accessories to highlight the plastic furniture. The furniture was too expensive to appeal to the mass toy market, and in 1965 the line was reintroduced as *Princess Patti*. The materials used to decorate the *Princess Patti* furniture were not as expensive as the *Petite Princess* line. With some nod to reality, the *Princess Patti* line included the, now rare, kitchen, bathroom, and TV set. Much of this *Fantasy* furniture is found individually packaged in boxes today. The lines included a four person family. Again in 1969, Ideal marketed a vinyl fold-up dollhouse together with plastic furniture made in Hong Kong. It did not include dolls. The furniture is hallmarked "1969 Ideal." Ideal was sold to CBS, Inc. in 1982 and ceased to be an independent toy company, although its brand is still strong today.

Ideal's dollhouse dolls were approximately the same 1:18 scale as their furniture, although the "tall" father and mother measured 5 and 4.75 inches respectively. The children were more to scale with boy measuring 3 inches and girl, 2.75 inches. These unmarked dolls were molded of a rubbery plastic and could be washed. Only their arms were jointed at the shoulders, held in place with a metal pin. This truly limited the play value of the doll. Their clothing, hair, eyes, and mouth were hand-painted. Father wore a double-breasted dark blue suit, but his shirt and tie were unpainted. His shoes were painted brown. He could also be found sporting a gray-blue suit with brown shoes. Mother wore a dark red two-piece outfit with red shoes. She has also been discovered in a mustard yellow dress with matching shoes. The boy doll was dressed in pale blue shorts, a white sleeveless shirt and white shoes. Sister matched in the reverse – a white top with a blue vest, a white skirt and white shoes. Other colors for the children's outfits have not been reported. Adults: $35/each, Children: $45/each.

Ideal's four plastic babies from left to right: an unclothed "frozen" hard plastic baby measured 2.5" tall. It had hand-painted features and was marked Ideal/USA on its back. He cost 10 cents in 1948 or could be found included in some of Ideal's boxed furniture sets. A harder to find baby was Ideal's jointed 2.5" doll with a painted sun-suit. He had moving arms and legs and was not marked. Apparently, he was only sold in 1948. Ideal's most common baby is very much like Renwal's. Molded in hard plastic his arms and legs rotate in their hip and shoulder sockets. He was 2.5" tall and his hair, eyes, and white diaper were spray-painted. This doll could be found in many of the later boxed furniture sets that had a cellophane window. In 1949, Ideal offered for one year only *The Smallest Baby in the World.* This unclothed hard plastic doll was only about .875" and was packaged in a cardboard box with a 1.25" hard plastic bathtub. Babies are often found today still enclosed in the cardboard box. Baby and bathtub were not hallmarked. Babies, $3-10/each. *Smallest Baby,* $15-20 MIB.

Reliable of Canada sold a line of dollhouse furniture similar in scale to Ideal's. In fact, many of the Reliable pieces were near exact copies of their Ideal counterparts. While Reliable did not market a family of dollhouse dolls, they did sell plastic babies, closely resembling Ideal's. The small pj baby, second from the right, is much like one made by Thomas. $3-10/each.

Trilby was a 5" hard plastic three-face doll sold by Ideal in the 1950s. She was not truly a dollhouse doll, although not completely oversized for a large scale dollhouse. The box stated that the doll had three facial expressions –sleeping, smiling, or crying. *Trilby* was dressed in a molded snowsuit either pink with blue trim or blue with pink trim and held a molded rattle. There was a pointed cone on top of her head which was rotated to make *Trilby* wake from sleep to either radiantly smile or sadly cry. $25 MIB.

Peggy was made by Ideal in the mid-1950s. She was a 5.25" inflexible, hard plastic doll on a stand with painted undergarments, hair, eyes, mouth, and shoes. Peggy was originally packaged with 8 outfits and a hat. These items were called her "Snap-On Magic Wardrobe." The clothing was hard plastic and snapped onto the doll. Unlike paper doll clothes with tabs, Peggy's clothing stayed in place. Her outfits included two bathing suits, two overcoats, a hat, pajamas, two school dresses, and a party dress. With changeable apparel, Peggy added nice play value to a large dollhouse. *Peggy* was later marketed by Lido with fewer outfits. It is unclear whether Lido's doll was made for the company by Ideal or whether Lido purchased the molds from Ideal and made the doll themselves. Ideal's, $30, Lido's, $20.

In 1964 Ideal introduced a four-member family to complement its Petite Princess and Princess Patti lines of furniture. Made of vinyl over a wire frame with cloth costumes, adults measured 5.5" and children 3.75". Mother and daughter were wigged, while the males had painted, molded hair. Facial details were painted. They were hallmarked "Ideal" on the bottom of their removable vinyl shoes and some of the clothing had cloth labels. $35 MIB Family.

Plastic Art Toy Corporation of America

While Renwal and Ideal became the dominant suppliers of high-quality plastic miniatures in the immediate postwar period, they were outlived by a line of furniture and dollhouses produced by The Plastic Art Toy Corporation of America and marketed under the name Plasco with a little drummer boy logo. The Company was formed on January 1, 1945, in East Rutherford, NJ, perhaps as the marketing arm of Columbia Protektosite Company. Columbia Protektosite was known as a pioneer pre-war producer of plastic toys. During the war they apparently were able to obtain significant quantities of scrap cellulose acetate and produced a line of wood-toned dollhouse furniture. After the war they do not appear to market the toys, but rather to produce the molding from which some of the Plasco toys were made.

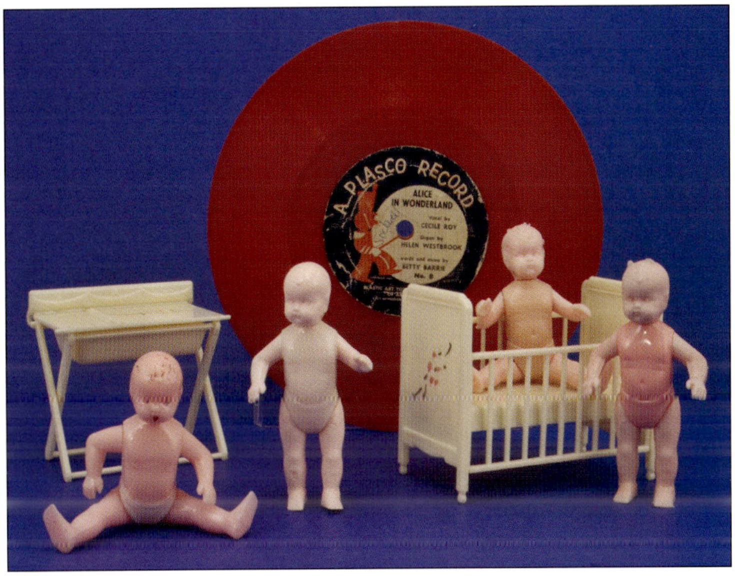

Plasco's 3.25" dolls were marked "Plasco USA" on their backs. Babies were originally sold in the Plasco boxed nursery set. These early babies were hard plastic dolls with painted features and diapers. Arms, legs, and head were moveable. In 1950, when the company changed the style of its cellophane boxes, Plasco began to include this baby in each of its furniture sets. Babies were also sold separately. While utilizing the same mold design, Plasco experimented with the plastic they used. Some of the variations seen in the baby are hard plastic with a white molded chest and diaper, and later a rubbery vinyl baby with a pink or blue chest and coordinating diaper. Much later, apparently after the molds were sold to other companies, the Plasco name was removed from the baby with the pink and blue details. $3-5/each.

Plasco advertised its line of kitchen furniture in 1946, announcing that they had retained a renowned industrial designer, Eugene J. Lux, to design a "streamlined and smartly modern" eleven-piece set of appliances and cabinets that could be used by a little homemaker wanting to play house or by an adult wanting to design a full sized kitchen. By 1947 Plasco was offering a full line of *"Little Homemaker"* dollhouse furniture in boxed sets. The inside of these early boxes were decorated to resemble walls and floors of a room or patio and could be used as room settings for the furniture. Within a short period of time Plasco began to sell its furniture in cellophane topped boxes. At times they included a small red 78 rpm phonograph recording of a children's song with appropriate titles like: *Playing Together, Setting the Table, I Want a Dollhouse,* and *Buddy's Garden*. Around 1953 Plasco moved to East Patterson, New

Jersey, continuing to make its distinctively designed furniture. Through the 1960s, furniture was offered without the Plasco name or drummer boy logo as Little Miss Homemaker Furniture in "House and Garden Colors" by Plastic Toy & Novelty Corp of Brooklyn, New York, either a successor to the original Plasco or a purchaser of their molds. This later company was acquired by Consolidated Accessories Corp. in September 1970. Miniature furniture and babies made from the original Plasco furniture molds have been found, apparently produced by Hong Kong, Brazilian, Australian and Spanish companies.

Plasco never produced a doll family to reside in the unique dollhouses it made and sold. They did however make a baby that measured 3.25" tall and was approximately 1:9 scale that was eventually included with many of their boxed furniture sets.

Louis Marx & Co.

Louis Marx was one of the first toy makers to seize on an "enlightened" (and self-serving) idea that a child felt more love and reassurance if he or she received a weekly 29¢ toy rather than $20 worth of toys for a birthday or holiday. He aimed at making quality toys at the lowest possible prices, thus breaking the more traditional approach of giving children a few, high-quality, expensive toys. By following this philosophy, his privately held Louis Marx & Co. became the largest postwar toy manufacturer, dominating the industry for nearly five decades. He set the standard for lithography of tin toys. He pushed the market towards low-cost molded plastic figures. He drove consumer choice, and helped encourage an attitude that toys needed to be constantly updated. He helped establish mass merchandisers as the consumer's source for playthings - his and others. His methods and products were copied by many, but, of course, he never hesitated to make a close "replica" of a competitor's toy.

Born in Brooklyn on August 11, 1896, to German immigrant parents, Marx was surrounded by a community and friends that cared for each other, without regard to financial status. Although Marx never felt that his early life was "tough", he finished high school by the time he was 15, poring over books about "how to become a $5,000 a year man". He was anxious to start work and make a financially secure mark. Soon after graduating from high school he was hired as an office boy with the well known toy maker Ferdinand Strauss. He quickly caught the eye of his bosses and within four years became the manager of Strauss' New Jersey production plant and a company officer. Not only his creative genius, but also his business sense, began to flourish. His philosophy of mass manufacturing was maturing, and his debate with Strauss management, urging them to focus on manufacturing rather than retail sales, resulted in his termination. After a quick tour in the Army between 1917 and 1918, he joined a Vermont wood-products company. He developed a line of miniature dishware and toys that caught the eye of a buyer from F.W. Woolworth. Sales increased from 15,000 units to 1,500,000 units in two years, adding a further cornerstone of his business philosophy — selling to mass marketers.

Despite having reached his $5,000 a year salary goal, Marx sought his independence. He and his younger brother, David, established a toy distribution company at 200 Park Avenue in Manhattan. Acting as middlemen between manufacturers and large chain retailers, their profit derived from finding ways to drive down the cost of the toys. They would take a design and reengineer it so that it could be produced either with the same features at a lower cost or with additional features at the same price point. If a retailer was interested, the Marx brothers would then find a manufacturer to produce it. In 1921 they began making their own toys when they purchased the dies for two mechanical tin toys from the ironically bankrupt F. J. Strauss Company. Marx immediately repainted, renamed, and reintroduced Strauss' rather tired mechanical monkey and minstrel with great success. Within two years, Louis Marx was a millionaire and began to expand and further develop his philosophy of controlling costs by controlling the key aspects of production. He acquired four manufacturing facilities in Girard, Pennsylvania; Erie, Pennsylvania; and Glendale, West Virginia.

Marx' refined his thinking about the toy business as his company grew. He believed that there were six factors that should be used in assessing a toy: familiarity, surprise, skill, play value, sturdiness, and comprehensibility. He saw dolls as inherently fulfilling the elements of familiarity and play value. He added surprise and sturdiness to his offerings.

Marx was able to survive the Depression because he could produce toys that could be cheaply sold by dimestores and mail-order companies in this financially tight decade. Not the inventor of the Yo-Yo, he produced a cheap tin version of Ronald Duncan's toy. He made tin trains that were unpackaged and were simply lined up in dimestore bins to compete with the far more expensive Lionel and Ives tinplate trains. He entered into licensing arrangements to produce Walt Disney, Popeye, Superman, and Charlie McCarthy tin wind-up toys. By 1940 Louis Marx & Co. was the world's largest toy manufacturer. The impending war saw Marx shift his metal working expertise to military goods and totally cease toy production.

Marx' greatest success immediately followed the end of the war. Well positioned to produce tin toys as before the war, he had maintained close personal relationships with the principal toy buyers of the mass merchandisers and mail-order retailers: F.W. Woolworth, S.S. Kresge, W.T. Grant, Sears & Roebuck, Montgomery Ward, J.C. Penney. The toy world was changing, and plastic toys could be produced more cheaply than metal. Marx, the ultimate "copycat", wasn't going to be outmaneuvered by his competition. Playsteel and T. Cohn were first to the market with tin dollhouses, although neither initially came with furniture or dolls. Marx assembled his team and designed, not only a house, but a houseful of furniture and a family of dolls. His 2-story colonial dollhouse was introduced to the market in 1949 selling completely furnished for $3.98, 71¢ below T. Cohn's unfurnished house. It was a huge success and Marx slowly dominated the dollhouse market over the next two decades, driving his competition from the field.

By 1959 Louis Marx and Co, Inc. was producing toys in over 19 countries, allowing the company to build on local strengths to support its growing business. Marx felt that German workers were the best producers of intricate mechanical toys, and Japanese workers were superior in producing small hand-made toys. After a crippling strike at its principal Glendale plant in 1962, Marx' new motto became "Hong Kong better, Hong Kong cheaper." He shipped more and more work offshore as United States union wages made his toys less competitive.

As Marx grew older, the company began to lose its dominance. Once convinced that a toy sold itself to a child, Marx had done little advertising, depending upon large retailers to create the demand for his toys. Television changed buying patterns as children were exposed to a vast array of toys. His close-knit design and production teams began to retire or were lured away by competitors like Ideal Toy. Foreign markets had different buying patterns than the American market and Marx was not able to readily expand into them. In April 1972, Marx sold his company to Fischer Price, then owned by Quaker Oats, for $51 Million. Quaker Oats was in the process of buying a number of toy companies, stripping them of much of their creative talent and lowering the quality of the product in cost-cutting moves. Quaker ran the company into the ground, and sold it in April 1976 to the former British subsidiary of Marx, Dunbee-Combex, for $15M. The new company was unable to successfully reestablish itself as Dunbee-Combex-Marx and declared bankruptcy in 1980. The Marx name was licensed to a number of companies. Unfortunately, Louis Marx, the genius who fulfilled the dreams of decades of children, lived to see the demise of the company. He died on February 5, 1982, at the age of 85.

The 1949 Marx Colonial Dollhouse was packaged with three "chubby" unmarked vinyl figures: a sitting boy and girl, each slightly over 1.5" and baby with arms out, just over 1". In later years, Marx sometimes included a small baby with its hands up. The figures were suitable for sitting on furniture and play yard pieces. Their clothing, facial features and hair were molded into figures with no painted highlights. These dolls were packaged in a brown paper bag marked "People," found in the box along with the house and hard plastic furnishings. Marx packaged these three or four small figures with his dollhouses for decades. $3/each.

The fourteen figures first introduced by Marx in its 1953 L-shaped ranch. The "thin" polyethylene figures, produced in a range of solid colors, were sized from 1.125" to 2.75". The dolls were well-detailed and had good play value. $2/each, $30-35/set.

First appearing in 1951, an expanded eight-member "chubby" family had a mother, father, and four children: boy, girl, diapered toddler, and baby in one-piece pj's. There were also seated grandparents. The flesh-colored figures ranged in size from 1.5" to 3.25". The extended family fit well in the larger dwelling, either on the main floor, on the patio, or doing laundry in the utility room. Scale was not important to Marx and these figures were sold separately in 1951 to complement any standard sized dollhouse. This set of eight vinyl dolls sold for 79¢ in the Sears catalog. The figures were not marked, but it is possible that when the dolls were new they had stickers applied on their back or underside. $5/each, $50 set.

Marx got around the fact that his figures could not be posed to sit or kneel by creating figures in action poses. Among the characters were baseball players, babies who played in the sandbox, and a girl playing dress-up. Others included a girl drying dishes, a boy brushing his teeth, and a girl petting a cat. $2/each.

A second type of family was introduced to complement the 14 figures of the L-shaped ranch. Their molded stands had labels incised on the underside indicating their position in the family: father (smoking a pipe), mother, sister, and baby (holding a block). They ranged in size from 1.5" to 3". The stands enabled the dolls to be easily placed around the house. $3/each.

Seated pink, blue, or ivory boy and girl dolls were enclosed with Marx' dollhouses that included the outdoor swingset. If a house included a pool, it came with a 2" boy posed to dive from a diving board and a 1.875" girl sitting on the edge of the pool, contemplating the water temperature. $2-3/each.

Marx introduced a third style family, also on marked stands, in the 1960s made from polypropylene. They were quite shiny and lacked molded detail. Father carried a book, having curbed his smoking habit, and his clothes reflected updated 60s styles. Mother had a new stylish pageboy and a shorter dress. Sister was holding a doll. Only baby remained the same. In the 1970s, some of the Marx dollhouses came packaged with this family, now hand-painted, indicating that they were produced in Hong Kong. $3/each unpainted, $5/each painted.

Three seated polypropylene figures were added to the third style family and packaged with the *Marx Imagination, House of the Future* in 1965. $3.

Marx' 1955 *Babyland Nursery* was packaged with seven new figures. The hard plastic nurse was 2.5" tall and stood on a base. There were six babies approximately 1", each a unique mold. Three were sitting and three reclining. $5/each, $50/set.

The 1956 *Little Red Schoolhouse* featured ten new figures in nine poses. A 2.625" teacher wore glasses and was holding a book in one hand and a piece of chalk in the other. She had been assigned nine students. There were two identical seated boys with hand raised and one seated girl with a book. The other figures were standing on bases, engaging in various classroom activities. Each child was approximately 2" tall. $5/each, $65/10 figure set.

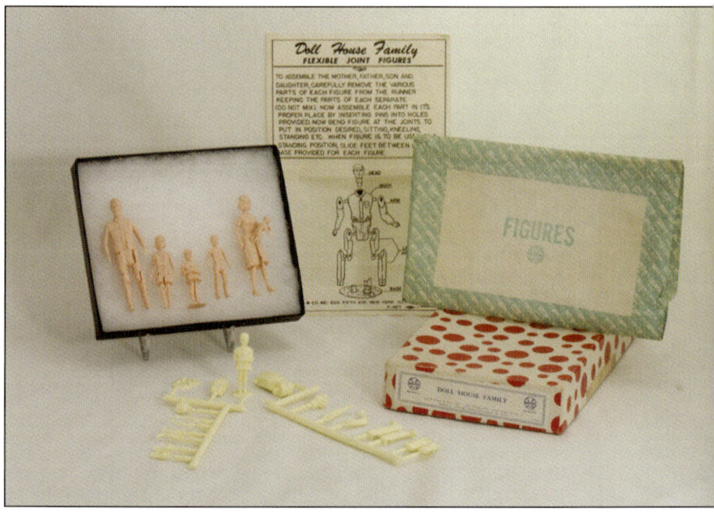

Introduced in 1961, Marx *Flexible Joint Figures* were assembled at their joints, enabling them to sit and kneel, a first for Marx. Easily assembled, a child snapped a protruding knob on one piece into the appropriate hole on another. Younger sister and baby were in one-piece. Father and mother were just over 3"; older sister, 2.125"; brother, .875"; stationary younger sister, about 1.625"; baby .875". $10 MIB.

Appealing to owners of newer 1:18 dollhouses, *American Family Twistoys* of 1963 were packaged by Marx in a plain, brown cardboard box and sold for $1.77 in the Sears catalog. Dolls had plastic heads and torsos with over-sized hands and shoes. Their arms and legs, resembling toothpicks, were wire covered with thin plastic tubing. Father and mother were approximately 4.5"; brother and sister, just under 3"; baby, 2". Cloth clothing was a new addition, but seams were not finished and lapels and decorations were glued in place. Hair and facial features were painted. The dolls had a gold sticker on their backs "Marx Toys, made in Hong Kong." Finally flexible, a Sears ad read: "Bend to pose em." $3/each.

In the revamped version of the *Twistoys*, marketed occasionally as the *Jones Family*, or more often as the *Brown Family,* dolls' torsos were hard plastic. Arms and legs were a wire armature covered with flesh-colored fabric. Heads on the mother and father were soft plastic and swiveled; boy, girl, and baby had a hard head. The hard plastic hands and shoes were scaled more normally. They had painted hair and facial features and cloth clothing. Father even had tiny buttons on his jacket. Mom wore low-heeled boots and baby was wrapped in a pink blanket. The plastic faces on the boy, girl, and baby looked almost identical to the "Twistoy" children. This boxed family, also produced in Hong Kong, appeared in the 1966 Sears catalog, offered at $1.89. They were sold in a colorful gift box with all family members pictured on the box cover. $25/set MIB.

After their introduction in the mid 1960s, the Brown family members, underwent numerous costume changes. $5/each.

Four dolls complemented the 1964 Marx Little Hostess/Amanda Ann furniture line. Mother and father, just under 4", were seated. A teenage standing daughter measured 4.25". A 4" maid was carrying a decorated cake with mocha frosting. The dolls' attire was colorfully painted, as well as their hair and facial features. Each doll had a mold mark reading: "Marx Toys, made in Hong Kong." At the front of the picture are miniaturized, 1.125" versions of the dolls that were included in the clear *See and Play"* dollhouse in 1968. $30/set for larger dolls, $3/each for small dolls.

Louis Marx was a larger than life individual, known for shaking hands with a friend or new acquaintance, reaching in a pocket and handing the individual a small toy. Doing business in a much different era than today, he was known to pass out a small vinyl reclining nude. In 1964 he expanded on the concept, introducing a set of scantily clad 1:24 scale "American Beauties" or "Bathing Beauties." Marx downsized the "Bathing Beauties" to create some of the dolls for his 1968 *See and Play* dollhouse as seen in the front of the picture. Bathing Beauties, $5/each. Reclining Nude, $25. Small dolls, $3/each.

The figures that Marx produced to inhabit his dollhouses witnessed many changes between 1949 and 1972. After experimenting with injection-molded polystyrene figures in his non-dollhouse playsets, Marx engineers decided on vinyl acetate as the material of choice for his first dollhouse figures. The rubber-like material would lose some detail when the molding dies were cut, and later when the dies were re-plated after chemicals in the material had attacked the die surfaces. Since plastic was a new material, Marx was constantly changing its formulations to produce a more desirable result, looking for ease of production, lower cost, and better quality. Eventually, the company adopted polyethylene for its figures. The figures stood better and had crisper detail. Marx designers and collectors refer to them as 'thin figures' to differentiate them from the more chubby vinyl figures. A waxier finish gave better mold release, cutting down on waste and scrap. Eventually Marx moved to polypropylene, a more engineered soft plastic, for reasons of cost and production efficiency. The material did not hold detail well when molded and had a very shiny finish.

The firm of Derham and Associates created the original sculptures that were used to make the molds for the vinyl dolls. Phil Derham, meticulous and detailed, could take up to a month to sculpt one figure. The models were turned over to Newark Tool and Die Company to be cut over a period of months into metal molding dies. Needing another source for the growing number of figures used in Marx playsets, the company turned to an Ohio toolmaker, Joe Ferriot of Ferriot Brothers, as their molder. Joe Ferriot initially used models sculpted by Derham, but he was impatient with Derham's slow production. Ferriot decided he would design the figures in addition to molding them. He developed a special plasticized wax as the media for his prototypes. The material would melt away as molten metal was poured into it to form a mold cavity. This transfer casting method reduced cycle time in half. Ferriot was an artist who specialized in depicting action in his figures. The Marx staff depended on his skills to add dimension and detail to the playsets. Later Marx supplemented Ferriot's output with companies formed by modelers trained by Derham, HMS Inc., and Bill Lemon's Nomel Plastics.

Marx included its first three dollhouse dolls in its 1949 Marx Colonial Dollhouse. In 1951, Marx sold an expanded house with a larger family and numerous accessories. Marx was constantly updating his miniature real estate to approximate the real world. In 1953, he produced a popular L-shaped ranch house. It included fourteen new figures: a governess with her brood of 13 youngsters. Sometimes the 14-piece set was packaged with the seated boy, girl, and baby from 1949. Later this 14-piece set was re-packaged with two parents and two kids molded on flat stands. As time went on, in order to spread the cost of design, Marx would use his figure sets over and over, sometimes differing the combinations. For example, this large set of family and children was also included in the Marx Zoo playset.

As dollhouses reflected a more affluent lifestyle, so did the figures. Four playing children were included in houses with outdoor playground equipment and swimming pools. The same children were also included with the Patio and Pool boxed accessory set as pictured in the Sears catalog in 1959.

In the 1960s, Marx added another set of dollhouse dolls with a marked base. These dolls appear to be made of polypropylene. When sold with the Marx Imagination, House of the Future in 1965, three new seated figures were added. A 1969 Wards catalog pictured both the older and newer sets of family figures in different Marx houses.

In the mid-1950s, Marx made three playsets that used the same basic building: the *Babyland Nursery*, the *Pet Shop,* and the *Little Red Schoolhouse*. Marx changed the lithography of the buildings to illustrate his theme and added appropriate furniture, accessories, and figures. The Marx *Pet Shop* was released in 1952. In addition to a great variety of pets, Marx included four vinyl dollhouse family figures. These were four of the same vinyl figures that were issued in 1951. This family was another example of Marx' reuse of his designs. The *Babyland Nursery* was issued first in 1955 with seven new figures. The third playset, the *Little Red Schoolhouse*, was marketed in 1956. The figures for this set were also new.

When collecting Marx 1:24 scale figures, it is hard to categorize them as dollhouse or non-dollhouse related. There are figures in the Marx Skyscraper playset that would be appropriate in any of his dollhouses: businessmen molded with and without their fedoras, ping-pong players, mother taking her toddler for a walk on a leash, man toweling off after a workout. The Sears store playset is filled with men and women, many dressed in hats and coats, having just come in from the outside. A mother pushes a child in a stroller. Farm sets have families generally dressed in work clothes ready to do their chores. The Super Circus and Marx Zoo playsets have figures borrowed from the dollhouse sets, and new figures showing families off on an outing.

In 1961, another new plastic family appeared in the Wards catalog. This six-member grouping was called "Flexible Joint Figures." Packaged in a white box with red circles, father, mother, older sister, and brother came still attached to a molding sprue in nine parts including a stand.

The early 1960s were successful, yet changing years for Marx, as they moved away from playsets. In 1963, both Sears and Wards were selling a larger scaled family called "American Family Twistoys." In the mid 60s, this family was revamped. Sometimes they were identified as the Jones Family, but more often were known as the Brown Family. Montgomery Ward advertised the family as "ready to move into almost any dollhouse." Well into the 1970s, after Marx had sold to Quaker Oats, catalog outlets like Harriet Carter, Lillian Vernon, and Price Imports carried this same five-member family, boxed in sets without the Marx logo.

In 1964, Marx introduced a brand-new line of *Little Hostess* plastic dollhouse furniture, apparently to compete with Ideal's *Petite Princess*. Unlike its simple 50s style furniture, this new line had pieces with moving parts and was designed with more sophisticated youth in mind. At least in England, hard plastic, non-poseable figures to complement the line were sold by the Marx subsidiary, Combex, under the name Amanda Ann.

Acme-Thomas

As Marx gained fame as the Toy King, another pioneer, Dr. Islyn Thomas, became "Sir Plastic." Thomas was born in Maestag, South Wales, in 1912. In 1923 his father, a miner, moved Islyn, his mother, and sister to the United States and the coal fields of Eastern Pennsylvania. Thomas first took up the trade of tool and die making. After graduating from trade school in Scranton, Pennsylvania, he took a job as a toolmaker with Consolidated Molded Products Corp., then one of the leading plastics molders in the world. He continued his education and by 1938 was named Chief Engineer. A primary focus of Consolidated was the automotive industry. They were able to cut the dies for relatively simple projects, but for more complicated jobs, companies like Newark Die were the leaders, and would work with Consolidated in designing molds that would be used to cast the products. Thomas gained further knowledge of the plastics industry from Newark Die, as well as a wife, when he married the founder's daughter. While working at Consolidated, Thomas helped a small-plastics "middleman," Benjamin Shapiro, who formed Acme Plastics Manufacturing Co. in the mid-1930s, by designing dies for a toy film-strip viewer, an airplane, and 3 small boats.

Thomas' perfect 50s family was molded as one-piece figures from the rubber-like Vinylite, and was sold in six-piece sets with both parents, a 1.25" baby, one of two older children, and one of two younger children, together with one of the three pets. Although introduced by 1950, this unmarked series of dolls was sold as "Playtime" figures in 1956. Older boy and girl measured 2", and younger brother and sister with raised left hands were 1.5". The dancing mother and father were approximately 3.5". These two figures were later made in colorful hard plastic attached to a 2.625" round red disc. The disc is threaded so that when you wind and pull the attached string, the dolls actually dance in a circle. This toy was marked "Thomas Toy" on the base. Like Louis Marx, Thomas could create multiple uses for his toy components. Family, $30 MOC. Dancing disk, $30. Individual figures, $3/each.

Thomas toys were not designed for "little homemakers" simply to admire. The company's vinyl figures could actually swing, slide, bounce, stroll, and rock on its playground and nursery pieces. When Thomas packaged his outdoor and nursery pieces, a selection of these dolls was often included, all sized to fit in the seats of strollers, seesaws, and Ferris Wheels. Figures,$3/each.

This 1955 set was made by Thomas for Campbell Soup's *Campbell Kids* toy line. It included eight plastic hinge-top school desks with integral chairs as well as a real blackboard, paper cutouts of textbooks, and teacher's desk cut into a cardboard display box with detailed lithography of a classroom. The eight Thomas students had painted clothes, hair, and facial detail. The teacher was their dancing dad with a painted brown suit. Molds were typically sold from one plastics company to another as they began to wear or when a new line of toys was introduced. In later years Aldens sold a small school set utilizing the Thomas molds. The figures were a bright yellow polyethylene and were packaged on a point-of-sale blister card. $375/set MIB.

Thomas made two sizes (1.25 and 1.5") of a small diapered baby. There were also two larger diapered babies (2 and 3") sometimes called little toddlers or "Tommy Tots." Diapered babies can be found on cards with crochet needle, thread, and instructions to create a dress. Other carded babies included suggestions for uses of the dolls as cord pulls, shower favors, and pins. Carded sets: $15.

Often drawing upon competing companies' designs, we see both a Thomas and Reliable of Canada pajama boy wearing his Doctor Denton's with a dropped seat. The Thomas boy holds his right arm over his stomach, while the Reliable baby holds his left. The Reliable baby was sold with the pictured Reliable outhouse. $10.

A late 1940s set of dolls, made by Thomas, were costumed as if on their way to a Halloween parade. The six-piece set included three boys and three girls dressed as a Lady Liberty like "Miss America", a majorette, Gretchen the Dutch girl, Hansel the Dutch boy, "Scotch Ladd", and "Kaptain Kiddy", a pirate. Dolls, originally molded in vinyl, are often found mounted on separate cards printed with appropriate landscapes and poems. A complete set of Thomas costumed dolls was later produced by Alden's in a harder polyethylene version, packaged on a blister pack display card. $15 MOC, $5 loose.

Thomas made combination vinyl and hard plastic dollhouse dolls in a larger scale. The boy and girl, standing in front of a Thomas cardboard house, measured 3.5". Hard plastic, colorful clothing served as the torso. The head was attached and rotated. Limbs were connected within the torso with elastic string. They were marked "Thomas" on their back. In this era of close copying of designs, a British firm, Poplar Plastics marketed an unmarked pair, dressed slightly differently. $10/pr. MOC.

In 1942 Islyn was recruited to become the General Manager of the plastics division of Ideal Toy and Novelty. While Ideal was primarily producing war materials at that time, Thomas used the contacts and knowledge gained at Consolidated to acquire unused toy molds and huge quantities of scrap plastic left over from making military parts. Developing a method to separate different plastics, he was able to utilize the scrap to make a limited line of plastic toys that were eagerly gobbled up by the market, at relatively high prices. As the end of the war neared, Thomas went out on his own, forming three companies aimed at capitalizing on his vast knowledge of this "miracle" material, the most well known being Thomas Manufacturing Corporation. In 1945 he renewed his relationship with Benjamin Shapiro and together they operated Acme Plastics Manufacturing Co. Thomas Manufacturing began to design a whole new line of toys, molded by Hungerford Plastics Corp. and distributed by Acme under its name. In 1950, Thomas Manufacturing had finally acquired its own molding capabilities and was thriving. Islyn Thomas bought out Shapiro's interest in Acme and started to market a broad range of toys under the Thomas name.

Thomas, having furthered his education in plastics engineering, continued to grow his reputation in the plastics field. He wrote the classic textbook in the field of injection-molding. He helped establish plastics manufacturing facilities in the United Kingdom after the war. He was part of President Truman's War Production Board and a member of the Commerce Department's advisory committee on Toys and Games Manufacturing. He was President of Newark Die while still leading Thomas Manufacturing, perhaps prompting Louis Marx to shift his die making from his competitor, Thomas, to the Ferriot Brothers in Ohio. In 1960 he sold his interest in Thomas to Banner Plastics and "retired" to the life of a plastics consultant and Welsh-American cultural leader. In 1975 Queen Elizabeth recognized his industrial efforts, when he was named an Officer of the Most Excellent Order of the British Empire –"Sir Plastic." He died in May 2002.

Collectors of baby boomer dollhouses and dollhouse furniture find that toys manufactured by the Thomas Manufacturing Corp. are worthy companions of the dollhouse toys and figures produced by the four companies which dominated the plastic miniatures market from 1945–1960, Renwal, Ideal, Plasco, and Marx.

Thomas' principal line of dollhouse sized figures was a "Donna Reed perfect" 50s family. Mom in her flowing gown linked arms with Dad in his double-breasted suit, while big and little brother, big and little sister, two different babies, and the family's two dogs and cat sat and watched. Children and babies in the "Playtime" series were sold to complement many of the Thomas products. The seated boy and girl, sold as the Playtime Twins, found their way into the classroom set made by Thomas for Campbell Soup's "Campbell Kids" toy line. The children in the Campbell's school set had hand-painted clothing, hair, and facial features. Generally, however, only a few of the Thomas figures had painted eyes and mouth. The figures were not marked.

The "Playtime" family could be purchased on a colorful 5x7 cardboard decorated with a living room backdrop. The figures were stapled onto the card. Dolls and pets were also sold singly on smaller individual cards with a partial living room scene. Often these cards included a poem about the attached figure. Author Bill Hanlon has an interesting segment on his web site about Islyn Thomas. He suggests that stapling the toys onto cards may have been an early Thomas solution to the problem of shoplifting from open dimestore bins and counter displays.

For the dollhouse collector who likes to do more than just look and rearrange furniture, the Thomas line is a great addition to a collection. Despite its wonderful play value and low 10-59¢ postwar prices, there are many well-preserved examples to be found today by collectors.

All the plastics pioneers affected the concept of dollhouse dolls. Dollhouses and their inhabitants became toys, not display pieces. Many would say plastics "spoiled" small dolls, making them unworthy to collect. In fact, this "revolutionary material" helped make dollhouses and miniature dolls available to children (not adults) of all economic levels. The miniature dolls reflected the period in which they were made. They wore up-to-date fashions and performed modern activities. They did not depend on sewing and painting to give them life, but rather on the highly developed artistic skills of modelers who gave them every minute detail.

Chapter 7

From the Cottage to the Factory

After the close of World War II, the worldwide toy industry continued to develop on a two-pronged path that had been paved before the war. In the United States toy giants like Marx, Renwal, and Ideal continued down the highway of mass production and mass retail distribution. The other road was taken by individuals applying well-developed individual talent and creativity to modern materials in order to make high-quality, handcrafted toys.

Shortly after the war, hand-made dolls produced by talented men and women made their way to the market. American entrepreneurship took a number of different paths in the immediate postwar period. Unlike their European counterparts, who fell back on their artistic skills in order to survive a war-wrecked economy, these crafts persons found a booming American economy. The first priority, however, was to find employment for all the men returning from military service. Rosy the Riveter was expected to leave the factory and stay at home. Many enterprising women helped provide for their families by developing cottage industries to produce beautiful, highly detailed dollhouse dolls. They weren't constrained by the materials they chose. Some used hard plastic or vinyl for the bodies, some covered wire armatures, others stuffed cloth, or used pipe cleaners. The dolls were dressed in hand-cut clothes with varying degrees of finish detail. Some dolls had hand-painted features. Neighbors were often enlisted to make clothing, to paint details, or to assemble the dolls, being paid "by the piece."

Some doll makers moved their businesses from their homes and built small factories to make their toys. The move to the factory was certainly not a trend unique to the postwar period. Companies like Fred K. Braitling had operated small doll factories before the war. Besides output volume, the common denominator seems to have been a desire to control all stages of production, rather than depending upon outsourced material and labor supply. The move to factories also reflected in some cases materials being used. Modern owners would have found it unfeasible to mold plastics and rubber in home workshops where volumes of chemicals would need storage and electrical usage would be high, just as pre-war owners could not work leather or metal. Workers with special skills were needed, and in the booming postwar labor market there was no need to market those skills on a piecework basis.

The small doll companies continued to be family owned and managed, and owners were very much part of the artistic, production, and marketing processes. These companies faced a number of business risks: they generally did not have broad product lines that gave them flexibility as market demands changed; their products were still hand-intensive with resulting high labor costs; with high overhead costs they did not have the volume to withstand pricing pressure supplied by the toy giants; their distribution channels were not well-developed, or well-defined. Their greatest risk, however, was the fact that the business was usually dependent upon one or two individuals who provided the creative and/or business leadership. When those leaders passed away or left the business, the business did not survive, unless there was a second generation with the interest and training to pick up the vision of the founders. Dolls produced in small family owned factories and in postwar cottage industries are among the most endearing dollhouse inhabitants.

Not only were extended dollhouse families produced, but also dolls depicting tradespeople, historic figures, and nursery rhyme characters. Toy distributors and middlemen were anxious to represent the artists, helping them to move the dolls to market. Dolls could be found in high-end toy and department stores, or sometimes they were sold by their makers at regional crafts fairs and local gift shops. Judging by the number still found in excellent condition today, they were highly prized additions to the dollhouses of the era and are now some of the most prized possessions of collectors.

Ethel Strong and her Twinky Dolls

Imagine, walking next door, wandering through a living room filled with bins of feathers, lace, and fabric, and visiting your Grandmother, who is sitting by a large window quietly painting and dressing little dolls. After a chat with your most favorite person, you go home with a lollipop and the doll of your choice. These were early memories of Lee Forsythe, granddaughter of Ethel R. Strong. An artist, entrepreneur, and miniaturist, Mrs. Strong brought her talents to the doll world and created the family of dolls known as "Twinky."

Born in Portland, Maine, in 1888, Ethel Wyman married Anson Strong in 1916, settling in Lynnfield, Massachusetts, just north of Boston. Typical of women of that era, she was schooled in liberal arts subjects. She spoke several languages and was an accomplished painter and musician.

She had already begun using her talents before the war to assist in supplementing her family's income. She started a gift shop in her home, Windmill Studio, featuring decorated cards and envelopes as well as hand-painted jewelry, wood carving, and miniature oils. Her association with Chester Waite, originator of Lynnfield dollhouse furniture, reinforced an early interest in toys and miniatures. Lee Forsythe remembers her grandmother as never able to sit idle, even painting the decorations on Waite's miniatures as she sat tending the garden produce stand in front of her New England farmhouse. Unable to obtain Waite's furniture as a result of WWII gas rationing, Ethel Strong turned to other ventures.

A New York toy distributor and agent suggested that miniature dolls would have a strong market. Unable to find bisque and frustrated with fabric, Mrs. Strong finally decided on plastic as a medium for her doll family. Since plastic was a war-scarce material, her plans were temporarily postponed.

At a Boston Gift Show in January, 1946, Mrs. Strong was introduced to George Bauer of Leominster, Massachusetts, a

Ph.D. in material science and an employee of the Commonwealth Plastics Company, maker of plastic buttons, novelties, and toys. Dr. Bauer's wife, Christina, a painter and sculptor well known for her pewter jewelry, offered to carve the models that would be used to produce the molds for a household of dolls. By fall of 1946, assisted by the Bauers, a five-member family was introduced. A neighborhood Girl Scout, Esther Ham, named them "Twinky Dolls." In a 1952 interview for Janet Pagter Johl's book, *Your Dolls and Mine*, Mrs. Strong described the Twinky dolls as a "fulfillment of a teenage ambition" to "think up a doll that could be special and a little different from just being a doll." She went on to explain, "I always wanted my doll to be one that could be played with and enjoyed by a child."

The injection-molded plastic parts for the dolls were subcontracted to Bauer, then shipped to Ethel Strong for assembly and decoration. Mrs. Strong quickly recognized that she needed help in finishing the dolls for sale. In 1947, following her conviction that women could exploit their talents by working at home, she received a permit from the Commonwealth of Massachusetts authorizing her as an employer for "Industrial Home Work."

Mrs. Strong designed costumes for the dolls. The concepts were then translated into small patterns by her friend, Dot French, to be reproduced as finished clothing by neighborhood women.

Initially, Mrs. Strong, utilizing her own artistic ability, decorated the feet, hair, and faces of the dolls. There was far more skill required in painting the faces, and she eventually asked young girls to assist her in painting the hair and shoes. Her family joined the effort. Anson Strong made small stands for the dolls out of lead plugs and stiff wire. Her daughter, Rhoda Buttrick, designed the company logo. Mrs. Strong handled the business details herself, whether it was filling her distributors' orders or, in 1948, writing to seek permission to make dolls in Girl Scout and Brownie uniforms. While a full-fledged cottage industry was developed, it was not sufficient to meet the volume demands of major toy marketers and Mrs. Strong apparently had no interest in mass production.

Mrs. Strong tried various marketing approaches. Networking gave her access to New York toy distributors like Block House and A. L. Larimer. Dolls reached 85 cities in 25 states, being sold in small gift and hobby shops.

Mrs. Strong wasn't just a businesswoman, however. She was a kind and thoughtful person. In the book, *In Praise of Dollhouses,* the authors tell of a daughter requesting replacement clothing for a cherished family of Twinky dolls. The clothes were sent to young Dorris Callicott without charge as a Christmas present from Ethel Strong.

First introduced in 1946, Twinky dolls quickly gained recognition. A mother might appear in a dress or a skirt and blouse. Father wore shirt and slacks and sometimes a crocheted vest. Young girl generally wore a cloth or crocheted dress that might match her mother's. Shirt and slacks or shorts made up the boy's costume. Babies were dressed in gowns or buntings. The dolls were not meant to have changeable outfits as glue was often used to add accessories like belts or hats. As their popularity grew, the dollhouse accessory company, Grandmother Stover's, advertised and distributed the dolls for a short time in 1950. Apparently, the demand for the dolls was so great that Mrs. Strong could not keep up, and this association was discontinued after six months. Mother and Father, $120. Boy and girl, $75.

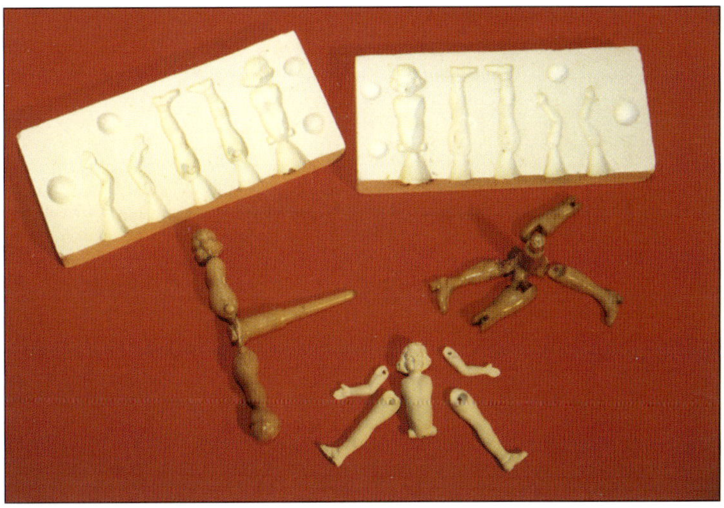

After some experimentation with materials, using Christina Bauer's molds, the dolls were eventually molded in butyrate acetate. The unbreakable plastic dolls were either snapped, pinned, or strung together with light elastic cord. The 2" baby and 4" boy and girl were molded in five parts – body, arms, and legs. The 5 1/2" mother and 6" father were each molded in seven parts with hinged legs allowing them to sit normally with bent knees. The unique designs of the adults' knee and hip joints encouraged a child's play. Boys and girls shared the same limb parts, while the parents' lower legs were different, allowing for gender appropriate shoes. The forearm of the father was more muscled than the mother's. Close tolerances and complexity of the parts led to a high level of manufacturing defects and rejections that were only discovered during assembly. *Dolls, molds, and parts from the collection of R. Lee Forsythe.*

As time went on, Mrs. Strong expanded the Twinky family by adding additional members and a complete household staff. The line further diversified with the addition of fairytale characters and holiday figures. Children were dressed for skiing, football, baseball, and as majorettes. Mrs. Strong added a military line in full uniform. A bride dressed in a beautifully detailed gown was married to a groom dressed in white tie. Nationality dolls were added, starting with a Dutch family and including Swiss, German, Scots, Spanish, and Mexican. In all, nearly 100 different designs were produced. For the more elaborate character dolls, Ethel herself sewed the costumes.

At first, when producing dark skinned ethnic dolls, Mrs. Strong painted the entire doll body. When this proved time consuming and unnecessary, she generally decorated only faces, hair, hands, and feet. The African American baby was molded in dark plastic while the Native American, African American, and Hawaiian doll bodies were totally hand-painted. On the Hawaiian dolls the shoes of the standard molded legs were simply painted over creating an amusing "barefoot" effect.

The financial details of the business helped to explain its eventual demise. In March 1953 relations with Mr. Bauer became strained over manufacturing defects. Perhaps facing investment in new molds, Bauer wrote that he could not produce an order for 250 dolls unless Mrs. Strong would commit to buy 1000 pieces. Selling at retail prices between 65¢ for a baby and \$3.00 for an elaborately costumed adult, margins were narrow. A competent businesswoman, Strong decided that she could not continue to profitably sell the dolls and carry a large inventory of parts.

Neighborhood women produced the clothes for the basic family, on a piecework basis. Records show that prices paid for a dozen men's coats was \$1.25. During the production years, at least twenty neighboring women made these costumes in their homes. *Patterns, drawings and clothes from the collection of R. Lee Forsythe.*

The company logo designed by Ethel Strong's daughter, Rhoda Butrick. *Drawing from the collection of R. Lee Forsythe.*

When Ethel ceased production in 1953, she packed away bags of unassembled parts and boxes of clothing, thinking the dolls a failure. Over the next twenty-five years of her life, while continuing to produce crafts and miniature paintings, she passed on her artistic legacy and became an inspiration to her granddaughter. Some years ago, Lee Forsythe started to experiment with paints and techniques to see if she could replicate the features once applied by her grandmother. There was a ready source of finished original clothing to go with the unassembled doll parts. With Lee's talent for hand sewing, she was able to authentically dress the dolls. She even found a large roll of the original elastic cord used for stringing the dolls. Mrs. Forsythe began selling a limited quantities of these "second generation" Twinky dolls, authentic and original in almost every detail, except for the use of a less glossy paint for the cosmetic details. To differentiate the first from the second-generation dolls, she painted two small vertical lines on the dolls' backs. Lee maintains that she can tell the difference in the facial details between the two, but it is clear that a special talent was passed to another generation.

Looking back, Twinky dolls were hardly a failure. Rather, they remain as beautiful examples of craftsmanship, finely detailed from molding to painting to costuming.

The family dolls were augmented by a wide variety of character dolls, providing opportunity for creative play. Here his wife and children greet a serviceman just returning on a Playskool Pullman. Serviceman, $200. Mother, $125. Children $75.

Mrs. Strong often exhibited her dolls at large crafts fairs like Topsfield and Boston's Minuteman. *Photo from the collection of R. Lee Forsythe.*

The expanded line of Twinky dolls contained a full household kitchen staff. In packaging the dolls, Ethel Strong sometimes mounted with thread on a light paper covered cardboard backing. The breakfast nook is by Chester Waite, of the kind hand-decorated by Ethel Strong. Maid and cook, $175. Chef and maid, MOC, $450.

There was whimsy in the Twinky line, as well. Here, fairytale figures, such as Little Bo-Peep and Little Red Riding Hood, together with the fictional character, Little Lord Fauntleroy, joined a clown and a cowgirl from the western family. Child sized character dolls, $150.

True to her New England heritage, Ethel Strong added John and Priscilla Alden and their children to the line. American Indian dolls, authentically costumed by a family friend, Martha Bayard, whose husband was a member of the Narragansett Indian tribe, joined them for Thanksgiving. The faces and lower arms and legs were painted to give a dark skin to the standard Twinky mold. Wigs were added, an unusual element for the dolls. *Dolls from the collection of R. Lee Forsythe.* $200/each.

A Twinky man dressed as Santa and a Twinky boy, similarly clothed, delivered Christmas skis to children clothed for winter play. Santas, $150. Skiers, $125.

The Holy Family fit nicely in a commercial crèche. The added Arab boy tends the sheep. Holy Family Set, $500. Arab boy, $150.

A white tie formal wedding party graced the line. Here bridesmaids and a flower girl dressed in net fabric gowns joined the suited Aunt, Uncle, and bearded bartender. Bride and Groom, $200. Bridesmaids and bartender, $175. Aunt and Uncle, $150. Flower girl, $100.

The Spanish family was among the nationality dolls produced by Ethel Strong. Complete family, $550.

A mother and father of the Colonial family generally wore powdered wigs. Here the young Colonial son talks with dolls dressed in the less formal fashion of common Colonial folk. Adults, $175. Boy, $150.

A stern nun presided over a school Christmas party, evoking memories of the author's childhood. Nun, $200. Children, $75.

A yacht skipper and debutante returned from watching America's Cup races. The hat and purse are modern additions, but the well-detailed yachting cap is original. Skipper, $200. Fancy dressed woman, $125.

Ethel Strong produced dolls costumed to represent literary characters of the day. Here the characters of Annie Fellows Johnston's *Little Colonel*, Mom Beck, Colonel Lloyd, and the Little Colonel stand in front of their plantation home. *Little Colonel from the collection of R. Lee Forsythe.* Adult characters, $200. Little Colonel, $150.

Babies were dressed in a variety of clothing, from bunting to Christening gown. The skin of African American dolls was painted, although some were cast in a dark plastic. The nurse, standing in front of a hand-painted screen similar to those produced by Chester Waite and Tynietoy, looked over the nursery. Nurse, $175. Babies, $60.

The Winsor Doll Company

Once upon a time there were two little sisters named Polly and Jessie. Each little girl had a dollhouse, and they played with them every day. One day while their mother was helping them make cushions for the little sofas, the girls asked, 'Mother, why can't you make us some families for our doll houses? We want dolls that will stand and sit and hold things and ride in our little cars and sweep with our little vacuum cleaners. We want a father who can climb ladders and help the mother wash windows, and a mother who can really hold the baby, and everything.' So the mother thought and thought and she asked the father to help, and they worked and worked, and found they could make dolls that would do all those things.

One of the benefits of having a talented and artistic mother with tremendous energy and creativity was the ability to have your wishes granted. Polly and Jessie were, in fact, real little girls, the daughters of Marion and Paul Winsor, Jr. of Cohasset, Massachusetts. Their request helped start a cottage industry that made thousands of miniature dolls. Marion Louise Joyce Winsor always gave credit to her inspiration, including a printed copy of the above story with each of the little Winsor dolls she sold.

While raising three sons, Paul III, Malcolm, and Chris in rural northern New Jersey during the Depression, this talented woman helped create fun and fantasy for the children while at the same time putting her artistic talents to work. After making a family trip to New York City and attending a puppet theater production of Hansel and Gretel, she engaged the family in making marionettes and building a real puppet stage. She encouraged each of the children to take a part in productions given to family, friends, and schoolmates, whether it was operating the puppets themselves or handling the stage lighting. As the family moved, first to Rowayton, Connecticut, and then to Cohasset, Massachusetts, Marion continued to introduce children to the world of marionettes, holding formal and informal workshops for neighbors and other young people of the community. As she taught children, she fostered their creativity, not by instructing them on the "right way", but by helping them explore many routes to the desired end. The children were never told a "correct" or "incorrect" decorating material or construction method. When one little boy made a puppet many times larger than the puppets being made by other children in Mrs. Winsor's workshop, it became a giant that could be used in staging Jack and the Beanstalk. Another child's particularly animated crow caused a slight rewrite to the Wizard of Oz. She built youthful confidence when reminding her young puppeteers just before curtain time, "Don't forget, you know more about what you are doing than anybody out there!"

By the early 40s when the two older boys had gone off to college and WWII naval service, the Winsor family had grown with the addition of the two daughters featured in the dollhouse story. While Polly and Jessie were too young to take part in the puppet workshops, they were always nearby, obviously absorbing the creative play of the puppeteers. As a girl, Marion had enjoyed playing with a dollhouse made by her father. On one of her frequent excursions to an antique shop, she found a large dollhouse that had both a stairway and an elevator, and bought it for her daughters' imaginative play. Subsequently, a second dollhouse, possibly made by Marion's father, was added so that each girl could enjoy her own miniature home. Sometime in 1946 or 1947, the girls remember calling upon their Mom to provide those inhabitants.

As she made dolls for her own children and for a few neighboring children, she realized that there was an emerging market for such dolls to complement the popular plastic furniture of Renwal, Ideal, and Plasco. Encouraged to broaden her scope by Betsy Allen, a cousin of Paul Winsor, who sold expensive imported greeting cards to high-end gift shops throughout the Northeast, Marion energetically engaged her entire family, and began to experiment with design and material. While the primary objective was to make dolls that could "do all those things", they had to be dollhouse scale and easy to reproduce. Marion related in a January 19, 1956, *Christian Science Monitor* article that she realized the important trick was to make the dolls look "handmade, but not homemade."

To meet demand Mrs. Winsor engaged friends and neighbors, as well as her family, as she operated from a workshop in her home and developed the cottage industry that became the Winsor Doll Company. Heads were strung on a stiff wire and painted with a matte flesh-colored paint that dried overnight. The next day eyes of blue, brown, or green were added, then eyebrows, then mouths. In addition to Marion's painting, a neighbor with well-recognized artistic ability, Ruth Pratt, decorated many of the heads, following Marion's pattern. Her son, Joel, maker of the Giant puppet, remembers trays of painted heads staring up at him as he entered the family dining room.

Grace Catrambone, originally engaged to help Mrs. Winsor clean her home, was drafted to help sew clothes that had been designed by the family, following patterns cut from manila folders. Clothing was made in bulk. Chris Winsor remembers sewing long chains of trousers that could easily be cut apart after sewing. Other acquaintances assisted in production, assembly, and packaging, being paid by the piece, as common in all cottage industries. Even Marion's young daughters had after school tasks. The girls were paid a penny a chair to paint over Renwal plastic rockers on which grandparents were seated!

The process for constructing the dolls started by cutting two pieces of pipe cleaner to appropriate length. A .375" band of flocking was removed from one end of each, with the clean end then being inserted into a hole in the shoe mold. Molten lead was poured into the mold, and after it cooled the shoe and leg were removed. Legs were inserted into pants, if appropriate, and then twisted at the hip. A wire for the arm was inserted through sleeves of shirts and blouses and then attached by twisting one of the leg wires around it. The other leg wire was threaded into the pre-drilled hole of the head and glued. Theatrical hair was glued on the bead covering the hole and wire end. Cotton stuffing was added around the middle to fill out the body. The dolls were then slid into cellophane bags, together with a copy of the story relating the dolls' inspiration and closed shut with a small brass clip. The overall length of finished dolls was 5.5" for an adult, 3.5-4" for a child, and 1.75" for a baby.

Early in the 1950s, Marion's interest started to broaden beyond the repetitive production of the dollhouse family dolls: father, mother, son, daughter, baby, grandmother, and grandfather. It grew to include western characters, Pilgrims, and Gloucester fishermen. Dolls were dressed in pajamas and as brides. Christmas and Easter dolls were made for the holidays. The dolls' primary market was upscale gift stores throughout the Northeast. Dave Churchill, a tenant in the basement apartment of the Winsor's home, carved wooden fishermen figurines, and introduced the Winsor doll to New England shop owners with whom he did business. Mr. Winsor's New York City based cousin, Betsy Allen, did the same to her gift shop clients in the Northeast. The Winsors traveled to Boston and New York to promote their work at trade shows.

Mrs. Winsor continued to shift her emphasis, producing small "scenes" with the wooden head dolls. Her whimsy was evident in her line of boys seated on driftwood. Her humor showed in the dozing figures of "The Long Sermon." Groups of caroling children stood on a snowy street. Marion made a number of larger dioramas as well, including colonial room settings, nativity crèches, and schoolrooms. One schoolroom, a representation of the first public school in Cohasset, now resides as an exhibit in the wonderful Cohasset Historical Society. A more modern schoolhouse is in the possession of Polly Winsor, appropriately, a university professor.

In 1952, Marion and Paul signaled in a Christmas letter to family and friends that they were finally tiring of the wooden heads and wanted to have time to do other things. In fact, the dollhouse dolls were phased out over the next few years. The Christmas letter suggested that one of their new projects would be making more expensive dolls. Marion began to work in clay and ceramics fashioning one-of-a-kind doll sculptures about twelve inches tall. A Benjamin Franklin doll under a glass dome was purchased for display by a Boston bank. A similar doll appeared on a library shelf in a magazine advertisement for a financial institution or insurance company, much to Marion's delight. Marion presented the actress Ethel Waters with a doll representing her character in the play, *Member of the Wedding*. She fashioned an ice skating scene under commission of a family who had provided photographs of the family members to be used as the models. She made a doll of her granddaughter dressed just as she was in a photo sent to her by her son. Not all dolls were one-of-a-kind nor of actual people. Priscilla and John Alden dolls were supplied for sale at the gift shop at *Plimouth Plantation*. Scenes of old men playing checkers or a grandmother reading to her granddaughter were also produced. In later years, Marion shifted to making well regarded one-of-a-kind figures entirely of clay that she fired in her own kiln. In her search to learn more about firing and glazing techniques she received guidance from potters at the well known Dorchester Pottery. She drew her inspiration from many sources, even keeping a clipping file of photos of interesting faces "with character."

Marion Winsor, like so many of the doll makers and miniature artisans of this period was, obviously, a remarkable woman. The concept of a cottage industry gave her the flexibility to be a mother, a teacher, a puppeteer, and artist. She found time with her husband and children to "construct" a house along the seashore by moving historical buildings to the site. She once related that she would find time to mold the heads of her dolls sitting up in bed before she fell asleep at night. She ran a company that made more than ten thousand dolls. She fulfilled her artistic leanings and found satisfaction by making fine dolls until her death in 1972.

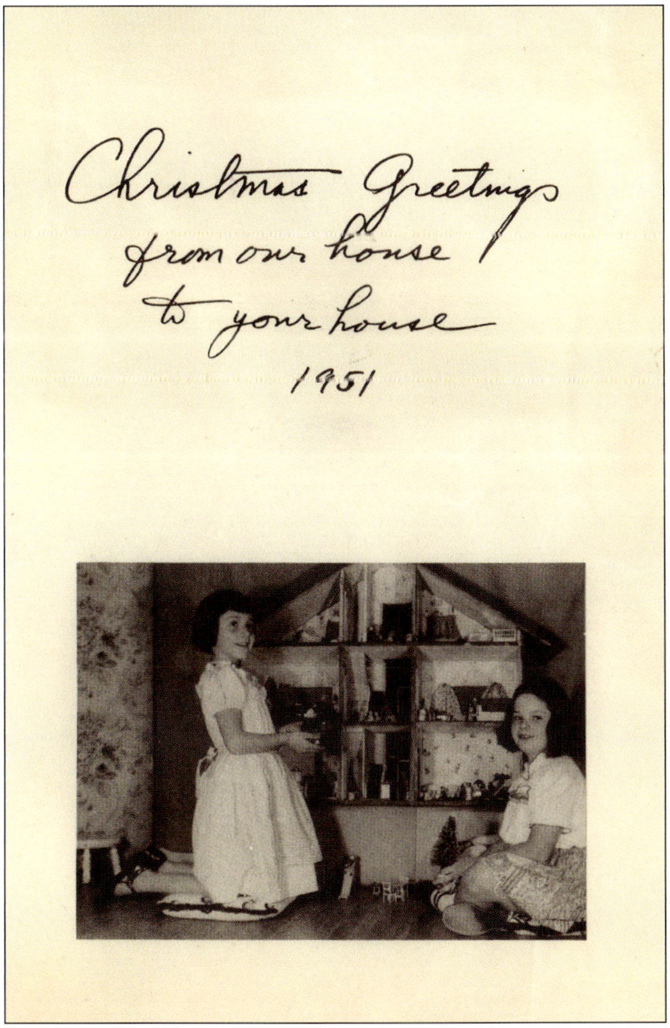

One of the houses the Winsor girls used for their imaginative play was primarily furnished with postwar plastic furniture. They lacked a family of dolls to create the sense of make-believe and magic they observed in puppet performances. The sisters' request for a family that "could do things" was granted when Marion Winsor began to make wooden head dolls. *Christmas card courtesy of the Winsor family.*

Marion Louise Joyce was born in 1899, growing up in Quincy, Massachusetts. She showed early artistic talent, but was denied formal art training. She did, however, become a newspaper reporter and newsletter writer in Quincy. She met and married Paul Winsor, a telephone planning engineer originally from Weston, Massachusetts, eventually settling along the shore in Cohasset, Massachusetts. *Photo courtesy of the Winsor family.*

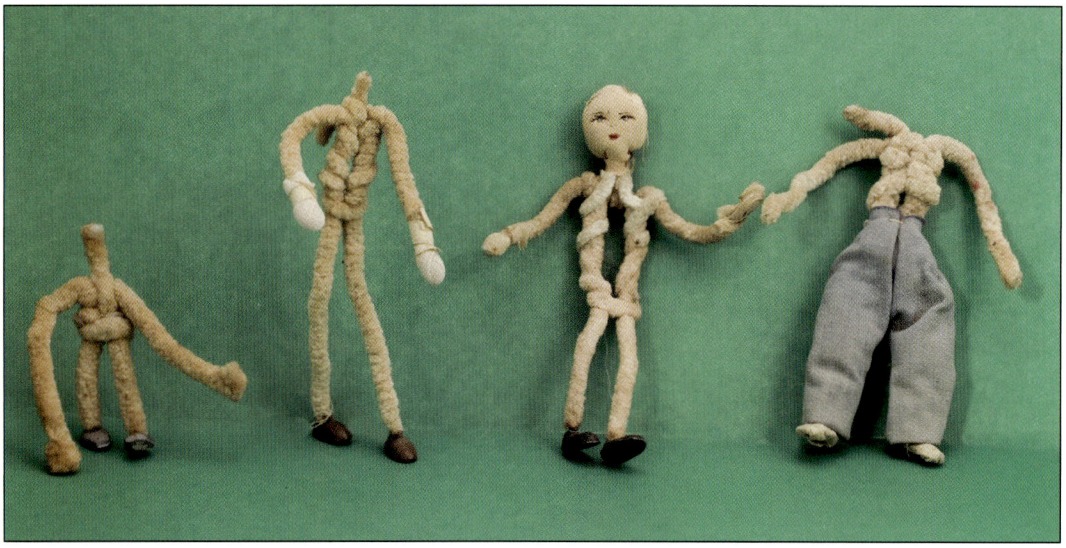

Pipe cleaners were ultimately found to provide the best internal frame for the first of Marion Winsor's dolls. The material was completely flexible and could withstand a great deal of bending and straightening. When it was found that feet made from pipe cleaners could not properly support the dolls, lead shoes were added. The shoes were poured into maple molds carved by Marion's sons Mac and Chris. As the hot metal burnt out the molds, more were carved. Mr. Winsor helped in procuring the raw materials. He found a maker of flesh-colored pipe cleaners that would supply spools of the product meeting the exacting color standards of Mrs. Winsor. The core of the pipe cleaner was a specialty metal, Monel, apparently chosen for its rust resistance and formability, despite its higher cost. A woodworking shop was found in Boston to supply wooden beads for use as heads. So long as the Winsors were willing to commit to purchasing 10,000 beads, the woodworker agreed to supply them with a hole drilled through the middle to facilitate attachment to the pipe cleaner frame. *Dolls from the collection of the Winsor family.*

At first, Marion Winsor made a basic family: parents, various sized toddlers and babies. At least two different sized heads, adult and child, were purchased to meet the minimum requirement. It is not clear whether the smallest bead, used for babies, was included in the bulk purchase. Marion Winsor's artistic sense and attention to scale extended to her choice of clothing fabrics. Cloth was chosen not only with patterns that would look correct in miniature scale, but with weaves that would not be out of place. *Dolls from the collection of Patti Cooper.* $30/each.

One set of dolls was a knitting grandmother and grandfather reading a newspaper, each sold seated in Renwal plastic rockers. Unfortunately Renwal's rockers were not originally supplied in a wood-like color, so the girls would paint blue and pink rockers brown to meet their mother's eye for realism. The rockers were painted in a two-step process. Fronts were painted one day, backs the next, after the fronts dried. *Dolls from the collection of Patti Cooper.* $50/each with chair.

In the early 1950s Marion Winsor branched out from her basic family offering. Capitalizing on the then current popularity of Westerns, Cowboy and Indian dolls were made, as were Daniel Boone and Davy Crockett dolls, carrying small wooden rifles and dressed in fringed suede-like material and coonskin caps. *Dolls from the collection of the Winsor family.* $65/ each.

Since Cohasset, Massachusetts, was close to Plymouth, families of Pilgrims were made for sale in local gift stores as souvenirs. The cottage in the background is one of Marion Winsor's later ceramic works, portraying a Pilgrim mother and daughter outside their *Plimouth Plantation* styled cottage. *Dolls from the collection of the Winsor family.* Dolls, $65/each. Cottage, insufficient examples to determine value.

Gloucestermen carrying small telescopes were dressed in yellow sou'esters and slickers representing New England's seafaring heritage. *Doll from the collection of the Winsor family.* $65.

A Winsor daughter baby-sits for a range of nursery figures. *Dolls from the collection of the Winsor family.* $30/each.

Typical of many doll makers of this time, Marion Winsor offered a bridal party. *Dolls from the collection of the Winsor family.* $65/each.

Marion Winsor's dolls, tending their garden, had expressive, hand-painted faces. *Dolls from the collection of the Winsor family.* $65/each.

Marion Winsor often dressed little girl dolls in two sizes representing her two daughters. Polly and Jessie actually had matching brown snowsuits and scarves as worn by the two dolls on the left. Just putting the finishing touches on a snowman also made by Marion, is another toddler doll. *Dolls from the collection of the Winsor family.* $65/each.

Holidays were celebrated with appropriate dolls. Here two children dressed in bunny outfits hunt for Easter eggs. *Dolls from the collection of the Winsor family.* $65/each.

The Winsor Doll Company began to make wooden head angels to hang from Christmas trees. Made from a stiff tulle fabric and not requiring legs or lead feet, the angels either carried a wire wand with a silver star at the end or a folded paper carol book. The angels found a national market, being carried by FAO Schwarz. An angel was the subject of an annual Winsor Christmas card as shown in the inset. *Dolls and Christmas card from the collection of the Winsor family.* $75/each.

Marion combed the beach next to her house and found small pieces of driftwood upon which she seated boys with fishing poles dressing them in clothing made from material scavenged from thrift stores because it appeared more authentically weathered and worn. *Dolls from the collection of the Winsor family.* $125/each.

A well dressed grandmother seated with her sleeping granddaughter in a wooden pew in a presentation piece known as "The Long Sermon." *Dolls from the collection of the Winsor family.* $250 w/dome.

On the left, dolls representing Marion, Paul, Jessie, and Polly Winsor and others sing Christmas carols. The family dolls appeared in one of the annual Christmas cards. *Dolls from the collection of the Winsor family.* $125/pr.

The Winsors sent an annual Christmas card, often with a picture of their children or the dolls: retired grandparents, a Nativity scene, a snow shovel boy, and carolers. *Christmas cards from the collection of the Winsor family.*

Two of Marion Winsor's dioramas: at the top, a Pilgrim roombox fully outfitted with period furniture and dolls; at the bottom, a school room diorama, including a pet rabbit in a cage next to the blackboard. *Dioramas from the collection of the Winsor family.* Insufficient examples to determine value.

A collection of Marion Winsor's ceramic pieces showing differences in size, materials, and construction. *Dolls from the collection of the Winsor family.* Insufficient examples to determine value.

Tiny Town

While Ethel Strong and the Winsors were starting their doll companies on the East Coast, another doll maker was busy creating a new series of dolls on the West Coast - "Tiny Town Dolls." The published history of Tiny Town dolls is rather scant, and much of what is known is not well documented as to source, but it seems certain that the dolls first originated in the late 1940s produced by Alma LeBlanc. In January 1948 LeBlanc, doing business in San Francisco, California, as Lenna Lee's Tiny Town Dolls, registered the trademark "Tiny Town." It is generally said that Alma LeBlanc had worked as a face painter decorating Nancy Ann Storybook Dolls, and had decided to branch out on her own.

For some period of time she operated in a mixed residential/commercial area at 305 Sixth Avenue in San Francisco, but at least, some of the work was outsourced in a cottage industry approach. The daughter of the gentleman who made the doll frames and feet for the Tiny Towns, Joy Sorenson Reis, remembers Ms. LeBlanc as "very glamorous in an eleven year old girl's eyes, speaking with a lovely French accent and always well dressed." It is believed that Tiny Towns were made at least until 1955, and possibly as late as the 1960s, although it is sometimes stated that the company changed hands at least twice, and it is not clear who succeeded Alma.

A Tiny Town catalog cover reads: "Their heads move and their arms and legs are flexible." Construction of the dolls was based on a pipe cleaner frame. Like the Winsor dolls, pipe cleaners were set into a mold and lead was poured into the mold, setting the pipe cleaner and creating the legs and feet, which were then painted. Legs were thread-wrapped. After Joy Reis' father, Kay Sorenson, delivered the doll frames, they were then assembled, dressed, and painted by Ms. LeBlanc and probably others, including her daughter Mary.

Dolls had thread-covered arms matching Mr. Sorenson's legs, and it is possible that he did the wrapping step for the entire doll. Their hands were felt and looked like mittens. According to long-time collector Lynne Wright, dolls are often found with rust spotted hands, apparently a result of using a pipe cleaner without a rust resistant core, unlike the Monel core material used by Marion Winsor. Doll bodies were stuffed cloth, surrounding the frame. Felt covered, stuffed heads were hand-painted.

As Ms. Wright pointed out, the faces differ, indicating that more than one artist worked on faces during the dolls' history, although no comparative study has been published attempting to create a timeline for face styles. Dolls had thin semi-circular eyebrows that varied in length. Girl dolls had heavy painted eyelashes. Eyes were circular, usually a black dot surrounded by blue or white. Some dolls had larger eyes than others. There were two indented dots in the felt face and a small bump for nostrils and nose. Some dolls had rosy rouge applied to their cheeks. Unopened mouths were painted shades of pink or red in a Cupid's bow shape. Mohair wigs, supposedly purchased from Nancy Ann Abbott's supplier, were used for hair in a variety of styles and colors. Some of the dolls could be purchased with a choice of hair colors, blond, brunette, black, or red. Dolls' clothing was made of various fabrics, including cotton, felt, and corduroy, with trimmings of ribbons, burlap, and lace. Like Flagg dolls, a lot of felt was used. Some of the dolls' shirts were made of horizontally wrapped yarn. The clothing, very neatly machine sewn, was not easily removable. Dolls had accessories like cloth flowers, lassos, jump ropes, and paint palettes, to illustrate their character. Shoes were generally white metal, but pink and brown were used on the dollhouse mother and father.

The majority of Tiny Towns were about 4", but there were larger 4.5", 5", and 6" dolls produced. Other than the dollhouse family dolls, and except for size and hair color variations, there were basically only two dolls made, girl and boy. They were dressed in over 105 costumes, however. The dolls were offered in different series, at one time numbering seven. Dolls' names and costumes changed, as did their places in series. A partial listing of dolls and series names can be found in the Appendix. Dolls were packaged in colored cardboard boxes with white or clear lids. The box generally contained the Tiny Town brochure listing of available dolls. The brochure's cover design changed from time to time, as did the listings. The box might have been marked with the name of the doll inside. Sometimes the doll's name was stamped in ink on the bottom of a foot, although markings rubbed off. Some dolls had an original gold foil wrist tag with the company name on one side and the doll's name on the other. One brochure instructs that dolls could be cleaned by scrubbing lightly with a wet toothbrush and soapy water. A doll would surely have suffered from such treatment.

Tiny Town Dolls were sold in high-end gift shops and department stores throughout the country including, among others: Leamington Oakland Gift Shop, San Francisco's White House Department Store, The Merry-Go Round in New Rochelle, New York.

For a short time after Tiny Town dolls began to be produced, Kay William Sorenson, a tool and die maker by trade, cast the dolls' feet in his basement hobby. With the help of his daughter, Joy, pictured on the left with her cousin Lois, he wound the pipe cleaner legs with a flesh-colored thread on a small winding machine that he had developed. When a batch was finished Mr. Sorenson would deliver them to Alma LeBlanc, occasionally taking Joy along on the trip across the Bay. *Photo courtesy of Joy Sorenson Reis.*

Tiny Town also made a dollhouse family of four that is very hard to find. Father at 4.5" and mother 4.25" were slightly taller than standard dolls, and their faces were much thinner. Girl and boy were smaller, only 3.5". These dolls were perfect for fiberboard dollhouses popular during this time period. $75/each unboxed.

A 4" Tiny Town ballerina with red hair in red tutu dances next to an almost 5" tall ballerina. The shoes on the taller Ballerina were more detailed with more lifelike painted ribbons attaching the shoe to the ankle. Comparison of the detail of the eyes indicates that either a different artist decorated the doll, or the taller doll was made for a more upscale line. Note the marks on the dolls hands resulting from the use of non rust resistant pipe cleaners. Ballerinas were also made with brunette hair and six additional tutu colors. $65 not boxed, $125 MIB. *Large Ballerina from the collection of Hilda Pitman. Original large Ballerina photo courtesy of Hilda Pitman.* $125/each MIB.

A well dressed, brown haired, Tiny Town doll marked "School Girl" on her foot. The name on the foot does not always accurately represent the name of the character. $65 not boxed, $125 MIB.

Standard Tiny Town dolls were approximately 4" tall. Here "Brother" and "Mickey" (minus her hat) danced to the tunes of a 50s jukebox. $65 not boxed, $125 MIB.

The "Little Artist" came complete with brush and palette. $65 not boxed, $125 MIB.

"Story characters" was the name of one of the many series made by Tiny Town. Here, Bo-Peep searches for her sheep. The dolls often had a gold foil hang tag on their wrists with the Tiny Town trademark on one side and the doll's name on the other. *Doll from the collection of Hilda Pitman. Original photo courtesy of Hilda Pitman.* $125 MIB

Not only did the faces of dolls vary, but so did the costumes and hair color. Two different Irish Colleens from the "Nationalities" series, one with black hair, the other a redhead, were dressed in different shamrock decorated regional costumes. The differences in dress and hair color was probably the result of a good marketing concept to drive collectors desire to "have the whole set." *Doll from the collection of Hilda Pitman. Original photo courtesy of Hilda Pitman.* $125 MIB

Typical packaging for the Tiny Town dolls. Sometimes the doll's name appeared on a tape label affixed to the end of the box or stamped on the bottom of her foot. The boxes contained a small brochure listing currently made dolls. Helen Siebold Walter of Staunton, Virginia affixed her shop's label when she resold a box holding a red ballerina.

Tiny Town dolls were often sold in high-end gift stores. Here the Morton Gift Shop, located in Atlantic City's Hotel Morton, advertised the dolls for $2.00 each in a November 1949 *House and Garden* magazine.

Tottie Dohme on Manhattan's East Side advertised twelve different Tiny Town dolls, "perfect sized for the doll house" in a November 1950 *House and Garden*.

The Flagg Doll Company

One of the best examples of a company that operated a small family-run factory manufacturing creative, quality dolls was the Flagg Doll Company of Jamaica Plain, Massachusetts. A husband and wife team, Charles and Sheila Flagg, were the founders who complemented each other in producing small dolls easily identified and sought after today.

Sheila Markham, was born in Haverhill, Massachusetts, in September 1916. At one time she designed shoes, but was working in a war production factory in Boston when she met and married Charles E. Flagg, Jr. Charles, a native of Brookline, Massachusetts, was an electrician wiring warships outfitted at the Boston Navy Yard in Charlestown. When the war ended, the Flaggs looked for a way to combine Sheila's interest in clothing and costumes with Charles' mechanical and business skills. Sheila had previously worked for a doll maker who suggested that she go into business on her own, and this became their goal. A straw stuffed doll was their first attempt, but something more substantial and less craft-like was needed.

They first had to design a process to make and clothe a new concept doll. That task fell to Charles who chose flexible vinyl as his medium. He worked with a two-piece mold. The plastic was pumped from a barrel and squirted through a gun into one side of the mold. A wire armature was then placed into the material and vinyl was pumped into the second mold. After the two sides were wired together, they were baked in an oven, also of Charles' design, for about 25 minutes. After baking, molds were immersed in water to cool. Charles often worked in the oven room, casting the dolls if his caster did not show up for work. The couple leased space in a dreary factory at 91 Boylston Street in Jamaica Plain, a Boston suburb.

A small assembly line took over. Dolls were removed from the mold. A good friend of Sheila, Joan Ceci, trimmed the seam flashing. Depending on order volume, two or three painters would add facial details. Sheila did a lot of the face painting, sitting right on the line.

Doll clothing was designed by Sheila, and her cloth prototypes were converted to a pattern on cardboard stock. A metal cutting die was then built to match the pattern. The patterns and dies were hung from a wall so that they could be accessed quickly to fill an order. Charles had designed and built a hydraulic press into which the dies were placed. Material stacked 20 or so layers high was put in the press so that clothing could be stamped out in quantity. Clothing pieces were placed in boxes labeled as to part and intended doll. A group of two or three women sewed together costume pieces like legs on pants.

Costumes were ingenious in design. Whenever possible they were cut so that an article could be stapled to the doll with one small staple passing through the body clasping front and back. The stapling machines, designed by Charles to be foot operated, allowed six costumers to have both hands free to hold clothing in place. All work was done at the factory - no activity was outsourced. In fact, it was considered unusual when pre-formed wigs were imported from Asia to be used on a line of display dolls.

As a family-run business, even the children got to try their hand at doll making. Their father would often take them to Boston's Franklin Park Zoo on Saturday mornings, stopping afterwards at the factory to "catch up on a little work." Daughters, Leslie and Penny, first painted toenails and fingernails on dolls before graduating to painting faces. Neither daughter was allowed to be a "costumer" after Leslie stapled her finger on the foot-powered machine. One person in the factory boxed dolls, a thankless and unpopular task, as it was difficult to place the feet in the pre-cut tab openings. The Flagg's youngest child, Charles III, was often the nominated "boxer."

Flagg dolls, first featured in advertisements of distributors like Afco Products and Q-T Novelty, appeared in the back of Fall 1947 issues of magazines such as *House and Garden* and *Vogue*. Not only did distributors appeal directly to mail-order consumers, but Q-T Novelty offered the dolls to retailers at the 1948 New York Toy Show. By 1951, Charles Flagg was handling his own wholesale and retail sales. Pictured clockwise from lower left: September 1947 *House and Garden* retail ad placed by QT Novelty; 1948 *Playthings* wholesale ad placed by QT Novelty; Afco's October 1949 *House and Garden* retail ad; November 1966 *House and Garden* Flagg retail ad; November 1968 *House and Garden* ad; Flagg's November 1951 *House and Garden* ad offering mail-order dolls directly to retail customers.

Sheila Flagg's artistic ability was tapped to design the dolls and costumes. Marion Schmuhl in her December 1993 *Dolls* magazine article, "Pliant Playthings of the Past", mentions that Sheila modeled in soap, while Sheila's daughter clearly remembers her mother modeling in clay. Comparing the greater detail of later dolls with the simplicity of early dolls would seem to resolve the inconsistency. Metal molds were made from the models. From time to time Sheila would change the molds to reflect changing hairstyles. Sheila, much like Joan Beringer, considered herself a costume designer, more than a doll maker or artist. Not much of a traveler, her inspiration for costumes for foreign doll lines was drawn from the C volume of World Book Encyclopedia, copying and adapting the designs under the "Clothing" heading to her doll. She taught her daughters to sew and they sewed their own doll clothes, although more so for *Ginny* dolls than Flagg Flexible Dolls.

Charles Flagg was not just the technical force of the company, but also directed the business and marketing aspects. Charles, an avid photographer, took all the promotional photos for advertisements and brochures, sometimes tying up the family's dining room table for months as he took photos and prepared layouts. By January 1950 the business was prospering enough that it was incorporated in Massachusetts under the name Flagg and Company, Inc. By the time the 1951 New York Toy Fair was held in February, Flagg and Company was handling its own sales directly, placing ads in *Playthings Magazine* and in mail-order sections of popular magazines.

Flagg produced several lines of miniature dolls in different scales, starting with dollhouse sized dolls. By August 1950, capitalizing on a growing market for well dressed collectible display dolls, the company added lines of 6" - 8" dolls, some dressed as dancers, historical figures, athletes, or bridal party members. The display dolls were clearly Sheila's first love, allowing her to capitalize on her interest in costumes. A large contract was entered into with Radio City Music Hall to supply Rockette, skater, and ballerina dolls. Cowboy and cowgirl dolls were produced as souvenirs of Pike's Peak. A baseball player was dressed in the uniform of the Los Angeles Dodgers and sold at the ballpark, soon after the team's 1957 move from Brooklyn. A 7" Wardrobe Doll, Renee the Campus Queen, with 15 interchangeable outfits, was introduced in the late 1950s. A line of 3.25" fairytale dolls was added in 1952. The dollhouse sized dolls expanded by additions of community dolls like policemen, teachers, and mailmen, although their costumes were not nearly as elaborate as the display dolls. Flagg ads boasted of 40 different dolls in 1950, doubling to 80 in 1953 and topping out at over 100 in 1957. The noted Flagg collector, Jeannie Beaumont, in her valuable on-line *Flagg Doll Guide* has catalogued over 150 doll varieties in the larger doll lines alone.

The target market was not just children, but also doll collectors and schools. Interestingly, the dollhouse dolls, like those of Joan Beringer, found a niche with psychologists and psychiatrists assisting in the diagnosis and treatment of troubled children. The principal selling point of the dolls was their poseability. Dolls could be purchased in stores or through the company's mail-order service. Flagg and Company instituted its own "Doll of the Month Club." Children were encouraged to acquire complete collections of dolls. A list of offered dolls was included in each box, although there are variations that never showed up on a list. Mindful of the need for shop owners to find profit in selling the dolls, in 1950 the company offered retailers the opportunity to purchase add-on doll stands to be sold at 10¢ for a small stand and 20¢ for a larger one.

Sheila Flagg had a fascination with dancer dolls. Her 6.5" display dancer was elaborately dressed for a ballet role. Her small dancers were 2.875" tall, shorter than the children of her family sets. Large ballerina, $50 MIB. Small dancers, $35 MIB.

A larger scale 5"-6" boy and girl were introduced in 1948. They looked just like the small dollhouse children, but no parents were ever added to the line. Extremely rare today, they were advertised for only one year. Large dolls, $75 unboxed.

Flagg dollhouse dolls were made in 1:18 scale to complement the very popular postwar Keystone, Playsteel, and Marx dollhouses as well as the era's popular 1:18 scale plastic dollhouse furniture. Extended families included grandparents. Adults were 4" tall and children, 3". $25/each MIB.

Flagg dressed its adults to represent various professions. Here a doctor and nurses care for the 1.5" babies. Babies were sold as pink-bootied girl and blue-bootied boy together in a box, or one baby was included with the extended family. Dark skinned African American babies were also made. The babies had a molded hairline that was not painted. They wore white cloth diapers attached with a small safety pin. Profession dolls, $40 MIB. Babies, $5/each unboxed or $12 for a MIB set of two.

Flagg included a complete household retinue: maid, chef, and stereotypical African American "mammy." The mammy doll was first cast in a dark colored plastic with a kerchief molded to her head. The maid in the purple dress and later Mammies had a slightly lighter skin tone than the early mammy. The chef is not mentioned on any printed listing of dolls. $40 MIB.

Village professionals included, from left: a grey-haired crossing guard in dark blue uniform, bow-tied fireman, mailman with bag, and light blue uniformed policeman. These dolls each had molded hats. $40 MIB.

Nuns in at least two different styles of habits were produced. The title "teacher" was marked on a box containing an undifferentiated mother. $40 MIB.

The New England heritage of the Flaggs was shown in their Pilgrim family set. Fathers' hats were molded on, and painted buckles decorated the shoes of the men and boys. The man and the woman were sold separately in boxes marked "Puritan Man" or "Puritan Woman." The entire family was also sold in a large box. $45/ each MIB. Boxed family $200 MIB.

Large 6-8" display dolls were Sheila Flagg's first love. The detail of the costume of the larger Native-Americans included beaded moccasins. The papoose on the back of the large woman doll is a normal, dark skinned 1.5" baby. The 4" Native American dolls are similar to the dollhouse doll, but the women have specially molded hairdos. Costumes vary in color. Large dolls, $50 MIB. Small dolls, $35 MIB.

Western themes were common in the 1950s. Flagg made cowboys and cowgirls in their dollhouse line. Interestingly, Sheila Flagg did not make nationality dolls in this size, except for the "Senorita." A small "Frontiersman" and "Frontierswoman" were made in the 3.5" fairytale line. $35 MIB.

The "farmer" and "farmerette" were also packaged in early editions without their hats as gardeners. $35 MIB.

The pixie and clown had their own molds with a lot of hand-painted detail. The pixie was not made in a large scale, although clowns are found in both scales. Large clown, $50 MIB. Small pixie and clown, $40 MIB.

The Flagg wedding featured a bride, groom, bridesmaids, and flower girls dressed in four colors, including pink, green, blue, and yellow. A minister presided over the wedding. $35/each MIB.

The larger 1:12 scale dollhouse dolls were introduced in the late 1950s or very early 60s, perhaps to serve the school market, as they fit well with the larger houses of companies like Community Playthings. This scale never had the same popularity as the1:18 dolls, and was never expanded. Boy and girl dolls were approximately 4.25" tall and father and mother around 6". Baby was the same 1.5" baby of the 1:18 scale family. These dolls were manufactured the same as the smaller scale dolls, hand-painted with simply styled cloth clothing. Hairstyles were a little different. The girls' hair bows were replaced with short bangs. An African American family was part of the line. Dolls were generally sold in a boxed family set. $100 MIB.

Flagg made a series of 3.5" dolls called Mother Goose or Fairytale. They were made with the same plastic covered wire armature as dollhouse dolls. They were introduced in 1952, available in a series of fifteen. The dolls were $1 each or $13.95 for the set of fifteen. These cartoon-like dolls had very chubby bodies. Eyes had both a blue background and black dot, and sometimes the eyebrow was just a dot with a solid line on either side of the eye for emphasis. Noses were molded into the plastic. Some feet were painted and some were not. Dolls were sold in smaller versions of the cardboard window boxes. Maid Marion, Robin Hood, and Friar Tuck were examples of the children's stories featured in the line. $25 MIB.

By 1960, business saw a slight decline as children's playtime became dominated by television, and more "modern" playthings replaced traditional. The labor-intensive production process squeezed profits. Charles Flagg's business acumen kept the business sound, but the company suffered a severe setback when he died suddenly of a heart attack in February 1965 at the age of 50. Sheila Flagg was thrust into the role of company President, and within 3 years faced a factory move a few blocks to 6 Bismark Street. The move accommodated the expansion of the Jamaica Plains subway station. Although the new factory was more efficient and in better condition, she still faced the same business pressures that Charles had felt. Making a profit became more difficult. Sheila and Charles were an extremely close couple. Charles drove Sheila, a non-driver, to work each day occasionally cajoling her to take her place on the line, because they had a big order to fill. Without his support and complementary expertise, she lost interest in the business and lacked the ability to reposition it in changing times.

Finally choosing to exit the business, in 1973 she sold the company to a retired military man, Ralph D. Eames. Eames tried to reestablish some of the marketing channels that had languished, convincing Radio City Music Hall to again carry Flagg dolls. He addressed cost by cutting the product line drastically. In the mid 70s the company slipped a note into its packages informing buyers that the large nationality and costume dolls would soon be discontinued and that the retail mail-order business would be stopped. The note correctly predicted: "We suggest you take very good care of the dolls you have as they are now collectors items." He focused on serving educational and psychotherapy markets, primarily with a very abbreviated dollhouse line. By 1985, the factory was operating on a part-time basis and Eames made the decision to cease production. Sheila Flagg had passed away in April 1979 and did not see the closing of the factory at the end of 1985. After almost 40 years, the doll molds were destroyed, ending one of the longest life spans of a miniature doll originated by an independent postwar entrepreneur.

Flagg and Company saw the value in offering a broad line of 1:18 scale dolls. A basic family consisted of father and mother, approximately 4" tall; brother and sister, approximately 3"; baby, 1.5" tall. This same-sized baby was used to accompany both the 1:18 and 1:12 scale doll families. An extended family was produced including grandmother and grandfather, stereotypical "mammy", maid, cook, and nurse. By the mid 50s Flagg had added at least 35 models to its 1:18 dollhouse dolls.

Dolls' hair, facial details, and shoes were hand-painted. Hair colors ranged from blonde to black, with all colors in between. Lips were painted various shades of red. Noses were molded into the face. Lines were molded into the hand for fingers with a separate thumb, although the detail was not always released from the mold.

Dolls in 1:18 scale have been observed with a number of different face types. The very first dolls had nearly flat, oval faces with round dots for eyes, a short paint stroke for eyebrows, and red circular or oval lips. Eyes appear to be a single color, but a close look shows that there is a black pupil obscuring most of a very dark blue background. Eyes of the mammy had white backgrounds and black dots, creating a wide-eyed look. Paint used on early dolls is duller than later dolls. Early bodies and limbs were thicker than later models, lending some evidence that the earliest versions were modeled in soap, not clay.

A 1948 *Playthings* magazine announces a "new and improved line", and there appear to be slight changes to members, including thinner, slightly more angular faces. Unlike the original mother, subsequent females had shoes painted well below the ankles. Eyes are the same black on dark blue. Some of the dolls have rosy cheeks. Advertisements show a mixture of mold styles.

Hairstyles and facial paint differed over the many years of Flagg Company production, as they focused on keeping up with the times. The next major variation, instituted in late 1948, affected all dolls in the line. They had thinner faces and their jaws and noses were more pronounced. Women and girls had wavier hair. The girls' hair bow was molded on the right side of the head as opposed to being simply painted on. Bodies were not as thick as early versions. Fathers sported a pompadour, and brothers a forehead curl. The background blue of the eyes was quite light, allowing the pupil to stand out. A still later version of the dolls is most commonly found today. This final version had fatter, triangular faces. Eyebrows were longer and lips were shaped. Women dolls had wavy page boy styles and girls had bangs and a painted hair bow. Men's hair was more closely cropped without a wave, and boys' curls were replaced with Elvis-like pompadours. Pictured in an ad from a 1959 Marshall Field Christmas catalog, they continued with only minor painting variation until the company closed.

All in all, there are at least five different mold varieties of grandmothers; four of mothers, girls, fathers, and boys. Three grandfathers have been observed. There were two different babies, easily distinguishable. The earlier baby has shorter arms outstretched to the side.

Mother Goose served as the inspiration for a number of dolls. Left to right are Little Boy Blue, Bunny Girl, Bo-Peep, Mistress Mary, and Jack-be-Nimble. Costumes, stapled onto the doll, were nicely done, given the dolls' size. Some of the dolls hold plastic, metal, paper, or fabric implements like Jack Be Nimble with a candlestick, aiding in identification. $25 MIB.

In 1948, a 4-piece family of Mother, 2 children, and baby could be purchased for $4.25. Father added $1.50. Prices varied over time, dropping as low as $3.65 for a 4 member family without a baby when Flagg first started direct sales. Individual dolls ranged from $1.15 for children, to $1.50 for adult family to $2.25 for more elaborately dressed dolls. In 1961 a complete set of five 1:12 scale dolls, packaged in a window-style box, sold for $5.98 in a store in Des Moines, Iowa. Undressed family dolls were also available by mail-order from Flagg. Besides an active direct mail-order business, dolls were sold in catalogs of retailers like Marshall Field and specialty marketers like Community Playthings, catering to schools.

A listing of the known dollhouse sized and fairytale dolls can be found in the Appendix. The list can never be considered complete, however, because uncataloged "specials" are occasionally found, in boxes with handwritten identification.

The four known varieties of mothers had observable differences in hairstyle, facial shape, and eye coloring. Earliest dolls also have thicker arms and legs, suggesting that they were modeled in soap, not clay. Pictured from left to right is the progression of mother dolls. $25-35 MIB. Older dolls bring a higher price.

Fathers and boys show variations as well in their facial size, hairstyle, and painted eyes and eyebrows. Pictured from left to right is the progression of father and boy dolls. $25-35 MIB. Older dolls bring a higher price.

Not only did the girl dolls have variations in hair style and facial detail, but later dolls had molded hair ribbons added. It is also clear that the faces of earlier dolls did not have clearly molded chins and cheeks. Pictured from left to right is the progression of girl dolls. $25-35 MIB. Older dolls bring a higher price.

In later years, grandmothers were simply the mother doll with hair painted grey. In early years, however, the grandmothers had unique molds. The grandmothers with eye glasses were quite rare and seemingly discontinued, possibly because of the difficulty in molding the glasses. Grandfathers were generally the father doll with grey hair and bushy grey eyebrows. Later versions had painted moustaches. Pictured from left to right is the progression of grandmothers and grandfathers. $25-35 MIB. Older dolls bring a higher price.

Charlie and Sheila Flagg formed a successful complementary team, he handling the marketing and designing the production system; she designing the dolls and their costumes. They, like other remarkable doll makers in the immediate postwar years, looked to tradition to design and costume their dolls, but quickly adopted modern materials to construct them. Their innovation and craftsmanship helps to explain why the dolls of the small postwar dollmakers are desirable additions to dollhouse collections.

Dolls were sold originally in a solid white two-piece cardboard box with blue lettering. Some early dolls have been found packaged in boxes with a Brookline, Massachusetts address. It is possible that the Flaggs initially ran the business from their home, before all activity was transferred to Jamaica Plain. Boxes generally have a rubber stamp on one side identifying the doll inside. Sometimes the name was handwritten, suggesting, perhaps, that it was a trial piece or a short run. Later the company used cardboard boxes with cellophane windowpanes enabling the buyer to see the doll being purchased. The dolls were attached by their legs and at the neck to an insert in the box. The first variety of this "window" box was two-piece and a later one-piece box with flaps that opened at the top and bottom was also used. A two-piece box with clear plastic top, embossed with Flagg designs, was introduced towards the end of the line. Boxes list the attributes of the doll as: bendable, educational, hand-painted, hand-dressed, washable, with removable clothes.

Chapter 8

Many Others Tried

The postwar trend of chain store toy distribution and point of purchase counter displays helped contribute an abundant supply of low-priced miniature dolls suitable to inhabit the tin and fiberboard dollhouses prevalent in the market. A company did not need to have a broad doll or miniatures offering to compete. Dolls merely had to be compatible in size and style to the offerings of major toy makers.

Some of the companies were moderately sized toy makers that appeared to be capitalizing on the popularity of dollhouses by creating a limited product line. They did not expand their lines, nor stay in the market for extended periods, especially as the popularity of dollhouses began to wane. There were a number of small family or artist run businesses making higher quality dolls, however, that did not seem to be able to develop the distribution channels necessary to create a long term place in the market. Europe continued to develop doll makers who made well-crafted hand-made miniature dolls.

Materials used by these niche suppliers differed little from the dolls being made by their larger or more recognized competitors. Plastic continued as the material of choice for all or part of the doll. Solid vinyl and rubber dolls could still be found. While many of the dolls were molded in a "frozen" position, poseable dolls with pipe cleaner bodies, and dolls with basic shoulder and hip joints were also available.

Gerber Plastic Company

In 1948, Gerber Plastic Company created a set of vinyl, female play dolls. These dolls were designed and advertised to fit postwar plastic dollhouse furniture. A 1948 Gerber ad in the trade publication *Toys and Novelties* showed a doll sitting in an Ideal dollhouse chair and one lying in a Renwal bed.

Gerber Plastic Company dolls came molded frozen in two positions – standing and sitting. Standing dolls were 2.5"; sitting dolls, 2.75". The molded vinyl dolls were advertised as being flexible, washable, and unbreakable. Initially, they were available with hand-painted facial features at a retail price of 10¢ each. If their outfits were also painted they cost 20¢ each. Hair was either blond, brunette, or red. Eyes were blue, lips, pink or red. Sweaters and skirts were combinations of yellow, blue, red, and green. Some dolls had painted socks and shoes. Dolls were individually wrapped in cellophane bags. They also came in a colorfully designed boxed set that held two sitting and two standing dolls. The lithographed bedroom backdrop had slots holding the dolls and created a life-like room setting. This set sold for 98 cents in 1948. The dolls were hallmarked "Gerber Plastic Co., St. Louis, USA." $10/each, $25/ 4 piece set MIB.

"Seiberling Rubber"

A family of four solid rubber dolls and a nurse were frequently found housed in post-war dollhouses. Approximately 1:18 scale, they were molded in one piece and lack poseability. While their manufacturer is not known, collectors sometimes refer to the dolls as "Seiberling." Former Seiberling Rubber employees have stated that the company never made dollhouse dolls. Noted rubber toy collector and author, Dave Leopard, having searched his extensive records for Archer, Seiberling Latex, Sun Rubber, and Auburn Rubber, has been unable to identify their source. Mr. Leopard suggests that each of the major rubber toy companies would have had capability to make the dolls. It is possible that a toy company contracted with one of the rubber companies to make the dolls for sale under a different brand. He also points out that solid rubber dolls were made in postwar Britain and found their way into the American market.

The dolls occasionally attributed to Seiberling Rubber. Father is 4.375"; mother 4.67"; girl 3.375" and boy 3.25". Their hair, facial features, and clothing were molded into the design. Molding material was a hard black rubber, so the skin, clothing, and details were all painted on. Father wore a tan suit, and his tie might be blue or red. Mother has been found wearing a two-piece suit of blue, green, or pink and her shoes were fashionably painted to match. Daughter wore a pink dress with blue flowers or blue dress with pink flowers with matching shoes and socks. Younger brother wore tan pants and shirt; his belt may have been red or brown. Father and son had brown hair, while mother and daughter were blonds. All dolls had painted brown eyes and eyebrows and red lips. A 4.75" nurse accompanied the set. More difficult to find, she was outfitted in a white painted nurses uniform and cap, stockings, and shoes. Her hair was brown. The left arm of the nurse is bent with her hand resting on her waist, while the mother is exactly opposite with her right arm bent. Dolls are found today in poor to very good condition depending on how much paint has chipped off. $10-15/each.

Allied Molding Corporation

Allied Molding Corporation, first appearing in 1948 trade ads, specialized in hard plastic molded toys: vehicles, animals, and a small line of 1:24 scale dollhouse furniture. Based in Queens, New York, the company maintained a year round Manhattan showroom on Broadway, near the Toy Building. Allied made 3 different dolls to fit with their toy line. Allied furniture molds or copies of the molds were later used to produce similar hallmarked lines for Kleeware in the United Kingdom and Pyro in the United States. Pyro did produce the baby, but it is not known whether either company made similar boys and girls.

To accompany their furniture and sit in their Ferris wheel and vehicles, Allied Molding Corporation made a tiny plastic seated 1.75" boy, 1.625" girl, and 1.125" thumb sucking baby. They were molded in pink, ivory, and blue hard plastic. Boy and girl were included with Allied's dollhouse furniture sets. Allied furniture was hallmarked, but the dolls were not. Pyro later made a similar baby. $3.

Beton

Beton, originally known as Bergen Toy & Novelty Co., had its beginnings in New Jersey in 1935. Originally, the company made small lead cowboys, Indians, soldiers, and animals. Later they produced a dollhouse family. By 1938 they were among the first companies to convert to plastic. Figures could be purchased unpainted or painted, and were sold in header bags and in boxed sets. In the intensely competitive postwar toy world where copying and low-priced overseas manufacturing was common, Rel Plastics of Patterson, New Jersey, undertook a corporate roll-up strategy and acquired Beton together with Plasco towards the end of the 1950s.

In the early 1950s, Beton made a set of hard plastic figures that were part of a set called "Railroad Folks", suitable for 1:24 scale dollhouses and train sets. They were hand-painted and stand on an oval molded base that was marked on the underside "Beton, made In USA." Father was the tallest at 2.875"; mother, 2.5"; boy 2.375", and girl, just over 2". $5.

Peco

Peco, or Product Engineering Company, primarily a die casting concern, made its headquarters in Portland, Oregon. Their toy figure offering included pirates, cowboys, Indians, frontiersmen, combat soldiers, and a set called "Little Women Dolls." The dolls, molded in Vinylite, were designed by John Benneth, a talented clay toy sculptor who had made his own toys since childhood. What made Peco's models unique at the time were the removable accessories that Mr. Benneth designed to accompany the figures. The dolls made their debut at the New York City Toy Fair in 1953, and in 1954 were selling individually on a card in 5&10¢ stores at 25¢ or four to a box for $1. Later these same sets were sold with paints so that the figures could be decorated. Other companies quickly copied Benneth's idea of including the add-on accessories and began selling similar figures at a fraction of the cost. Despite Peco's higher quality, they could not compete and discontinued production in 1956.

T. Cohn/Superior

The single patio Spanish styled tin dollhouse with red tiled roof is among the most recognizable of the Baby Boomer dollhouses. Produced by T. Cohn of Brooklyn, New York, it was introduced in time for the 1948 Christmas season. The house was sold furnished with Plasco or Renwal furniture and in an unfurnished version. Scale matched nicely with the furniture of Renwal, Plasco and Ideal, and the dollhouse is now often found with an eclectic mix of postwar furniture. Windows were made of metal and opened, casement style. T. Cohn continued to market a slightly smaller scaled Superior line throughout the 1960s, introducing several additional house styles. Houses produced before 1957 were packaged with hard plastic, solid colored furniture marked Superior. After that time, the houses were sold with inferior 1:24 scale soft plastic furniture, reportedly made for Superior by Marx. In the late 1950s or early 1960s, Superior introduced a five-member family to complement its dollhouses. Mother, father, brother, sister, and toddler boy were each molded in one piece from polyethylene soft plastic. Each of the figures, with the exception of the seated father and the toddler, had bases that helped them stand. Superior thoughtfully added a dog for the children to play with.

The soft plastic dolls made by T.Cohn/Superior to inhabit their later lower quality tin dollhouses had realistic expressions. Mother was 2.625"; Brother, 2"; sister, 1.75", toddler,1.25". A sitting father is missing from the set. $3/each.

The four Pecos Little Women Dolls were approximately 3.25" tall. Each Vinylite figure was a different solid color. *Rally Queen* was a sportswoman. Her accessories included a tennis racket, bullhorn, team pennant, binoculars, and sports hats. *Dottie Debutante* was dressed for an evening on the town. She was accessorized with bracelets, cape, and purse. *Hattie the Hatter* was, as her name suggests, hooked on hats. *Peggy Pigtails* portrayed a schoolgirl. Her accessories included her dog Spunky, a doll, schoolbooks, and lunch box. As their designer, John Benneth, realized, the detachable accessories made these dolls delightful for dollhouse play. $60/set MIB.

Susy Goose Toys

Located in Michigan, the Kiddie Brush & Toy Co. through its subsidiary, Susy Goose Toys, produced a set of plastic family figures. First introduced in 1954, these figures accompanied various playsets marketed by Susy Goose. They would be very suitable for dollhouse play, and resembled Marx' and Thomas' softer plastic dolls of the early 1950s.

Susy Goose's "Smith Family" consisting of father, mother, girl, boy, and twin babies, were the travelers who stayed in the "Friendly Folks Motel," a metal, lithographed, and furnished, highly desirable playset. Father was 3.25", mother 3", daughter 2.25", and son in sitting position, 1.5". The twins were 1.25". They were molded in cream colored soft plastic. Standing dolls had bases for stability. Figures were nicely sculpted with the girl holding her doll and father's hands shaped to carry the luggage in and out of the motel. $15-20/each.

A grocery store called "Susy's Superette," also made by Susy Goose in 1954, included some of the family figures as well as a grocer, a cashier. and a bag boy. The bag boy is missing from the scene, apparently out on a delivery. $15-20/each.

Premier Products

A Brooklyn, New York, based company, Premier Products, known in the 1950s primarily for its spaceships, issued a four-piece set of 3" spacemen. Apparently to have a point-of-sale "girls toy" to complete their line, they also released a set of plastic "school girls."

Premier Products "Back to School" dolls are 2.5" tall, suitable, although not precisely scaled, for play in a 1:24 scale dollhouse or school. Selling for 29¢ a set, they were packaged in a plastic bag with a cardboard header labeled "Back To School." The dolls were molded in various poses, curtseying, jumping rope, walking with books, and strolling. The dolls were just over 2.5" tall, cast with different outfits and hairstyles. Molded in unpainted solid colors, examples have been found in pink, brown, and bright yellow. $5/each. $30/ set of 4.

Carol-Lee Dolls

Created in the late 1940s to early 1950s, these vinyl dollhouse dolls were 1:24 scale, appealing to owners of the smaller scale dwellings beginning to appear on the market. Not much is known about their creators, a husband and wife team, residents of Littleton, Colorado, who died in an accident in the 1980s. The five-member family was packaged in a box marked "Carol-Lee Dollhouse Dolls, Denver, Colorado." Possibly, they were also sold individually.

Carol-Lee dolls were hand-painted with non-toxic, washable paint. Dolls, jointed at the hips and shoulders, met the creators' belief that children needed flexible dolls, as opposed to the non-poseable figures being sold with 1:24 scale houses common at that time. Father was 3.375", mother 3.25", older boy 2.25", girl 2.125", and young boy 1.5". Eyes, eyebrows, and shoes were painted black. Lips appeared to be dual-colored as a result of the color bleeding when applied. Males had black painted hair and females, yellow. Clothing was a combination of colors in a darker color scheme. Borrowing from the Renwal doll slogan: "They stand, they sit, they kneel," Carol-Lee's packaging states: "They stand, they sit, they carry." $10/each. $60/set of 5 MIB.

Trim Molded Products

Located in Burlington, Wisconsin, Trim Molded Products created a family of five stand-up plastic dolls that came packaged with "The Doll House Family Cut-Out and Coloring Book." In the front of the book, ready to cut out, were colored outfits with tabs for all five dolls. A second set of clothing was printed without colors so that the purchaser could paint or decorate them as desired.

Trim Molded Products advertised that their plastic doll family was perfectly sized for the average dollhouse. Father was 5", mother 4.75", boy 3.75", girl 3.625" and baby measured 2.5". They were molded of a very thin plastic. To stand, their feet were inserted into a 1.25" round plastic base. Faces and clothing were molded into the plastic. The set of five sold for 29¢. This toy was advertised in Life magazine as having been play tested and approved by World Toy House of St. Paul, Minnesota, a toy distributor apparently holding itself out as a rating agency! $25/set, uncut MIB.

Five-Inch Dressable Dolls

There were many small-plastic dolls during the 1950s not perfectly scaled in all their proportions for a dollhouse. Targeted for the inexpensive "display counter" market, many were imported and featured jointed arms and/or legs. They could be found with or without blinky eyes or hand-painted detail. Generally, they had simple cloth clothing or were sold undressed, often in sets for do-it-yourself costuming, featuring cloth, patterns, and even small hand sewing machines.

Of particular interest because of the breadth of its offering, however, was the doll marketed by a Los Angeles, California couple, Mr. and Mrs. Harry A. Wagner. The doll, probably imported, was a 5" hard plastic figure with jointed arms. The doll itself was not unique to the Wagners. Other firms, such as Cheerio of Canada, Hassenfeld Bros., and Standard Toycraft, sold similar dolls. What made it unique, however, was the fact that it was sold dressed in seventeen different outfits such as Little Red Riding Hood, a ballerina, and a play doll. Each became a member of the *Parade of Dolls*. Mrs. Wagner designed the costumes. The doll's facial characteristics, fingers, and shoes were molded and her eyes and lips were painted. Each doll sold for 29 cents in 1954. After Harry Wagner's death in 1954, the firm was purchased by H.J. Duffey & Associate, with Mrs. Wagner staying on in charge of design and production.

5" dressable dolls were popular offerings from a number of companies. Some were sold already dressed, while others were packaged as part of sewing kits. The doll on the left is unmarked, but closely resembles a Wagner, "Parade of Dolls" figure. The doll on the right of Canadian origin is marked on her back, "Cheerio". $5.

Pipe Cleaner Dolls

Simple pipe cleaner dolls were made to appeal to children who wanted additional play value inherent in a flexible doll. They did not have the artistic detail in either their decoration or clothing as those produced by Winsor Doll Company, but they were inexpensively priced. F.W. Woolworth marketed one such family. Hitting a very low price point, Woolworth sold father and mother for 29¢ and boy and girl for 25¢. They were initially sold individually packaged in plastic wrappers.

F.W.Woolworth's dolls had a pipe cleaner frame, painted plaster of paris heads and soft plastic shoes. The pipe cleaner frame extended through the shoes. Metal clips that pinch the pipe cleaners together served as hips and shoulders. Their upper torso was wrapped with cotton batting, but the legs and arms were unwrapped. Dolls had painted facial features. Female dolls currently found had blond painted hair. Male dolls had brown shoes; mothers' were yellow and daughters' white. Simply made clothing of various fabrics including broadcloth, silk, crepe, and muslin, was glued, as opposed to sewn, and lacked bottom hems. Father and mother were 4.5"; boy and girl were 3.25"; baby, wrapped in a blanket, was 2.375". The young girl was sold attached to a Jaydon piano bench ready for a recital. Extended family members have not been found. $5/each.

Grandmother Stover's Inc.

John Stover of Columbus, Ohio, created a thriving business named in honor of his grandmother. He sold a large array of miniature accessories to decorate and add play value to postwar dollhouses. Primarily packaging miniatures made by others, he also had a small cottage industry of local women to decorate the small items that found their way into his blister packs and boxed sets.

At some point Woolworth's dolls were sold with popular miniature furniture and accessories of the day. Variations include a male doll dressed as a chef holding a Playtown turkey. $10.

Four adult dolls at a card party were sold attached to Ideal card table chairs holding a hand of playing cards. Dolls were not marked but have "patent pending" on their shoes. $60/set attached to chairs.

A family of these dolls caught the eye of children's author Billie Avis Hoy, who apparently submitted a manuscript for a book to Junior Reviewers, the educational division of Riverside Press Publishers. With the manuscript were thirty-nine 5x7 black and white photographs of the dollhouse family placed in and about a 1948 Keystone fiberboard dollhouse. The theme appears to be "welcoming a new baby into the family." Apparently, the book was never published and the photos were returned to Ms. Hoy.

Another pipe cleaner frame family was in the market, sold by an unidentified manufacturer/distributor. They can be differentiated by the hard plastic lower arms and legs and plastic heads attached to their pipe cleaner frames. Father stood 5" tall and mother 4.5". Their facial features and shoes were painted. An additional piece of plastic, resembling a sole, was added to the shoe bottoms aiding the dolls to stand. Clothing was felt and crepe paper. The woman appeared to have crepe paper hair sprayed with a fixative. Additional family members have not been found. $5-10.

Another series of pipe cleaner dolls was marketed by B.S.& Co. With pipe cleaner frames and hard plastic, glossy painted heads, these dolls were not marked in any way. Father was 5" tall, mother 4.75", boy and girl were 3.75". Father and boy had the same size head, which made the boys' face appear oversized to his body. Father and son had painted dark hair. Likewise, mother and daughter had the same size face, but mother's appears to be too small in proportion to her size. Female dolls had yarn hair glued to the heads. Dolls had painted facial features. Shoes, painted as well, were black, brown, blue, and for the young girl, red, to match her outfit. Clothing was generally felt with wrapped yarn for the female dolls' sweaters. The dolls, made in the USA. by or for B.S.& Co, were initially sold in a cardboard box marked "Adjustable Dollhouse Dolls." $50/set MIB.

One of John Stover's first attempts at marketing dollhouse dolls was his 1947 eight-member extended family of cloth over wire frame dolls, reminiscent of Edith Flack Ackley dolls. The dolls' features were embroidered, and either real hair or yarn was used for hair. Included in the set were a mother and father, boy, girl, baby, nurse, African American cook, and maid. Adults were 5" tall; children, 2.5"; baby, 1.25". As with Ethel Strong's Twinky dolls, he offered the family for a very short time. Grandmother Stover's never marketed another complete family, although, at times it offered small babies. Small babies, $5-6. Cloth dolls have not been found in order to establish price.

Doll Artisans

There were doll artisans working in the period utilizing inexpensive base materials, but adding finely detailed costumes. Wood was still a popular media, as shown by the Reinmenyder dolls of Eagles Mere, Pennsylvania. Some United States artisans, starting with a pipe cleaner frame, added more expensive and detailed heads, limbs, and clothing. A fine example was the "Dainty Dollhouse Dolls" created by the Veta Doll Company of Pasadena, California.

A mother, father, and daughter hand carved in wood during the late 1940s or early 1950s by a Mrs. Reinmenyder of Eagles Mere, Pennsylvania. Father was 4.5"; mother, 4.25; girl, 2.75". Their costuming was quite elaborate. $50/each.

A 5" Little Lord Fauntleroy made in 1948 by Mrs. Reinmenyder stands next to a classic 6.5" carved "Hitty" doll. $225/pr.

Dolls of the Veta Doll Company were made in the style of bisque shoulderheads with shiny painted-over bisque faces. Their bodies were pipe cleaner frames with bisque lower arms and legs. It is not known whether the bisque pieces were purchased in kit form or created by the doll maker. Father was 4", mother 4.25", boy and girl were 3.25". Their faces had painted features. Mother and son had blue eyes; father and daughter, brown. Their charming clothing, made of felt, burlap, and organza, was old fashioned in design. Their shoes were painted on the bisque legs. $200/family set MIB.

Veta Dolls came packaged in a gold cardboard box with a white paper label. The label had a hand drawn picture of a house, fence, and two trees. It was lettered: "Dainty Doll House Dolls Veta Doll Company Pasadena, California." Inside the box were four slots, one for each doll. A four piece family: mother, father, daughter, and maid, was offered by FAO Schwarz in its 1947 Christmas catalog, for the then princely sum of $7.75. It was pictured with a Keystone dollhouse filled with Renwal's plastic furniture.

Chapter 9

As Europe Recovered and then Prospered

When hostilities ceased in 1945, all of Europe faced the formidable task of rebuilding a ruined economy and war-ravaged industrial capability. Unemployment was high as soldiers returned to civilian life after almost a decade of European warfare. Many women lost their husbands and sons in the war and were faced with the prospect of sustaining themselves in difficult times. Raw material supply was channeled to rebuilding infrastructure and to the basic industries that would provide employment and spendable income.

Unlike their American counterparts who generally were interested in supplementing family income in a booming post-war economy, men and women in England, Scotland, and Germany, drew upon craft making skills as a principal source of income. Following a long tradition of toy making, they began producing small dolls made from scraps, leftovers, and limited quantities of scarce material in order to survive. Various steps in the doll making process were farmed out to neighbors and relatives. Some produced the bodies, generally by covering wire armatures with paper, cloth, or yarn. Others made clothing from scrap cloth, sometimes from a family's curtains, carpeting or old clothes, or painted the faces and added finish detail. There were national and regional similarities between many of the dolls, as doll makers looked to their fellow countrymen and country-women for inspiration and collaboration. The dolls were dressed in everyday clothes as mothers, fathers, children, grandparents, doctors, nurses, policemen, mailmen, and maids.

The biggest problem faced by these cottage artisans was gaining access to markets outside their own country, as many of their fellow citizens faced similar financial constraints. The United States military personnel stationed throughout Europe provided an early market for the dolls. Doll makers would go door-to-door through the military bases selling dolls. They established outlets in PXs on the bases and in souvenir stands in airports. As time went on, military personnel would send them home as gifts or show them to friends and family back in the United States, developing an appreciation and demand for the dolls. Governments sponsored toy fairs assisting the doll makers in finding overseas outlets. United States distributors struck distribution agreements with these artisans, giving them broad access to a market that appreciated the uniqueness and workmanship of the dolls.

With the advent of the Marshall Plan investment in 1948, Western Europe's economy began to boom, and it saw unparalleled growth from 1950 to the late 1960s. Trade barriers within Europe were removed and export markets, particularly to the United States, increased significantly. A number of the European doll makers who started in the immediate postwar period benefited from this economic growth, obtaining capital to expand their businesses and gaining access to markets outside the borders of their home countries. Within the region, dolls were often sold at high-end gift shops, where they were sometimes purchased for collectible displays, souvenirs, or knick-knacks. Doll makers prospered as increased tourism gave exposure to their well made, unique dolls. European doll makers of the 1950s and 60s apparently were not trying to reach the same low-priced market segment favored by the major United States toy producers. American producers complained after visiting toy fairs like those held in Nuremberg, Germany, that European toy makers did not see need to turn their product lines over annually or to adopt the newest production materials. They were more content with quality and tradition. Europeans used more expensive materials and methods, allowing for great artistic detail. Subject matter was aimed at regional and national characters or fairytale scenes, not just the dollhouse market. Many of Europe's miniaturists and doll makers, with their focus on quality, produced their toys for decades, and some still prosper today.

Erna Meyer

The story of Erna Meyer and her wonderful doll creations illustrates a number of themes common to Europe's postwar recovery period. Erna Meyer, born in Bavaria in 1924, always had an interest in dolls. As a child, she tried to make her own flexible dollhouse dolls because hers would not sit on a chair properly. She studied to be a kindergarten teacher, but after the war ended in May 1945, she was not able to secure a job. Like many young women of the era, she depended on craftwork to make a living. Recognizing that local children had few toys to play with, she and some friends began to make small dollhouse dolls from available materials. In addition to selling the dolls to neighbors and relatives, Erna Meyer was able to exchange the dolls for cigarettes at nearby United States military offices, building on connections established by her aunt who worked there as an interpreter. Business boomed, and in October 1945, her father convinced her to officially register a firm and obtain a business license. As it was nearing Christmas, she exhibited samples of her dolls decorated as Santa and children in the window of a local pharmacy near her home. A sign in the window told people when and where to purchase the dolls. The next morning she was awakened by the sounds of her neighbors filling the stairway leading up to her family's third floor apartment. They were very anxious to secure her dolls for the holiday season.

Erna Meyer met her husband Friedrich Bernhard Bethge at Munich's 1949 Oktoberfest. Erna's mother took pity on a hungry student and invited him home to dinner. Marrying in 1955, they formed a wonderful team producing and marketing Erna Meyer dolls. *Original photos from the collection of the Erna Meyer Company and Frau Gabriele John von Freyend.*

Erna Meyer had a lifelong fascination with dollhouse dolls. The doll pictured on the left was made from wood by Erna Meyer as part of her examination to become a kindergarten teacher. Dolls on the right were made by Erna Meyer as a young teen in 1938 or 1939 as inhabitants of her childhood dollhouse. *Dolls courtesy of the Erna Meyer Company and Frau Gabriele John von Freyend.* Insufficient examples for valuation.

The original 1945 Santa displayed in the window of a local Munich pharmacy that started Erna Meyer's business. *Dolls from the collection of the Erna Meyer Company and Frau Gabriele John von Freyend.* Insufficient examples for valuation.

Erna Meyer's business followed the familiar design of a cottage industry, with family and friends as outworkers and staff. She ran the business of designing, finishing, and distributing the dolls from her home for eight years. Despite its initial success, business began to lessen in 1948 as a result of the currency reform imposed by the government to help control postwar inflation. Erna considered giving up her small business, but persisted after hearing about a Toy Fair to be held in Nuremberg in 1950 as an export showcase for locally produced toys. Traveling with Friedrich Bernhard Bethge, whom she had met at the Oktoberfest in 1949, she attended the fair to try and expand her market. At the Fair she made the acquaintance of Käthe Kruse and received some guidance from the legendary doll maker. Ms. Meyer and Mr. Bethge exhibited all of her dolls mounted on a board, catching the eye of buyers from around the world. She was able to secure numerous business contacts and successfully re-invent her company. Mr. Bethge, having joined the company to offset his school expenses, stayed on after he finished his studies, marrying Erna in 1955 and helping to expand the Erna Meyer Company.

Truly a cottage industry, home workers would arrive weekly to drop off clothing or completed dolls and pick up their next batch. If they lived a distance away, dolls and fabric were mailed to them. A small group of employees worked in the Meyer's home – painters and women who added finishing touches, as well as people to assist in packing and shipping. By 1953 Erna Meyer, needing more space, relocated to a larger building and then moved again, in 1955, within Munich. Here the company remained until March 2003. Today the company is located on Münchner Strasse in Dachau, Germany.

The Erna Meyer Company was fortunate, in that its success did not hinge solely on the presence of it founder. Erna Meyer Bethge's children, Michael and Gabriele, both joined the company in the 1970s and worked alongside their parents, learning the business. Gabriele, starting with the company in 1977, relates that her mother encouraged her input not only about the designs of the dolls, but also about the company's strategy and direction. They were close collaborators rather than competitive parent and child. Erna Meyer continued her life's work, designing and making dolls until her death in 1996. Her husband, Friedrich, died in 1998. Today, their daughter, Gabriele John von Freyend, owns and operates the business. The dolls are still made by hand as a cottage industry. Gabriele's hand is still quite evident in the finished product. She personally inspects every doll before it is sent to a customer. She designs all the dolls and their clothing, and makes the prototypes used by her cottage workers, now located in Eastern Europe.

Early dolls made as presents by Erna Meyer for her parents' wedding anniversary in the early to mid 1940s. Dolls stand in front of a 1:10 scale wardrobe made by Erna Meyer's father for her childhood dollhouse. *Dolls from the collection of the Erna Meyer Company and Frau Gabriele John von Freyend.* Insufficient examples for valuation.

Earliest Erna Meyer dolls were fabric wrapped over a padded wire armature frame. Their mitten-like hands were covered with skin-colored fabric. Feet were stuffed with cotton or wool to make a booty that was then covered with fabric. No cardboard sole was added to the shoe of these first dolls. Early dolls had long, oval shaped faces with hand-painted simple facial features: a dot for eyes, two dots for nose. Children were 9 or 12 cm, 3.5 or 4.75". Initially, clothing scraps and seconds were used to fashion the dolls' clothing. The Meyer family carpet was made bald, as its thick hair, "flokati", was plucked out to help decorate the dolls. *Dolls from the collection of Swantje Köhler. Photo courtesy of Swantje Köhler.* $150/each

By 1949 the trademark *Liliput* was used. "Heidi and Peter" were first generation dolls and carried the *Liliput* trademark. *Dolls from the collection of the Erna Meyer Company and Frau Gabriele John von Freyend*. $350/pr MIB.

A new style of doll was introduced in 1949, also in 1:10 scale. Adult dolls were approximately 6.75". There was a change in the face of the doll with slightly more visible molded features. As the war years faded into the background, better fabrics became available for clothing. The *Liliput* trademark was only used for a short period. It was discontinued after a claim of infringement was lodged by another toy making firm. *Dolls from the collection of the Erna Meyer Company and Frau Gabriele John von Freyend*. $300/pr.

Early 50s dolls were patterned with thin molded faces and ears. Handcrafted *papier mâché* was now used to shape the head of the dolls, which was then covered with fine skin-colored fabric, also used to cover the limbs. Shoes now had a sole of punched cardboard and came in various color variations. Clothing was carefully styled to the time. Boys in the picture wore tovel scooter hats, typical in Hamburg, Germany. *Dolls from the collection of the Erna Meyer Company and Frau Gabriele John von Freyend*. $150/each.

Erna Meyer dolls were featured in the illustrations of a mid-1950s children's book, *Im Puppenhaus. Dolls from the collection of the Erna Meyer Company and Frau Gabriele John von Freyend*.

Heidi and her best friend, the goatherd Peter, of Johanna Spyri's famous tale were popular characters throughout the company's history. This pair was made in the 1960s. Doll heads were now made from polystyrene foam covered with fabric. $75/each.

By 1961, Erna Meyer had developed distribution outside Germany. This December, 1961, *House and Garden* advertisement was placed by a doll shop, Gina and Selma, in New York City.

This family exhibited changes made in 1975 when cotton jersey limb covering was replaced with skin-colored foam. Dolls were being made in such great quantity that the company started using injection-molding for its plastic shoes. Children no longer had painted eyebrows. Forty home makers were making 90,000 dolls a year. *Dolls from the collection of the Erna Meyer Company and Frau Gabriele John von Freyend*. $65/each.

In 1957 dolls were made in 1:12 scale, more suitable for fine dollhouses of the time period. Adult dolls were 15 cm or just over 6", and children were 5, 8, and 11 cm, or 2, 3, and 4". This 1960s family, with polystyrene foam heads and cardboard soled shoes, were representative of the company's line. Eyebrows of the adult dolls had two painted lines. Eyes were now painted with a very round pupil and white iris. *Dolls from the collection of Swantje Köhler. Photo courtesy of Swantje Köhler.* $75/each.

Dolls of 1:15 scale were added in 1957, sized from 4.75" for adults to 3.25" for children. This smaller size was made until 2000. A 1990s casually dressed 1:15 scale family now had revitalized facial detail on their injection-molded heads. As one of her first projects after joining the company, Gabriele John von Freyend helped her mother design the jogging suits. $55/each.

Erna Meyer, collaborating with her daughter Gabriele von Freyend, kept fashions of dolls up to date. Doll heads were now injection-molded plastic, covered with cloth, replacing the more detailed polystyrene foam. These 1980 dolls, with a more orange-hued fabric covering, had less facial detail. They reflected a reduction in overall quality and cost, needed to meet dropping market prices. *Dolls from the collection of the Erna Meyer Company and Frau Gabriele John von Freyend*. $55/each.

Grandparents were common extensions to the basic family produced by Erna Meyer. A 1:10 scale grandfather, with cardboard soled shoes, is paired with an early 1950s 1:12 grandmother needing reading glasses. Both grandparents have highly molded facial detail. $100/each.

Household help complemented the Erna Meyer family line. Maid and nurse were post-1975 examples of foam wrapped limbs and plastic shoes. $65/each.

Between 1982 and 1994 a fourth scale, 1:18, was added. Adults were 4.25" and children 2.625". The newlywed dolls were styled like their larger 1980s counterparts. $50/each.

Erna Meyer dolls underwent numerous changes over their more than 60-year lifespan. The first 1945 prototype doll, pictured on the far left, had a simple oval head and rough cloth wrapped body. The second doll, from 1949, was smaller with greater facial molding detail such as ears and nose. A fine skin-colored wool fleece fabric covered its wire frame. As shown in the third doll, 1950 brought further changes. Kneecaps were added, and shoes now had cardboard soles. The head was handcrafted *papier mâché* covered with fabric with increased detail such as cheeks and a more prominent nose. This design still had molded ears. In 1962, the dolls changed further. Kneecaps disappeared and cotton jersey covered the arms and legs replacing the earlier wool fleece. The head was cloth-covered polystyrene foam. The fifth doll, with painted hair, represents a 1971 variation of dolls with plastic heads and hands. They were made until 1985 but were offered at a lower price point. They did, however, have injection-molded plastic shoes and skin-colored foam limb covering, added to larger dolls in 1975. The doll on the far right is an example of the fine porcelain dolls added in 1999, after Gabriele John von Freyend took over direction of the company. Dolls have porcelain heads, as well as lower arms and legs. *Dolls from the collection of the Erna Meyer Company and Frau Gabriele John von Freyend.*

Schoolrooms were a popular offering of the Erna Meyer Company. An early 1951 version, with collapsible desks was sold, but not made, by Erna Meyer, and the box did not contain any of her dolls. The pictured set came with the six seated dolls and teacher. The dolls' kneecaps date its production between 1950 and 1962. The two standing dolls are modern additions c. 1990. $500/set MIB.

Over the years dolls were produced in many different scales and styles. As with any series of dolls that has been in production for such a long period of time, the product undergoes a number of changes. Some basics have remained constant about the construction of the Erna Meyer dolls - the wire frame, fabric covering the dolls' faces, hand painting of the faces, stylized hands covered with fabric, and the total handcrafting of the doll, except for small compromises to mass production of injection-molded heads and plastic shoes. Even today change continues to keep the dolls up-to-date and appealing to the discerning tastes of serious collectors. In 1999, under Gabriele's leadership, fine quality, porcelain dolls were introduced. Adult dolls are 15 cm or just over 6" and children were 5, 8, 10 and 12 cm – 2, 3.25, 4, and 4.75".

Erna Meyer had earlier entered into a confusing collaboration with Käthe Kruse after their meeting at the Nuremberg Toy Fair. One story survives that Käthe Kruse purchased small dolls from Erna Meyer, which Käthe then placed in the arms of her dolls as miniature toys. Gabriele relates that Käthe Kruse felt that Erna Meyer was the only doll maker of the time making dolls of quality and character to match her own. It was possible, in fact, that Käthe Kruse decorated some of Erna Meyer's dolls, today leading to some confusion as to origin. Drawing upon the old relationship, with Gabriele at the reins, the company, from 1995 to 2001, produced a series of 6.5 cm pins inspired by Käthe Kruse's collection. Kruse's traditional Mimerle and Jorgel dolls were also made as 11 cm Erna Meyer dolls. In 1988, Gabriele joined forces with her parent's old friend, Bodo Hennig, the head of the Bodo Hennig PuppenmObel Company. The Erna Meyer Company produced a line of dolls "exclusively" for sale by Hennig. They wore clothing matching the style of his Art Noveau and Biedermier-like period furniture.

The production of the Erna Meyer Company was not limited to dollhouse family dolls. A wide range of fairytale dolls was also made during the 1950s and 60s. Pictured at left is Der Strummelpeter, Slovenly Peter, with uncombed hair and uncut fingernails. Hansel and Gretel, pictured at top right, talk with the wicked crone. At bottom center, a jester, a water carrier, Pied Piper of Hamlin, and chimney sweep, each illustrated popular children's fairytale characters. *Dolls from the collection of the Erna Meyer Company and Frau Gabriele John von Freyend*. $150/each.

The company, unlike others of the era, did not over-expand to meet demand. Holding on to its cottage industry production model and its commitment to high quality, it weathered economic cycles and is still recognized today as a premier producer of dollhouse dolls. In all, Gabriele estimates that there were 2,000 different dolls in 60 years of production.

They have proved among the most popular and enduring of all commercially made dollhouse dolls, once purchased by Jacqueline Kennedy for her daughter Caroline, and residents of the dollhouse of the authors' daughter.

A line of whimsical Mascottes was produced to hang from the rear view mirrors of cars. The hobo on the right had a few days' growth beard and the sailor playing the accordion had tattooed forearms. They were approximately 4.25" tall with fabric-covered *papier mâché* heads, dating them to the mid-1950s. Their feet were slightly oversized. *Dolls from the collection of the Erna Meyer Company and Frau Gabriele John von Freyend*. $150/each.

German regional themes were popular subjects for Erna Meyer. Three 4.25" boy dolls were dressed in the quasi-military costumes of the Munich student clubs. Dueling was common among club members, and dolls had forehead and cheek scars painted on their heads to prove their "manhood." *Dolls from the collection of the Erna Meyer Company and Frau Gabriele John von Freyend*. $150/each.

Munich, founded as a monastery in 1158, is symbolized by the small Münchner Kindle holding a large, soft pretzel. $150.

Erna Meyer created special character dolls. From left: a tennis player, an artist from the Schwabing neighborhood of Munich, a fashionable traveler, an American cowboy, and a fireman. One Christmas Erna Meyer's son awoke to find a whole squadron of firemen riding his new, large fire truck. *Dolls from the collection of the Erna Meyer Company and Frau Gabriele John von Freyend*. $150/each.

These 1957 regional costumed nationality dolls represent France and Italy. They were 1:10 scale. *Dolls from the collection of the Erna Meyer Company and Frau Gabriele John von Freyend*. $150/each.

Two sisters dressed in traditional Hungarian clothing had their names, Piri and Piroska, hand lettered on their aprons. It is possible that they were sold as undressed dolls by Erna Meyer to the Szálasi firm of Hungary to be authentically costumed and named. $65-75/each.

1:12 scale dolls, marketed exclusively by B. Altman and Company as George and Martha Washington, were packaged under the "Ermey" trademark during the late 1950s to mid 1960s. According to Gabriele John von Freyend, undressed dolls sold to Szálasi were dressed and wigged in aristocratic costumes as well. The 1:15 scale doll on the right, likely dressed by Szálasi, was made in the mid 1970s as indicated by his plastic shoes. Ermey George and Martha Washington dolls, $125/each. Szálasi dolls, $75/each.

Gabriele John von Freyend has continued the tradition of her mother by producing fine quality dolls. She introduced a line of exquisitely detailed porcelain figures in 1999. Doll heads are made at Munich's historic Nymphenburg Porcelain Factory. Her catalogs show that she honors the company's origins, focusing part of her offering on Santas and Christmas festivities.

Modern porcelain 1:12 dolls are beautifully outfitted in period dress. Gabriele John von Freyend carefully inspects, then arranges each outfit and wisp of hair before placing the dolls in their box for sale.

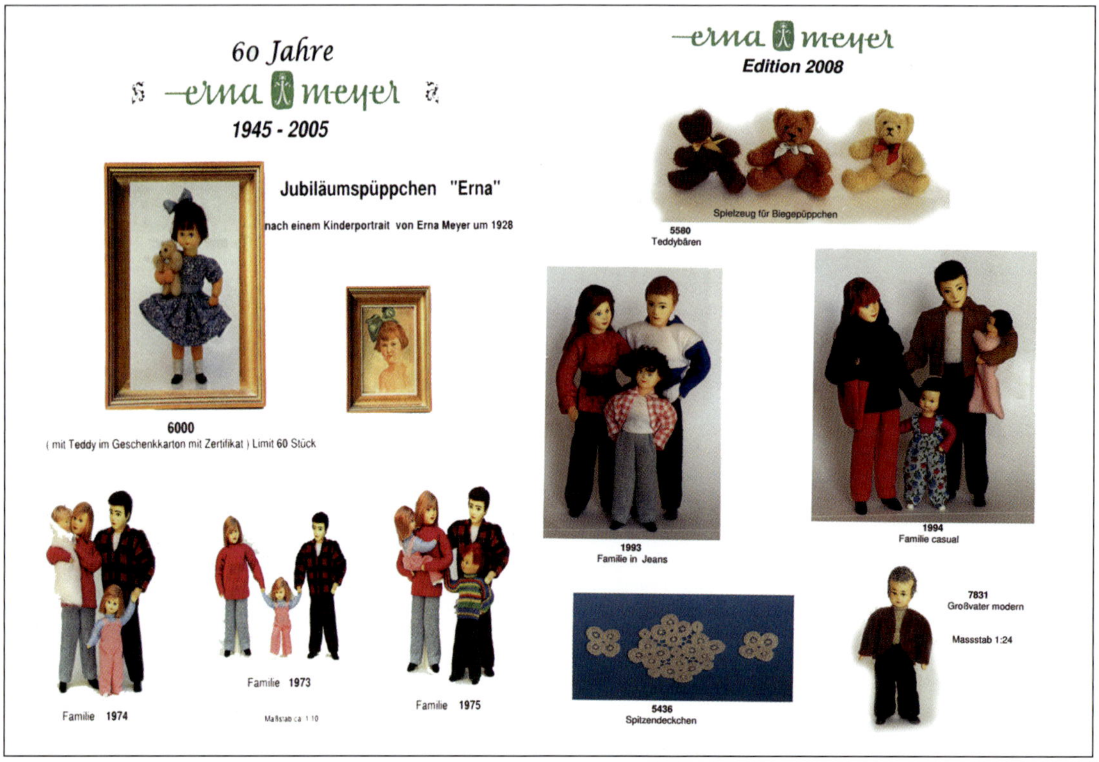

The Erna Meyer Company has operated for over 60 years. For its 60th anniversary, Gabriele John von Freyend issued a limited number of framed dolls holding an Erna Meyer teddy bear. The doll represents a portrait of her mother made in 1928. The Erna Meyer Company continues to make cloth-covered dollhouse dolls in 1:10, 1:12, and modern 1:24 scale.

Bodo Hennig

It was natural that many of the dolls made right after the war were produced in and around Nuremberg. Southern Germany had long enjoyed a tradition of toy making. However, the Erzgebirge area of Eastern Germany had long been known for its fine wood toy production. Skills were passed from one generation to the next and as the toys became more sophisticated, trade schools for men were established to train young men in toy development. Erzgebirge is well known for miniature room-boxes and stores, small dolls, nutcrackers, and elaborate layered Christmas displays made from wood from the forests covering the Ore Mountains. It was into this tradition that Bodo Hennig was born in 1928. Raised with good woodworking skills, during the war he assisted local farmers by making boxes for their products. In his spare time he dabbled at toy making.

Fleeing the Russian occupation of Eastern Germany, he settled in the Allgäu region of Southern Bavaria where he developed his hobby into his profession. In 1949, he exhibited his work at the first postwar International Toy Fair in Nuremberg. Although he did not sell any of his work, he learned what the market was seeking. By 1951, he had established Bodo Hennig PuppenmObel Company specializing in dollhouses and miniatures, and his attendance at the 1951 Nuremberg Fair was a great success. He secured a small factory and used home workers. His furniture was made of hard wood, especially maple, found in Bavarian forests. Slightly larger than 1:12 scale the pieces were appropriate for the small hands of young children. They were decorated in a variety of styles from brightly painted folk art to fine 19th century Biedermier styles. Throughout the next four decades Bodo Henning expanded his offerings to include metal and ceramic accessories, and by the 1970s was offering dolls to live in his dollhouses. At least three different lines of dolls were offered.

Bodo Henning maintained and grew his success over such a long period as a result of his well-recognized product quality and his conservative expansion policy. He continued his work well into his 70s. Employing more than 80 factory workers and 100 home artisans, the company expanded its production in 1998. Although he sold his company in 2002, it survives today making a wide range of dollhouse miniatures.

Bodo Hennig's catalog featured three different dollhouse doll lines. True to his woodworking tradition, Henning made a line of jointed maple dolls shown here on the top left. Dolls had metal shoes and yarn hair with hand-painted facial details. All were well dressed in cloth outfits. Adults stood about 5.5" tall, children about 4", and baby, 1.5". The extended family included parents, grandparents, boy, girl, and baby. Dolls on the top right were made by Erna Meyer for Bodo Henning, starting in 1988, and were presented as his "Belle Epoque" line. Well dressed in period costume, these cloth dolls were typical of the Erna Meyer style. At first there were nine dolls: a father, mother, maid, nurse, baby, older boy and girl, toddler boy, and girl. Dolls can be found in different costumes, creating more variety. Dolls were similarly sized to Hennig wooden dolls. On the lower left is the complete line of unmarked bendable dolls made by Hückel for Bodo Hennig, mostly dressed in modern styles appropriate to many of Hennig's dollhouses. Dolls were soft vinyl molded over a wire frame.

The facial details and hair of the dolls made by Hückel for Bodo Hennig was molded into the heads and then highlighted with paint. The shoes on some adults were removable, although they were molded as part of the leg on the children and grandparents. There were six dolls in the family: 6" father, 5.75" mother, 5.5" grandfather, 5" grandmother, 4.25" older brother and sister, 3.125" boy and girl toddler. Hückel made these dolls of one-piece plastic construction for Bodo Hennig. They were sold as families or individually. Clothing sets could be purchased for the dolls. $5-7.

ARI, EDI, and Preh

Some German companies with prewar roots survived the war and either reentered the doll market when the war ended or modified their manufacturing capabilities to make dolls. One such company, August Riedler GmbH & Co. KG, known as ARI, was originally founded in 1864. Based in the town of Königsee in Thuringia, Germany, Riedler initially made industrial parts from porcelain, but by 1872 had turned his skills to making bisque and porcelain dolls and doll heads. In 1908 his son and grandson took ownership interests in the business that had expanded to employ over 400 full-time and home workers. ARI was one of the manufacturers of the miniature all-bisque dolls common to the 1930s.

When Germany was divided after WWII, Thuringia and the ARI factory were located in East Germany. Unable to obtain the raw materials to continue to run the factory as a porzellanwerk, the company first adopted the new plastics and vinyls for their dolls. ARI made bendable dollhouse families, nurses, and nationality dolls. They were sold in boxed sets and individually. Even though the company was an East German company, it was able to keep open its distribution channels in the United States. The dolls were featured in the Q.T. Novelty catalog during the mid 1960s.

ARI operated as East Germany's largest privately owned company. Perhaps, its size or success led to its expropriation in the early 1970s by the Communist government and its transformation to a "peoples owned enterprise", renamed VEB Puppenfabrick Konigsee. The company continued making vinyl doll families, at least into the mid-1990s after the German reunification.

The company founded in 1919 by Jakob Preh in the Bavarian town of Bad Neustadt followed a much different path. Named Jakob Preh, jun., it specialized in the manufacture of electromechanical devices and radios. Jakob Preh died in 1945, just as the war ended. His widow and son, realizing that they needed to invest in new equipment and technology to keep the company running, purchased a large plastic injection-molding machine. Apparently the demand for the company's electric devices was not enough to keep the machine operating at its capacity, so in 1949 Preh began making small hard plastic dolls from styrene, marketing them under the trademark PlasticBaby, apparently the first German company to make dolls from the new hard plastics. All the dolls have excellent detailed molding and the plastic body material is of a heavy weight. Preh discontinued its doll production in 1960 when its industrial products filled its injection-molding capacity.

A series of small 3" hard plastic nationality and bridal pairs, slightly resembling the prewar bisque nationality dolls, were produced by a company known as Edi. The company name in script was a registered design mark under the German trademark system. Little else is known of the company or the time of its existence or production.

August Riedler GmbH & Co. KG, known as ARI, traced its roots as a porcelain doll manufacturer to 1872. This 3.5" white bisque doll, typical of dolls imported to the United States in the 1920s and 30s, has 1920s hairstyling. With painted facial features, hair, shoes, and socks she is wire jointed at shoulders and hips. A modern doll made from old ARI molds, she is marked with the triangular ARI trademark and the number 507. Modern recast, $20.

ARI's postwar soft plastic family was roughly 1:18" scale, with adults measuring 4 to 4.5" tall; children, 3.25"; toddlers, 2.25"; babies, 1.125". Boy and girl dolls appear to be the same mold, but with gender identifying clothing. Dolls were simply dressed mostly in felt, but also in cottons and knits. Most seams were glued, as opposed to sewn. The most commonly found dolls were soft, pliable vinyl, jointed at shoulders and hips. Hair was molded with painted facial features, shoes, and socks. Adults, $5. Children, $3.

ARI's postwar school set was made with a spectacled teacher carrying a leather book bag. She had six students, some of whom carried brown felt book bags. Generally numbered, dolls were marked ARI in a triangle on their backs and some identify their German origin. Seven doll set, $50.

Preh's "PlasticBaby" dolls, resembling prewar bisque dolls, were generally small non-gender-specific children, 3.5-4" with smaller babies. These dolls, jointed at the shoulders and hips, had molded hair and features, with added hand-painted details. Dark skinned African-heritage dolls of this size were also made. *Photo courtesy of Swantje Köhler.*

After the mid 1970s government takeover of ARI and its renaming as VEB Puppenfabrick Konigsee, the company continued to make dollhouse and slightly larger regional costumed dolls. $3-5.

PlasticBaby made larger dolls about 5.5″ tall, with childlike features. Girls had synthetic hair wigs, styled to fit their costumes. Larger dolls wore leather shoes and their clothing was more finely detailed. Dolls of both sizes were often clothed in German regional dress made from felt, patterned cottons, and even leather for their lederhosen. Dolls can be identified by the word PlasticBaby inside an elongated diamond shape molded on their backs. $15.

EDI's 3″ toddler-like dolls were dressed in regional costumes. Their arms and legs were strung together at the shoulders and hips. A number of different heads were used. While some had non-gender-specific forehead curls, some girls had a bun on the top of their head and some boys had short curly hair. A bridegroom had a molded top hat. Facial features, shoes, and socks were painted. *Dolls from the collection of Diane Hogan.* $10/pr.

Right hands on EDI dolls had pointing index finger with other fingers on both hands gripped in a fist with only the thumbs protruding. $5.

3" EDI dolls were sold by mail-order in sets of six for $3.50 as advertised in *House and Garden's* November 1952 issue.

Grecon

The British doll making industry was given a big boost when a talented Jewish refugee, Margarete Cohn, fled Germany and settled in London in 1936. She had already established herself as a doll maker after attending an arts and crafts school in Berlin towards the end of WWI. By 1919 she had obtained a patent for a doll's head and was producing dolls, some of which resembled people she knew. Using a contraction of her nickname, Grete, and her last name, she registered the trademark, "Grecon" and shifted from the production of bisque dolls to cheaper cloth dolls. Upon her arrival in London she quickly re-registered her trademark and exhibited a line of miniature dolls at a British Industries Fair. Working from her studio, she trained others to help her produce the dolls, establishing a cottage industry in London. Faced with restrictions on raw material, she used bits and scraps to create her small scale, wool-wrapped, wire armature dolls. Her business prospered, and an advertisement appearing in a September 1941 trade magazine, *Games and Toys*, indicated that she was able to continue supplying dolls right through the Battle of Britain.

Immediately after the war, Grete looked to find ways to expand her business and markets. In 1946, she showed her dolls at a trade exhibit at the Victoria and Albert Museum titled "Britain Can Make It". The exhibit was held to showcase Great Britain's productive capacity, and only overseas markets were targeted. She was apparently quite successful, as Grecon dolls could be purchased in the United States at department stores like Pittsburgh's Joseph Horne Co., and through catalog companies, like Mark Farmer Company of California. Beginning in 1952, A. Barton & Co., a London dollhouse and miniature manufacturer, became the distributor for Grecon dolls, a relationship that lasted until the late 1960s. The dolls could also be purchased in London's department stores, like Harrod's and Hamley's, and in small specialty shops.

Ms. Cohn made a basic dollhouse family consisting of a mother and father, older and younger children, and a baby, all in a variety of costumes. She extended it to include a grandmother, grandfather, nursemaid, maid, chef, chauffeur, policeman, postman, pianist, cowboy and cowgirl, bridal party, Scotch Highlander, Dutch dolls, uniformed military figures, English and Scotch guards, sportsmen, a hiker, a clown, and a wonderful coronation set made in the early 1950s in honor of Queen Elizabeth II. Ms. Cohn would also make unique dolls exclusively for small London shops and as souvenirs, making a definitive list of variations impossible. Some dolls became seasoned overseas travelers, as they didn't take up much space. During the early 1950s A. Barton advertised over 50 varieties of the dolls. After Ms. Cohn relocated from London to Sussex in 1959, her outworkers retired or left her employ, and the variety of dolls she produced narrowed to a nine- or ten- member extended family, which she continued to make into the early 1980s.

In her book, *Bartons Model Homes,* Marion Osborne, a well-recognized expert on Barton Toys and Grecon dolls, quotes from a mid 1980s letter from Grete Cohn to Chichester, United Kingdom shop owner, Hazel Baldwin, "I always regretted that my small business fell gently asleep, as I resented selling it, considering it a highly individual enterprise . . . I myself was only interested throughout my business activities to keep my production on a 'studio type'. I always disliked the glamour of a big concern". These wonderful "wooly" little dolls are generally found today well played with and obviously appreciated.

Margarete Cohn and her cottage industry staff produced Grecon dolls for almost 50 years, with little or no change in basic construction technique. A bendable wire frame was padded and then wrapped with wool yarn. Hands were formed by bending the yarn-wrapped wire into a u-shape, resembling a fist. Metal painted shoes were attached to the legs, giving better weight and stability, and allowed the dolls to stand upright. Dolls were approximately 1:21 scale. Mother and father measure approximately 3.375"; older children, 2.75"; younger children 2.125"; baby without shoes, 2". They might have lived in an Amersham dollhouse of the 1930s, a 1950s Barton Model Home, or a tin Mettoy house of the 1950s. Early adults, $70. Early children, $50.

Grecon dolls had padded net faces with hand-painted features. Some dolls even had yarn ears. Their hair was embroidered onto their heads in a stylized fashion. Clothing was made of felt, cotton, jersey, and wools in miniature pinstripe, hounds-tooth, and plaid. This set dates from the late 1950s, early 1960s. Adults, $60. Children, $40.

Great attention was paid to the detail of the clothing. Classy accents included yarn ties, miniscule buttons, lace collars, purses, yarn jewelry, net stockings, embroidered flowers, loop and eyelet eyeglasses, and tiny bead earrings. This family dates from the mid to late 1960s. Adults, $60. Children, $40.

Grandparents were a favorite subject of Grete Cohn. White bearded grandfathers were usually dressed in houndstooth trousers, grey vests, and black morning suits. Grandmothers had large wardrobes including everything from bathrobes to fancy gowns. Grandparents generally wore wire-framed spectacles. Grandparents, $60. Older pictured children, $50.

Grecon dolls were not merely dressed as families. Pictured from left to right: gardener, school girl, and monk. Character dolls, $75.

Dolls were made in two known scales. Here a 3.375″ nurse holds a 2″ baby and a larger 5.5″ nurse hold a 2.75″ baby. Small nurse and baby, $115/pr. Large nurse and baby, $145/pr.

Both the 1:21 scale and 1:18 scale dolls were dressed in regional costumes. From left: a pair of 1:21 scale Scots dolls, a 1:18 scale Bavarian man, and a small American Western pair. Small dolls, $75. Large dolls, $100.

It is not clear how the dolls were packaged initially. When A. Barton & Co. became a distributor, Grete Cohn delivered the dolls wrapped in tissue paper, one dozen to the lot. Barton's repackaged the doll family and sold it in a box with a black and white picture of a Grecon doll family with grandparents on the top. The box stated that the dolls could "stand, bend or sit." Inside the box was a Grecon father, mother, boy, and girl. *Photo courtesy of Marion Osborne.*

Grecon dolls were also made as souvenirs for London gift shops. A uniformed "Bobby" stands 5.5". $100.

Some dolls had rectangular cloth tags sewn onto the back of their clothing. Tags might say "Grecon Little People" or "Grecon Made In England." Paper tags have also been observed and foil tags were sewn onto the back of the clothing on some of the larger dolls. The foil tags read "Grecon, Made In England, London."

Tomac and Dol-Toi

After the war, yarn-wrapped wire figures resembling Grecon dolls were produced in the Glasgow cottage of a Miss Thompson. Like Grecon dolls, Tomacs had painted metal shoes into which wire frames were inserted. Wire limbs were wrapped with wool yarn, as were the bodies after a small amount of padding was added. Shoes of Tomac dolls were much larger than those of the Grecon's. Hands were made by simply bending the wire back in a "U" shape. The dolls' heads are one of the principal differentiations between the two lines. Tomac heads were built upon a Dainite rubber button, which, after padding and covering with a fine flesh-colored material, had a distinctive round and flat shape. Faces look as if their basic design might have been added with a rubber stamp enhanced by hand painting.

Besides dollhouse family members, Tomac dolls were dressed in a wide variety of costumes: Soccer players, bridal party, boy and girl scout, cowboy and American Indian, Scots boy and girl, London Bobby, Horse Guards, Beefeaters, Dutch and Bavarian children, pirates, and Royals.

Both Grecon and Tomac showed national pride in their doll lines. Here a Tomac Queen stands next to a Tomac Beefeater flanked by Grecon's Household Cavalry Life Guard, Bagpiper of the Scots Guard, Royal Navy Officer, Grenadier Guard, and Tower of London Beefeater Guard. $90/each.

Tomac's 3" tall cloth-covered, button head dolls were dressed in the fashions of the times. Material used for costumes was generally cotton, wool, and silk. Some details were added, especially to the legs, by using colored threads to represent socks and stockings. Sometimes a child might carry a favorite pet. Shoes were larger cast metal painted in different colors. $70/each.

Miss Thompson dressed her dolls in a range of costumes. Her Scottish nationality was reflected in the knickered golfer and the Tartan-clad Highlander. She dressed dolls in the costumes of other countries, as well. An American cowboy and a Dutch couple are pictured. $70/each.

Miss Thompson was mindful of some of the outposts of the British Empire, producing delightful dolls from the Caribbean islands. $70/each.

Tomac dolls had brown paper labels attached to their back reading either "Tomac Toys, Made in Scotland" or "Tomac Toys Bearsden Glasgow." It is rare to find a labeled example today.

Tomac dolls were imported to the United States and sold by mail-order, appealing to those of Scottish-American heritage. In a December 1952 *House and Garden* they were offered for $1.98 each or $5.75 for a set of three.

The story of these dolls becomes a little more complicated in the mid-1950s. The British miniatures firm, Dol-Toi, located in Stamford, Lincolnshire, needed a line of dollhouse dolls that would fit with their 1:18 scale furniture and accessories. In this period, it either purchased Miss Thompson's complete business or her stock of materials and patterns. There is some indication that Miss Thompson stayed on and assisted Dol-Toi, at least with the start-up of production.

Dol-Toi was a substantial family-run company by the time it began manufacture of the Tomac dolls. Originally formed on June 23, 1944, in Stamford, as County Caravans Ltd., it was headquartered in a former public house under the supervision of its managing director, Eric Green. In 1949, Clarence Ibotson, a trained woodworker, invested in the company and became a director, with Eric Green becoming chairman. In 1953, Eric Green resigned and Clarence's wife and Company Secretary, Muriel, became a director. In July of 1953 the company name was officially changed to Dol-Toi.

Dol-Toi prided itself on making dollhouse furniture that would last. For the most part, the dollhouse furniture was made of beech wood in 1:18 scale. Clarence's prior woodworking experience aided in the design and construction of many of the pieces. There was furniture for every room of the household as well as a large array of accessories. In an article appearing in a local newspaper, the *Lincoln, Rutland and Stamford Mercury*, Muriel explained a company philosophy, "we pride ourselves on trying to produce everything a full-scale house has." Clarence Ibotson remarked that right after the war "there were even fewer toys made for girls than boys so it was a ready market." With Muriel later designing dolls' costumes, the Ibotsons worked as a team and eventually used their four grandchildren as a test market to evaluate the appeal of their miniature products.

Not long after the purchase of Tomac dolls by Dol-Toi, the Ibotsons changed the design somewhat, replacing the cloth-covered button head with a plaster head that allowed for molded details. Sprayed-on flocking replaced yarn as hair. There was no change to the bodies, although the late, more detailed heads had smaller feet, replacing the original oversized lead feet. The earliest of the plaster heads, pictured on the left, had simple painted facial details, including plain black dots for eyes. Later dolls, pictured on the right, had more defined painted features, most with blue eyes against a white background. $50/each.

Scouts were a popular subject for the Ibotsons. Pictured are three 3.25"plaster head scouts. Plastic head scouts were also produced in the 1960s. $50/each.

Mrs. Ibotson introduced 3 and 4" "Miniature Dolls in National Dress for Children of All Nations" in 1960. About 20 dolls representing authentically dressed Welsh, Scots, Dutch, Eskimo, Argentine gaucho, Persian children, Cornish Pixie, and Cornish Maid were broadly advertised in trade magazines. Dolls were made first with plaster heads and later with plastic. *Dolls from the collection of Marion Osborne. Original photos courtesy of Marion Osborne.* $60/each.

In an effort to reduce cost and breakage, a further change was made to Dol-Toi dolls in the early to mid-1960s when molded plastic heads replaced plaster heads. The length and bulk of the shoes had already been reduced earlier. Plastic head dolls were not as well padded under their clothes. Nationality costumes and doll family clothing continued to be made as before. Upper left, differences between plaster and plastic construction is visible. Nations dolls were simply packaged in brown cardboard boxes and identified by attached paper tags with the Dol-Toi logo. *Dolls from the collection of Marion Osborne. Original photos courtesy of Marion Osborne.* $60/each.

Extended dollhouse families were dressed for inside living and outside play, as well as maids, nurses, and chefs. Adult dolls were made in a 1:18 scale, measuring 3.75" tall. Children ranged from 2" to 3.25". $25/each.

Dol-Toi tried to appeal to the broad range of ethnic minorities represented in the United Kingdom. An Indian subcontinent family was produced wearing non-ethnic clothing, as was an African heritage family. By this time costuming was simplified and appeared to be primarily made of felt. $25/each.

An aid to identifying the age of these dolls is the size of the cast metal shoe. The doll on the left is a Tomac doll with large, thick and fairly straight shoes. The next Dol-Toi is a plaster head with simply painted eyes. The shoes are fairly large, but are contoured between toe and heel. Next is a plaster head with painted eye detail. Shoes are smaller with some contouring. The plastic head doll on the far right has shorter and thinner shoes with a nicely rounded toe and narrow heel.

The Ibotsons enjoyed immediate success with their miniatures. In 1954, Dol-Toi relocated to a new, more efficient facility on Uffington Road in Stamford, and in 1957, expanded once again after they added dollhouse dolls to their product line. The Ibotsons traveled to promote Dol-Toi. Block House was retained as their agent in the United States, and Dol-Toi was exhibited at New York Toy Fairs. In the 1960s, one inventory of Dol-Toi food sent to the United States, had 60 food choices to pick from, assembled on plates, in saucepans, fry pans, etc. At 1:18" scale, Dol-Toi furniture fit well in the fiberboard houses of Keystone and Rich, but a trend had started towards 1:12 scale for higher quality kit houses finding their way into the market. Nonetheless, Mr. Ibotson with a zealous sales approach, showed how many of their accessories could easily coexist in either scale. Dol-Toi was also exported to Canada, Australia, Denmark, and Sweden and had representatives in Austria, France, Germany, Italy, and the Far East.

Dol-Toi's work force consisted of a combination of factory employees and home workers. Assembly work and sewing were the major tasks of the home workers. They wrapped the two-piece wire frame of the dollhouse dolls first with pipe cleaners, and then finished them with yarn. Dolls then went back to the factory to receive their heads and were out-sourced once again for clothing. The four adult dolls, grandmother, grandfather, mother, and father were considered large and were wound accordingly as one size. The older children made up the medium-size teenagers, and girl and boy toddlers were the smallest dolls. Home workers received a payment of 15p (about 37¢ at the then prevailing exchange rate) per packet of 10 completed fathers or grandfathers and 20p (49¢) per packet of 10 for all other dolls as they were more time consuming to wind than the adult males. A home worker might produce between 200 and 400 doll bodies a week at a rate of 20 to 40 bodies an hour, depending upon their complexity.

Costumes changed, however, as Mrs. Ibotson, with the help of one of her home workers, Mrs. Paton, expanded the line in 1960 adding a line to appeal to "children of all nations." A Father Christmas doll and a Christmas fairy ornament were produced for the Holidays. The company paid attention to its dollhouse dolls as well. At its peak, the company offered more than 50 variations of dolls. Dol-Toi marketed its international dolls and miniatures to schools as teaching aids. Mrs. Ibotson and Mrs. Paton made a bridal set to garnish an Ibotson son's wedding cake in colors matching the actual bridesmaids' gowns. Later, similar dolls were advertised for use by caterers!

Dolls sold in gift stores and department stores like Galt's for less than the equivalent of $1.00. They were packaged individually in cellophane bags and in boxed sets. Unmarked, they were parceled with small round paper labels, bearing the Dol-Toi logo.

The older son of the Ibotsons, Anthony, joined the company in the late 1960s and replaced his mother as a director in 1971. The family began to lose control in 1972 when new directors were added, including, Christopher Baxter, a director of Condor Toys. In 1974, Condor Toys took over Dol-Toi and the Ibotsons resigned. Dol-Toi retained its name but "Condor, made in England" appeared on the packaging. Condor Toys lasted until the end of 1978. In 1986, the dolls made a re-appearance under the direction of Peter Clarke. They were called Figertoi.

Other Dolls of the United Kingdom Style

Doll makers other than Tomac and Dol-Toi adopted Grete Cohn's popular 1:18 scale "United Kingdom Style" of dollhouse dolls. The style was adopted in other countries as well, perhaps with an eye to the British or United States markets.

Other British doll makers, creating a unique regional style, emulated method of construction, decoration, scale, and dress of Grete Cohn. Examples from Britain have been found with pipe cleaner frames, padded faces with crudely painted facial details, and roughly cast lead shoes. Men measure 4.25"; women, 3.75"; ring bearer, 3". Despite lack of fine detail in the dolls themselves, the costuming is special. $150/set.

A four-member dollhouse family with a butler and maid has been found made in "United Kingdom style," marked "Made in Hungary." Obviously a doll made for sale within Hungary would have carried some variation of the country's official name, "Magyar Köztársaság." $25/each.

Like "United Kingdom style" dolls, adults, of an approximate 1:18 scale, measured 3.75" tall and children, 2.625" tall. They were constructed from a wire frame and their limbs were thread-wrapped in pink. Dolls did not wear shoes but their feet were wrapped so as to represent footwear. Men's shoes were black; boy and girl had ivory feet. The maid's toe was outlined in black thread. Each foot was attached to a rectangular piece of paper-wrapped wood, stamped with their origin on the bottom. Their clothes were made from a variety of fabrics and their accessories were lace, felt, and embroidery thread. Dolls' hair was colored thread that had been exquisitely woven to create European chic hairstyles. Differing somewhat from United Kingdom style, faces were vertically wrapped pink thread filled with a soft material. Eyes were embroidered rectangles and a few small stitches formed the mouth. A touch of painted cheek blush was apparent on some of the dolls. *Dolls from the collection of Patty Cooper. Original photo courtesy of Patty Cooper.* $25/each.

British toy makers like Roddy and Air-Fix made a few miniature plastic dolls, similar in size and style to their American counterparts. The dolls were sometimes used as souvenirs.

Roddy produced plastic babies similar to those produced in the United States by Renwal, Ideal, Irwin, and others. Scots doll on the left measured 2.875". The undressed blinky eye baby measured 3". Airfix, a producer of the furniture seen in the background, manufactured the 4.25" hard plastic girl with jointed arms and simple cloth dress. Babies, $10-15. Airfix girl, $15.

Plastic was also used by United Kingdom doll makers. Here, Roddy dressed one of its 3" plastic dolls to honor the coronation in 1953 of Queen Elizabeth II. The doll is placed next to a Britain's copy of the coronation throne first commissioned by Edward I to hold the Stone of Scone upon which the ancient kings of Scotland were crowned. $25 MOC.

Lundby

Just as toys were scarce in the United Kingdom and Germany during the war and in the immediate postwar years, Grete Thomsen, a doting aunt in the village of Lundby, Sweden, couldn't find a suitable dollhouse or furnishings to give as a gift to her favorite nieces. As the story goes, taking matters into her own hands, she made a dollhouse for the children and added hand-made furniture and accessories, starting with an upholstered armchair made from curtain scraps. Neighbors and friends saw the house and asked Grete to make copies for their children. By 1947 she and her husband, Axel, realizing commercial potential in her skill, had established *Lundby of Sweden* with the aim of making a full line of dollhouses, furniture, and accessories. There is no documentation to prove precisely when the Thomsen's produced their first commercial dollhouse, but it is known that the department store, Ferdinand Lundquist, was one of its first major customers. Demand was so great that in 1948 the Thomsen's stopped making miniatures in their basement and moved to a small factory in nearby Lerum. Like many European toy makers in the postwar period, some production of miniatures emerged as a cottage industry with local craftsmen designing and making toys in their own homes. One such artisan, an interior designer, Per Börnfelt, merged his miniature furniture company, Lerro, with the increasingly successful Lundby after a 1959 fire destroyed the workshop in his parents' home. A new joint factory utilizing more modern mass production methods was built in Lerum and opened in 1962.

In addition to dollhouses, Lundby made furniture, dollhouse dolls, and accessories all designed to fit with 1:15 to 1:18 scale houses. Their products were sold in the United States through mail-order catalogs and miniature shops, and Lundby toys were distributed in more than 20 countries worldwide. The 1970s were highly successful years with Lundby making more than 100,000 dollhouses a year. To meet growing demand, Lundby established a global manufacturing network in 11 different countries. Victims of their own success, expansion into the United States, coupled with a cooling of the "traditional toy" market, financially squeezed the Thomsens. They sold their interest to Stefan Karlsten in 1982. Attempting to retrench, Karlsten moved production back to Lerum from Hong Kong, but the company suffered a bankruptcy in 1983. Lundby was able to reestablish itself in 1984 when the Swedish government came to its aid with significant financial support. Lundby went back to its roots, and while they employed more than a hundred workers in their factory in Olslanda, they had nearly 100 women working out of their homes in a reestablished cottage industry. Not content to be small and regional, Lundby acquired a Danish and a German firm as well as the British firm, A. Barton & Co. in 1984. They continued to market Barton's products under the "Caroline's Home Ltd." tradename.

Lundby first introduced a family of dolls scaled to complement their houses in 1974, exclaiming in their catalog: "Here come the Lundby dolls! You are bound to love mother Mona, father Robert, Peter and Marie." The mother was 4.5"; father, 4.75" and children 3.25". *Dolls from the collection of Sue Morse of the "We Love Lundby Club."* $40-50/family.

Lundby still made creative houses from high-quality materials, including wood cut from 150-year-old trees. Lundby can be credited with being the first to use modern wiring techniques in a mass-produced dollhouse. Later versions were available with an extension, making possible a whole new floor and a larger home. Lundby made furniture with opening drawers and doors and great play value for every room of the house. Through many ups and downs, Lundby was always innovating and keeping their toys up-to-date.

Lundby couldn't sustain its success, and facing bankruptcy a second time, it was acquired by ScanBox Danmark Group, the parent company of Brio Corporation. In 1993, Micki Leksaker AB, a former Lundby distributor, acquired production rights, then the Lundby name in 1997, re-introducing Lundby in 1999. Not merely relying on the past, it expanded the Lundby line, introducing new and up-to-date designs. Located in Gemla, Sweden, their products are distributed around the world.

Lundby first introduced a family of dolls scaled to complement their houses in 1974. These unmarked dolls were made of a soft vinyl material. Packaged singly and as a family, they came in a variety of colorful cotton, jersey, and knit outfits.

Lundby introduced a new line of dolls in 1979. Their catalogs proudly announced: "We have grandpa and grandma, brother and sister, mom and dad, aunts, uncles, cousins, and babies – whatever you want them to be, they can be. And whatever you want them to do, they can do. Use them to create your dreams!" The dolls were all dressed in cloth costumes, up to date and stylish for the period. In the early 1980s there were at least 27 costume variations, and in the mid 1980s each uniquely costumed doll had a different first name and catalog number. They were sold as a four person family of mother, father, boy, and girl as well as singly.

In 1983 Lundby made a short foray into a very simple undecorated wood house and furniture line, known as Lundbynette aimed at the German market. Complementing the line was a series of wood dolls, jointed at the neck, shoulders, hips and knees. There was a six-member extended family, each with yarn hair, painted features and quaint cloth costumes. The line was not distributed globally or available for long, and the dolls are scarce today.

In 1994, Lundby modified the original dolls slightly, with packaging indicating that they were produced by Lundby, for distribution by Micki Leksaker AB. The dolls varied from their predecessors slightly, the major difference being that the eyes were somewhat garishly outlined in black "eye-liner" and the Grandfather's fringe of hair was darker, while his mustache remained grey. The line featured three different babies, an infant in a basket with the same top curl of the earlier line, one diapered baby with a forehead curl, and one toddler without a curl. Dolls' costumes continued to be removable, but were less detailed and varied.

Micki Leksaker introduced a new series of dolls in 1999 and, at the same time, expanded the Lundby line. Mother and daughter had rooted and restyled light-colored hair, while the molded hairstyles of the father and brother were similarly updated. The grandparents remained the same. Three babies were in the line: the top curl baby in a basket and two diapered crawling babies, one with the former toddler's head and one with the forehead curl. New up-to-date costumes were added.

Micki Leksaker, in keeping with its constant improvement of the line, introduced newly designed dolls in 2004. The Lundby line, now over 60 years old, continues to appeal to collectors all over the world.

Lundby Type 1 heads were separately molded and attached to the bodies. Arms of each doll were molded as part of the body. Legs of the father and children were also formed with the body, although mother's legs were separate and joined to the body at the hips. There were grooves cut in the stomach and back of the father to allow him to bend at the waist without tearing. Female dolls had rooted synthetic blonde hair, as one might suspect of dolls with Scandinavian heritage. Father's hair was molded as part of the head and painted black. Similarly the boy's hair was molded and painted brown. Facial features, shoes, and socks were painted. *Dolls from the collection of Sue Morse of the "We Love Lundby Club."* $10-12.50/each dressed.

Type 1 Lundby dolls came in a number of costumes, changing year-to-year to match fickle fashion trends. This family is from 1977. *Dolls from the collection of Sue Morse of the "We Love Lundby Club."* $40-50/family.

Type 2 children were dressed casually for a variety of activities. *Dolls from the collection of Sue Morse of the "We Love Lundby Club."* 10-15/each.

A second type of doll was introduced in 1979. Improving greatly on the original design, bodies were molded in a harder plastic and separate limbs and heads were firmer vinyl formed around a flat wire aperture, allowing dolls to be bent in many positions. They were marked on the back "patent pending Lundby." The family became an extended one with the addition of a grey haired grandmother, Sophie, and a bald, grey fringed and mustached grandfather, George. Following their innovative approach to miniatures, Lundby also added a pregnant mother, Christine, in maternity clothes to the line. The dolls were renamed and their outfits updated. Lundby frequently added belts as a fashion accessory. Mother's painted shoes were changed from a mid-heeled pump to a mid-heel with a T-strap. Mothers and daughters had rooted hair; other family members had molded and painted hair. Interestingly, the hair color of the female dolls was changed to brown in place of Swedish blonde. *Dolls from the collection of Sue Morse of the "We Love Lundby Club."* Sophie and George, $15-20/each. Mother and Father, $16-18/each. Christine, $20-25/each.

The Type 2 family was expanded in 1981 to include a toddler, sitting in a high chair and a smaller blonde baby in a cradle. *Dolls from the collection of Sue Morse of the "We Love Lundby Club."* $5-8/each.

In 1982 Lundby added a diapered crawling baby with white painted booties and a baby in a traveling basket with a curl on top of its head. Through the 1980s the hair color of the dolls darkened and they were packaged wrapped in pink or blue bunting, with playpens, and in small playsets. *Dolls from the collection of Sue Morse of the "We Love Lundby Club*." $5-8/each.

In 1986 a baby with a little molded top curl. The baby on the right, similar to the baby introduced in 1982, was dressed more as a toddler. *Dolls from the collection of Sue Morse of the "We Love Lundby Club."* $5-8/each.

The 1994 dolls produced by Lundby for distribution by Micki Leksaker AB did not differ much from the Type 2 dolls, except for heavy black outlining around the eyes. *Dolls from the collection of Sue Morse of the "We Love Lundby Club."* $30-35/family.

The third type of Lundby dolls was introduced by Micki Leksaker in 1999. Dolls were molded in a firm plastic and were jointed at the shoulders, hips, and knees. Heads, now more angular, swiveled. Facial decoration around the eyes was softened. Lip color on the mother and daughter was changed from red to a bright pink, and their skin darkened. *Dolls from the collection of Sue Morse of the "We Love Lundby Club."* $12-16/each.

There was considerable variation in the fabrics and costumes, including a well-dressed bride and groom introduced in 1987, shown here on the left. A bridal couple was reintroduced in 2000, with an updated hairstyle and dress for the bride, although the groom seemed uncomfortable in his somewhat ill-fitting rental tux! *Dolls from the collection of Sue Morse of the "We Love Lundby Club."* 1987, $50-75/pr. 2000, $30-40/pr.

Costuming was important in the Lundby line. Here a Type 2 woman dons a knit suit. This costume, and a number of others sold in the mid-1980s, was removable, and Lundby sold separate outfits for the dolls. *Dolls from the collection of Sue Morse of the "We Love Lundby Club."* Doll, $16-18/each. Outfit, $15-20/each.

The 2004 Micki Leksaker catalog pictured its new line of dolls. There was significant change to clothing styles, even featuring costumes for a pair of female rock stars. Shoes were changed to reflect twenty-first century styles. Children had molded and painted sneakers and women went casual with clogs. All dolls had modern hairstyles - the father's hair was spiked and gelled. Grandfather had a full head of white hair and a well-trimmed beard. Grandma looked much younger and sports a pageboy haircut. Women and girls all had rooted hair with different mod hairstyles. *Catalog from the collection of Sue Morse of the "We Love Lundby Club."* $12-25/each.

Chapter 10

A Time of Regional Pride and Global Awareness

World War II ended isolationism. Not only had servicemen and women of many countries been stationed in far off locales, bringing home stories of their travels and adventures, but the world economy became increasingly interdependent. Threats of the Cold War gave everyone greater knowledge of world events because they saw that world affairs could directly affect them. Television opened windows on current events and foreign cultures in ways that print media had been unable to do. Increased affluence and growth of air travel made tourism a major industry, available to more than the "moneyed class." Western Europe's borders were easily crossed as roads and railways were rebuilt and improved. Children in all countries, including the United States, were expected to "learn their geography."

Doll makers everywhere took advantage of the increased global awareness and showed national pride. While some artisans were focusing on creating dollhouse families, others produced nationality dolls dressed in the authentic regional costumes of their home and neighboring countries. Others drew upon folk legends they had grown up with which were familiar to children all over the world.

Costume and storybook dolls as well as puppets had been made for many years before the war, but they were aimed primarily at local markets, well off travelers, and a few specialized overseas distributors like Kimport Dolls. It was in the postwar time period, however, that miniature dolls really found their way around the world. In the late 1940s, miniature European fairytale and nationality dolls were sold through the same outlets as their dollhouse counterparts. At first this was door-to-door, in small shops, military exchanges, and airports and then through overseas distributors lined up through personal contacts and government sponsored Toy Fairs. Dolls produced on other continents followed similar routes to the market with some interesting exceptions.

Not long after the European nationality and fairytale dolls began to appear in the United States market, American toy and doll makers such as Madame Alexander, Nancy Ann, Twinky, Tiny Town, and Flagg happily capitalized on the trend. International dolls of all sizes were produced, dressed in American visions of "exotic" costumes, and fairytale characters became the subjects of some doll makers as well. European countries were most often represented, although Mexican and Chinese costumes could be found. Native Americans, cowboys, cowgirls, Eskimos, and colonial figures usually represented North America. There were no changes to the design of the dolls themselves, only their costumes.

A few of the dolls sold were marketed as learning tools, and some were aimed at trying to capture or instill national pride. Many American and European made dolls were sold as part of collectible sets. Variety helped sustain the market by motivating a child to collect a whole series "just to have them all!"

The Regional Dolls of France and Bernard Ravca

France had long enjoyed a history of fine doll making. Societies dedicated to bisque and celluloid dolls helped advance the art and represented the interests of the French doll makers. Many doll makers had their studios in Paris' Montmarte, making fashion dolls for adult collectors. Dolls dressed in the regional costumes of France were likewise very popular and could be found in many sizes and styles.

Bernard Ravca was born in Russia in 1904 and emigrated to France with his family during the Russian Revolution. His dream was to become a doctor, but lack of funds when his father died, changed his plans. In the early 1920s, he got a job painting shawls, scarves, and doll faces. He did not like repetitiously creating the same faces on dolls. In 1924, he was asked to make a doll representing the character Marguerite from the opera *Faust*. He decided that by giving the doll a unique face as she might have actually looked, he could give it personality. He developed techniques to achieve his goal of creating unique dolls and opened a small studio in the Montmarte. At first he made cloth dolls in the likeness of famous people as well as a series of at least 65 different French peasant dolls in their regional costumes. Generally more comfortable in making the faces of younger people, he was challenged by an English lord to make a pair of "mature" dolls for his wife, celebrating their wedding anniversary. The dolls received praise and attention and his business boomed. Now Ravca turned his attention to making faces of older people.

He developed and perfected the art of making faces look old, showing wrinkles and character lines. His early dolls were cotton cloth-covered with American silk stockings to give the appearance of skin. Their faces were needle-sculpted with painted features. The body was a cloth-covered wire armature. Hair was spun wool. His technique of molding with breadcrumbs allowed him to endow his characters with lifelike expressions. No two dolls were alike.

He won a gold medal for his dolls in 1937 at the Paris Exposition in competition with dolls from 42 countries. When George VI and Queen Elizabeth visited France in 1938, Ravca dolls decorated their rooms and caught the eye of the Queen. In 1939, at the request of his government, he exhibited a large selection of his dolls, including his regional costume dolls, in the French Pavilion of the New York World's Fair. During the Fair, Germany invaded France. Ravca did not return to Paris, remaining in this country and raising money for the Free French by lecturing and exhibiting his dolls. In 1947, he married a well known doll artist from New York, Frances Elinor Diecks.

Painted face dolls covered with crepe paper were produced, decorated with simpler costumes made from cloth. A common element of the crepe paper dolls was their bright pink cheeks. Ravca dolls all had hair, shoes, and undergarments of crepe paper. Dolls were built on a flexible wire frame. The three pictured fairytale dolls, signed and dated 1941 on the reverse gold foil tag, were approximately 6" tall. Some were affixed to wooden stands, others on cardboard. The smaller fine lady measured 4.25", and was signed by Bernard Ravca on the base. Ravca also made French regional dolls from clothespins. Large dolls, $40. Small doll, $25.

Crepe paper could be formed over wire frame dolls to produce high fashion figures. The face of this 3.625" doll was painted on shiny paper, then glued to the stuffed crepe paper head. $15.

French doll makers had a long history of creating dolls dressed in authentic regional clothing. The wire framed, fabric-covered body of dolls in this collection measured 5". Figures had stuffed, hand-painted faces and hands of crepe. Yarn hair was arranged in regionally typical styles. $25.

French regional dolls had elaborate costuming, typical of that nation's doll makers. Shoes were made from a waxy paper resembling leather. The village or region represented was handwritten on a paper tag attached to the wrist. $25.

Like their counterparts in Germany, England, and the United States, later French doll makers made dolls from hard plastic. This 4.5" jointed *Posté* man with painted hair, face, and shoes was dressed in an authentic felt uniform with leather bag. $25.

Together, the Ravcas built a very successful business, prolifically producing a wide array of dolls, from life-size to miniature. While the majority of dolls created by Bernard would not be classified as dollhouse dolls, in a 1947 brochure about the artist, he is pictured surrounded by some of his smaller creations arranged in front of a large dollhouse made by Rich Toys. The couple's subjects ranged from Frances' ballet dancers and pixies to Bernard's actors, actresses, athletes, biblical figures, Native Americans, and historic notables. Common people with character were not neglected, as seen in his *Real People Dolls*. The dolls were sold at department stores where the Ravcas set up their display of more than 1200 dolls and through direct mailings to collectors with whom they had established relationships. Examples found their way into museums such as at the Traphagen School of Design. Over time, the Ravcas also made lines of miniature dolls that did not have the same attention to facial character. They were obviously aimed at a lower price market not served by their finer dolls.

The history of the dolls had a somewhat poignant finale. Towards the end of Bernard and Frances' lives they were trying to sell their collection of 1200 dolls to a single buyer who could afford to keep it intact and display it as a life's work. They were childless and without relatives they deemed "acceptable and qualified" to receive the dolls. In 1981 they started mailing their long term customers, offering substantial discounts on their stock of dolls. By 1984, they were liquidating their entire collection on a piecemeal basis at an 80% discount. Bernard went on to live until 1998, with Frances dying two years later.

Baps

One of the most representative craftswomen in the postwar recovery of the German toy industry was Frau Edith Von Arps-Aubert. A well educated, elderly war widow, Frau Von Arps looked for a business with which to support herself. Drawing upon skills learned before the war, she chartered a new company in 1946 under the name "Baps." Enlisting others in and around Nuremberg, she developed a cottage industry. Edith chose to make small wire-framed bendable dolls of familiar themes: dolls of Germany's regions and neighbors, and fairytale dolls. Frau Von Arps was prolific in creating her characters and animals. She had an inherent instinct about educating children, as there is probably no better way to reinforce a story in the mind of a child than to recreate it in many different ways. She also made storybook characters as small puppets. Her dolls were easily discernible with their cloth bodies and colorful, round cheeks. They were beautifully costumed, and many storybook characters had tiny accessories.

Frau Von Arps not only was the creative force behind the dolls, but she was quite adept at marketing them. At first Mrs. Von Arps and her friends went door to door on American military bases and sold or bartered dolls to families stationed there. Some families would buy whole collections of dolls to bring back to the United States after their tour of duty. In time dolls were offered in the PXs of the bases and at airport gift stores. Apparently, the contacts Mrs. Von Arps made served her well. By 1948 her dolls were being offered by specialty retailers, mail-order merchants, and department stores in the United States. In the 1960s, they were also available as a monthly choice selection from the World Wide Doll Club.

A wonderful story of Frau Von Arps' business prowess and creative foresight was told by Bob Morrell, of Glen, New Hampshire, in a 1990 speech given to the Newcomen Society. Bob Morrell had been called back to the Army during the Korean conflict and was stationed along with his wife in Nuremberg. Mr. Morrell was a natural entrepreneur who had just made a decision to sell his ice cream business in New Hampshire's White Mountains, but who had not yet decided what to do next. Sometime in 1951 or 1952 Frau Von Arps, selling her dolls door to door, met the Morrell's and told them of the loss of her family during the war. During their conversations the Morrells mentioned their career indecision and the fact that they would soon return to the United States. Reflecting on their quandary, Edith suggested that they build a fantasy village represented by the characters of her dolls, perhaps allowing them all to make a living! The Morrells bought an entire set of the dolls and returned to the States shortly thereafter. They opened their theme park, Story Land, on an 80 acre parcel of untillable land in 1954, one year before Disneyland opened. Originally featuring 16 small attractions, many based upon the Baps storybook characters, the North Conway, New Hampshire, park has continued to grow, and still operates today.

Baps dolls, including smaller puppets, regional and national dolls, and fairytale characters, had similar colorful clothing. Costumes were made of felt with embroidered detail, but cotton prints, taffeta, organza, and muslin, was also used. Dolls' shoes were metal, with or without a felt covering, or metal with paint detail. Some have a paper sticker attached to one shoe reading "Germany." Accessories were made of cloth, metal, paper, straw, felt, fabric and plastic. While the provenance of Baps dolls has been clearly traced to Frau Von Arps-Aubert, there appears to be some connection to another German doll maker, Ilse Ludecke. It is believed that Frau Ludecke, also of Bavaria, was a friend of Mrs. Von Arps who assisted in the sale of the dolls in the early years. Jean Grout, in her wonderful article on Baps in the Spring 2003 issue of *Doll News* magazine, speculates that Ilse's sister, Sophie, a seamstress, might have sewn some of the clothes for Baps dolls.

Dolls purchased on American bases in Germany were not packaged, although later dolls were boxed in a cardboard display box marked "Western Germany" or affixed to cardboard bases. The dolls sold in the 1960s through the World Wide Doll Club were in a mailing box.

There is little evidence that the dolls were made or offered for sale after the early 1960s, but while hard to find, they are not rare today. Frau Von Arps really knew how to appeal to children and they clearly treasured her dolls that piqued their imaginations and fantasies.

Baps dolls were sometimes dressed in regional clothing. Shown here is a Bavarian family. Dolls' construction was wire frame with metal feet. Frames were covered with cloth or paper and dolls limbs' were wrapped with a layer of flesh-colored felt. Some examples have been noted with thread wrapped limbs. The round or oval-shaped face of the doll was stiffly padded and covered with fine painted cloth. Eyes were either round or oval; cheeks, large and rosy. Faces on most dolls look to be stenciled, as they are so perfect. Features were less detailed in later versions of the dolls. Yarn was used for hair, and some dolls had ears of thread. Family, $200/set.

Featuring 16 small attractions, many based upon the Baps storybook characters, Story Land had over 15,000 visitors the first year it opened. The North Conway, New Hampshire, theme park has continued to grow, adding more attractions and rides all aimed at providing a fun family experience consistent with the family's original mission and vision.

One series of nursery rhyme dolls, about 4.75" tall, was adhered to a white cardboard box top with elastic thread. The side of this box identified the attached characters with a typed paper label. To the right of this label was a *BAPS* circular sticker. Story Land's Baps Inspired Cinderella Castle is pictured in the insert. $150/set MIB.

The 1950s collection of Baps dolls is prominently displayed with original hand-painted backdrops in the Story Land gift shop, giving credit to the creative vision of Edith Von Arps-Aubert. Peter Pumpkin Eater's house can be found in a shaded spot in Story Land Theme Park. *Dolls from the Conway, New Hampshire, Story Land Theme Park collection.* Dolls vary in value, depending on size. Generally, individual dolls are $50/each. Complete sets sell at a premium of 10-25%, depending on the size of the set.

Snow White awakens the Seven Dwarfs. Hand-painted facial details of each dwarf identified its character. *Dolls from the Conway, New Hampshire, Story Land Theme Park collection.*

Little Bo-Peep sadly cries over the loss of her five fleece covered sheep, despite the bells hung around their necks. *Dolls from the Conway, New Hampshire, Story Land Theme Park collection.*

Not all figures were based on human models. Felt-skinned Peter Rabbit is scolded by his Mother as Flopsy, Mopsy, and Cottontail look on. *Dolls from the Conway, New Hampshire, Story Land Theme Park collection.*

Baps puppets, which could be used in a cardboard Baps puppet theatre, were a product of the 1950s. Adult puppets were 4.25″ tall and children, 3.25″ tall. The head of the puppet was stationary and firmly attached to a stiff wire extending 2″ below the puppets' feet and ending in a small 5/8″ metal disk. Puppets' bodies were metal springs, covered with a cotton tube. Bodies were attached to the head with a single loop of thread that allowed the body to rotate around the wire. Costumes were similar to standard dolls' clothing. Felt covered shoes were attached to the bodies. The metal base was designed to fit into a groove cut in the floor of the puppet theatre, allowing movement for theatrics or play. The concept of the grooved floor apparently came from a large multi-story castle found in Frau Von Arp's doll and puppet filled store. This stereotypical "Little Black Sambo" set is missing one tiger. It was packaged without a stage. Puppets, $40/each. Complete sets sell at a premium of 10-25%, depending on the size of the set. Sets complete with stage and backdrops, $500+.

Baps dolls can be found in different sizes that may not relate to standard dollhouse scales. Size, without hats, was generally 5.25″ for adult dolls and 3.5″ for children. Slightly larger dolls have been cited at 6″ and 4″, respectively, and smaller 4.25″ adult dolls have been reported. Simple Simon, 3.75″ tall. The Pie-man, 5.25″.

Danish Pixies and Hans Christian Andersen Dolls

Northern Europe produced wonderful examples of high-quality miniature dolls drawing upon well-known folk tales as well as the fairytales of Hans Christian Andersen.

Different types of dolls, including paper dolls, had been made over the years to represent the characters in Andersen's delightful fairytales. In the 1950s Alice Jorgensen of Odense, Denmark, the birthplace of the poet, chose to portray the Andersen's stories with dolls constructed of a wire frame covered by thread. The stories represented in the line included: "The Little Mermaid," "The Steadfast Tin Soldier," "The Butterfly," "Little Tiny or Thumbelina," and "The Emperors New Suit." A small, translated copy of the fairytale was often included in the box with the doll.

Ms. Jorgensen also made a line of dolls, known in Denmark as pixies, little elves and gnomes, that usually make an appearance around Christmas time. Much of European toy and doll making centered in specific geographic areas, and artisans had opportunity to work near each other, gathering hints and drawing inspiration. This style of pixie dolls flourished and still lives on today, because of one such association between artists.

Alice Jorgensen sold many of her dolls at a small store, NumbSkull Jack just across the street from H.C. Andersen's historic home. In 1963, the shop's owner, Inge Stokkebye, came home to find her youngest daughter, Anne Beate, lounging about and reading a stack of movie magazines. As the company's advertising brochure tells the story, Mrs. Stokkebye announced, " 'This will not do. We must find some occupation for you. I need someone to make some pixies – this will be just the job for you'. 'Oh, but I can't do that – I have never done anything like that before!' Anne Beate answered, alarmed." After much loving help from her mother and a series of trials and errors, Anne came up with a design that she was happy with, seemingly drawing upon, but not copying, the designs of Alice Jorgensen's dolls displayed in her mother's shop.

Anne Beate's pixies were immediately popular, and more designs were added over the years. The implement they carried can fix the dates of the dolls' first introduction: a pair of skis, a book, rolling pin, axe, and lantern. There were over 60 members of the pixie family. Anne Beate also experimented successfully with making small dolls on the same wire skeletons, based on the fairytale stories of Hans Christian Andersen.

The pixie dolls enjoyed yet another extension to their wonderful life when, at age 74, Anne Beate Stokkebye sold her company in 2004 to Mette Markes Jepsen, who has carefully carried on the tradition with her company, Anne Beate Designs. Ms. Jepsen continues to run the business as it was in the past, as a cottage industry, although a quite extended one, with 25 women in Denmark and 20 in Vietnam helping with the construction and painting of the pixies. To help train her assistants, Anne Beate made about 15 models of the dolls showing various stages of construction. The models are still there, but Mette Markes Jepsen can rely on the memories of 8 women, aged 78 to 88, who have made the pixies from the very beginning in 1963. In fact, Ms. Markes Jepsen credits her oldest employee, Mrs. Morkedal, who has painted the pixie's faces from the very first, as her most productive. Over the years, Mrs. Morkedal has changed the style of the dolls' faces somewhat to fit her artistic inclination, but they still capture the delight of her earliest dolls. As with a true cottage industry she has trained a granddaughter to continue her craft, assuring continuity. Dolls are sold with a paper tag attached by string to their legs, identifying them as "Genuine Anne Beate Designs, handmade in Denmark."

With Ms. Markes Jepsen's newly added emphasis, distribution, and enthusiasm, the sales of Anne Beate Designs have tripled. Dolls can be obtained through at least two distributors in the United States. The company shows its products at fairs and exhibitions and they are featured on the company's website, www.annebeatedesign.dk.

Alice Jorgensen's Hans Christian Andersen dolls varied in size from 1.75" to 4.5", but were small enough to occupy a dollhouse or miniature fairy castle. Their heads were stuffed netting with hand-painted features. They had gorgeous yarn hair and clothing of various fabrics including wrapped yarn, netting, flannel, and burlap. Dolls came packaged in a cardboard box with red and white striped paper adhered to the box top. The box top was professionally printed with the doll's story title and, "A Hans Andersen Doll (hand-made); copyright Alice Jorgensen; Odense (the birthtown of the poet) Denmark." The story of the one-legged soldier and his ballerina was included in the box. $50/set MIB.

In the *Simple Simon* set. Simon measures 4.5". A beautiful yarn-wrapped goat was included. Clothing details were added to the thread wrapped frames. $50/set MIB.

A tiny 1.75" *Thumbellina* marked "Copyright, Alice Jorgensen, Odense Made in Denmark" on a paper label glued to the bottom of the green lily pad. $25.

The 2.625" *Little Match Seller* perched on small volumes of Hans Christian Andersen 's stories. The costume was well done, illustrating the rags of the small girl. $25.

Little Mermaid, entirely wrapped in yarn with thick, flowing, braided hair, sits on a small gold painted wood base. $25.

The elaborate *Emperor's New Clothes* set was mounted on a wooden base and was packaged assembled in Alice Jorgensen's red striped box. $150/MIB.

Alice Jorgensen's pixies were constructed similarly to Hans Christian Andersen dolls with thread and yarn-wrapped wire frames. Boys and men, wrapped entirely in grey thread, sported red cloth caps resembling familiar knit hats. Old men had long white beards. Women and girls also were wrapped in grey yarn, but wore red skirts made from the same material as their hats. Dolls, without shoes, were mounted on small, round, gold painted stands and were often posed for outdoor winter activity. Dolls ranged from 3.5" to 4" tall. A paper label on the bottom of the stand identified them as Alice Jorgensen Dolls. $25/each.

Anne Beate's very first pixies were a boy carrying a sack and a girl holding a bell. The girl pictured on the left, from 1964, is another early design. The doll was made with brown and yellow yarn hair. The family, obviously ready to make a batch of traditional rice pudding, was made between 1971 and 1973. The implements dolls carry help to date Anne Beate dolls' year of introduction. Adults measured 4"; children, 3.375". Individual dolls, $15. Boxed set, $75 MIB. *Doll on the left from the collection of Anne Beate Design. Photo courtesy of Anne Beate Design.*

Anne Beate pixie dolls were approximately 4" without their caps. Dolls consisted of a wire frame with stuffing in the body, which was then wrapped with thread of various colors. Hands and uncovered legs were flesh tones and various other colored threads were used for clothing: grey, blue, red. Females wore red cloth skirts with mothers having lace fringed white aprons. White bearded men wore red felt tunics. Faces were stuffed tubes of ivory cloth with hand-painted facial features. Some dolls had yarn hair, woven into different styles. $15/each.

Three features distinguish Anne Beate dolls from Alice Jorgenson's. Heads on the Jorgenson pixies had a protruding jaw, where the Stokkebye dolls follow the shape of the tubing used for the head. Ms. Stockkebye upgraded her dolls adding metal clogs to the unshorn Jorgensen pixies, and pom-pom ski caps actually knit from fine yarn. The Anne Beate dolls had small foil hang tags and the Jorgensen dolls often had a paper label attached to their base.

One of the 15 models, dating from 1966, used by Anne Beate to instruct her assistants on the proper construction of her pixies. *Model from the collection of Anne Beate Design. Photo courtesy of Anne Beate Design.*

Anne Beate Stokkebye made a line of 4" historic dolls dressed in costumes of Dutch immigrants who resided in the Armager area of Copenhagen. Dolls on the left are thought to be Armager dolls. Dolls on the right are confirmed members of the line. *Dolls on the right from the collection of Anne Beate Design. Original Photo courtesy of Anne Beate Design.* $15/each.

Anne Beate Designs followed the same lead as Alice Jorgensen in issuing a line of Hans Christian Andersen fairytale figures. *The Steadfast Tin Soldier* on the left is similar to Alice Jorgensen's, but can be distinguished by the pronounced jaws of the characters' heads. A scene from *The Tinder Box* is pictured on the right. *Dolls from the collection of Anne Beate Design. Photo courtesy of Anne Beate Design.* $25/set.

Souvenir and Craft Dolls

Souvenir dolls were made throughout the 20th century. Dolls dressed in national costumes were often given as gifts to friends and visitors from foreign lands. Within a country, a person might choose to collect and display dolls dressed in their homeland's regional costumes. For the most part, however, if you did not have considerable wealth and time to make extended overseas trips, it was unlikely that you would have been the direct purchaser of local dolls. The airplane changed travel patterns after the war, making short, affordable overseas vacations possible. The market for keepsake souvenirs grew as people other than the most affluent found time to travel. As tourists expanded their lists of possible destinations, local doll makers adapted their craft to produce dolls that could be easily packed by a traveler and serve as reminder of the country visited. Dolls ranged from cheap, poorly made examples, to sophisticated, well-detailed costumed models. Some dolls used commonly found materials for doll heads and bodies: cloth, hard plastic, vinyl, resin, ceramic, and wood. Others used locally found natural products such as nuts, shells, and straw. Some doll makers, especially European, are well known, but many dolls were the products of local villagers and craftsmen working in cooperative enterprises. Many of the dolls are larger than the focus of this book, but many are of a size that might fit in a dollhouse, miniature castle, chalet, or cottage.

The United Kingdom

While the United Kingdom had its wonderful small yarn-wrapped wire dolls by Grecon and Tomac, there was also a large market for souvenir dolls dressed as the Royals, Guardsmen, Highlanders, Welshman, and Irishmen. Cheaply made plastic dolls dressed in inaccurate costumes were common, although there were notable exceptions that deserve mention. Although Peggy Nisbet dolls were somewhat larger in size than dollhouse dolls, they set new standards that were copied by other, quality minded doll makers.

In 1952 Peggy Nisbet started her doll business in Great Britain by creating a 7" bisque character doll to commemorate the upcoming coronation of Queen Elizabeth II. Encouraged by the success of the finely costumed doll, exclusively featured at Harrod's Department Store, she decided to fill a niche for fine quality, accurately costumed dolls representative of the United Kingdom. At first costuming dolls made by others, principally 6" childlike dolls known as Rosebuds, she continued to search for a doll that would be unique to her. Through various times in the history of the company, she made dolls of resin, vinyl, and styrene, returning to fine-bisque in 1976 for a line of special dolls. Her character dolls often were made to commemorate a Royal event such as a wedding, investiture, or state visit of a visiting dignitary. A historic line of character dolls featured past kings and queens. She made dolls of British women street vendors known as "Cries of London", and dressed Guardsmen, Bandsmen, and Beefeaters in their ceremonial uniforms. By the mid 1970s she offered more than 200 different dolls in her catalogue. Then she experimented with a 1:12 scale historic line of articulated miniature dolls, and tried to produce a contemporary set that could be used in modern dollhouses. They were more complicated to make and less profitable than her "souvenir" dolls, and the line was quickly discontinued. Operating two factories, which also relied heavily on skilled "needleworkers" sewing costumes in their homes, Peggy Nisbet, her daughter, son, and husband all participated in the business. The story of this remarkable woman and her dolls is well documented in her autobiography, *The Peggy Nisbet Story*. Mrs. Nisbet died in 1995 at the age of 86.

Dolls celebrating the heritage of Ireland were not as plentiful as dolls from the rest of the United Kingdom. Doll making was often a communal craft, the dolls being offered to tourists, usually anxious to reestablish their Irish roots. One company, however, Jay & Co. Ltd. of Dublin, produced dolls costumed as everyday folk of Ireland's many counties and regions. Clothes were made of basic materials of Irish peasants: homespun wool, simple cotton, and hand knitted shawls. Dolls were offered by Kimport during the mid-1960s and 70s, and were being sold at least into the 1980s by Jay. Little else is known about this company.

Peggy Nisbet's small factory in Scotland made costume dolls with painted shoes, socks, and facial details. Dolls were dressed in authentic tartans with felt tams. Here, the dancing Scots Lad (Andrew T-63) and Lassie (T-169) from the "Happy Doll" line. All hard plastic, 6-6.5" tall. $20/each.

All-plastic 8" British Bobby from the "Tower Treasures" line (K-6) was typical of the souvenir type doll produced by Peggy Nisbet in England. $20.

Jay dolls from Ireland were authentically costumed. The pictured man from the Aran Islands even wore a miniature hand-knit " Fisherman's Sweater" and knit cap. Dolls were 5", 7.5", or 11.5" with 20-25 different styles of each size. Bodies were felt covered over a padded wire armature. Heads were heavily painted clay, often found chipped today. Dolls were mounted on wood stands, and many can be found with their original tags reading "Collectors Character Doll handmade by 'Jay' of Dublin." Tags also described the doll's origin, giving background on the region and time period. *Dolls from the collection of Millicent Lynch*. $20/each.

Italy & Greece

The inspiration for regional and souvenir dolls in Italy clearly rested with the wonderful Lenci dolls of Elena Scavini. Lenci dolls were first made during WWI when Elena, after losing a child, had turned to doll making to occupy her time. When her husband, Enrico, returned from the war, they quickly built the company into a well-recognized global entity with showrooms in the United States, United Kingdom, Germany and France. The trademark, "Lenci" was adopted in 1922 to replace "Scavini Dolls". Elena continued to grow the business after Enrico's 1926 death, but competition from imitators and the company's expansion into fine quality ceramics increased its debt, and she chose to take on partners in the late 1920s. By 1940 Mrs. Scavini sold her interest in the business to her partners, the Gerella Brothers, who operated under the name Ars Lenci.

Lenci doll heads were made of a single piece of felt stretched over a hard form that provided its features. A series of 8.25" miniatures, known as *mascottes*, was produced wearing costumes of the regions of Italy. A similar, but much rarer, line of mascottes, 6 ½-7", tall was also made. The striking feature of the Lenci dolls, most often copied, is their expressive faces, especially eyes and mouths. Dolls do not look straight on, but rather up and to the side, adding to the surprised expression created by their lips, formed as if they had just said "Oh!" Their brown or blue irises stand out against the white background of the eye. Small white highlights representing reflected light were added to the iris.

One Lenci imitator, Carla, made small dolls in regional Italian dress well suited for a dollhouse. Companies like Magis of Roma, Eros, or Treasures of Italy commonly offered inexpensive souvenir dolls. Dolls were dressed as clergy or in Swiss Guard uniforms. Others wore traditional regional costumes. Generally, 5.5 to 6" tall, some dolls had all-plastic unjointed bodies, while others had stuffed felt bodies with plastic arms. Synthetic wigs in various styles were used. All wore soft plastic shoes. Although some of the dolls had painted felt heads, others had plastic heads with a layer of flat paint added to resemble Lenci's painted felt heads. Hand-painted facial features furthered the "Lenci look."

Inexpensive souvenir dolls 5.5"-6.5" tall were produced by a number of Italian toy companies. Dolls were dressed to resemble the clothing of Italy's eleven regions and many of its cities. Foil labels identified the region and manufacturer. Often the dolls were made of plastic, but their faces were cloth-covered and painted in the "Lenci" style. Majis of Roma made the Milanese doll on the left. The three dolls on the right (Venice, Capri, Rome) were made by Treasures of Italy. During 1965, Prince Macaroni Company offered them in the United States as part of a twenty doll set. For $1 and a box top from a Prince pasta product, a doll could be yours. $10/each.

Lenci dolls were the inspiration for many souvenir dolls made in Italy and Greece. The most often copied feature of the Lenci dolls was their expressive faces. Dolls did not look straight on, but rather up and to the side, adding to the surprised expression created by their lips. Their brown or blue irises stood out against the white background of the eye. Small white highlights representing reflected light were added to the iris. A series of 8.25" miniatures, known as *mascottes*, were produced wearing costumes of the regions of Italy. Here a girl carried a pig to market. *From the collection of Lucy's Dollhouse.* $1000.

4.25" Carla dolls, made entirely of felt, covering a stuffed fabric body over wire frame, with synthetic hair wigs. The hand-painted dolls' faces, particularly the eyes, resemble Lenci dolls. Dolls had red, white, and green embroidered stripes on their shirts resembling the flag of Italy. $15/each.

Greek souvenir dolls are commonly found dressed in traditional costumes. Pictured is a pair of 7" non-bendable dolls made of plastic. Faces were fabric-covered with hand-painted details. $10/each.

Northern & Eastern Europe

Doll makers throughout Europe made regionally costumed dolls representing their own countries and those of their neighbors aimed at the increasing number of travelers anxious to purchase souvenirs. Every region of Europe had souvenir offerings.

Northern European doll makers made souvenir dolls as well. At left is a 4.75" Swiss couple, tagged Lucerne Unterwald. Their wire frames were felt covered. Faces were a silk fabric with painted detail. Hair was carefully added with embroidery thread. Dolls wore oversized felt shoes. In the center, a pair of Swiss dolls made in the "Grecon style" with thread-wrapped wire frames and cast metal feet. Mother was 3.75": daughter, 2.5". On the right is a Danish 3.75" couple, he from Sjzelland, and she from Bornholm. They were thread wrapped wire framed with metal feet and hands. $20-25/each.

Doll makers in many countries felt free to create nationality dolls of their neighboring countries. A Dutch family, c. 1957, purchased as souvenirs on a United States military base in Wiesbaden Germany, was cloth-covered over a padded wire frame. Adults, 3.75": children, 2.125"; baby 1.5". $50/family set.

Eastern European countries celebrated their heritage, even under Communist rule. 4.5" Polish women had painted, molded, clay heads and soft plastic hands, legs, and shoes. Their wire frames were poseable. Doll on the right is from the Lalki region. The 4.75" musicians made by a Krakow arts and crafts cooperative, perform the "Tatra Robbers Folk Dance", characteristic of the Podhale region of Poland. Individual dolls, $10. Musicians $30/set.

Among the most recognizable nationality dolls are those produced by Joli of Poland. Made entirely of wood with fine thread hair and cloth costumes, they were offered by mail-order for $1.50 pair in an October 1956 *House and Garden*. $10.

Not only did Hungarian doll makers make dollhouse dolls in the "Grecon style," but also thread wrapped nationality dolls. The 3" woman and 2.125" pair, made for export, were dressed and decorated in their native costumes. $10/each.

Peasant dolls had been made in the Soviet Union as early as 1920, just after the Revolution. Judging by the English labels, they were made for export. Older dolls often had woven straw shoes, where later dolls had shoes crocheted from yarn. Older dolls had painted cloth faces and bodies. Later postwar dolls, such as the one pictured, had composition heads and cloth-covered padded wire frames. Sizes varied greatly, but many, such as this 4.25" figure, were of dollhouse size. Small older dolls $60-100. Small postwar dolls, $25.

Japan

Japan has long had a history of dolls, or *ningyo*. In fact, Japan is one of the earliest cultures to make dolls expressly for children. As early as the 10th century, pairs of play dolls were made, and by the 12th century, children began to keep dollhouses occupied with little figures. The making of dolls reached a peak during the Edo period (1603-1867). The designs of many current dolls were established during this period. The Edo dynasty dolls were elaborately made with multiple media used for each doll. In the mid-17th century, a pure white material made from crushed clamshells and glue, *gofun*, was used to coat the heads of both male and female dolls before facial features were painted on by hand. Wooden *kokeshi* dolls were carved by farmers in Northern Japan, unable to afford more expensive materials. Stuffed silk skinned dolls, with or without *gofun* heads became popular in the 1920s and 1930s. Individuals made elaborate kimonos of different periods of Japanese history. Dolls may have had different interchangeable wigs appropriate for the time or season. Similar sets of dolls with multiple kimonos and *Kabuki* theater masks were also made.

Simple dolls of northern Honshu, *Kokeshi,* were made solely of wood by farmers who could not afford the scraps of cloth with which to clothe them. They were often thought to commemorate children who had died. Sold as temple souvenirs to pilgrims, they were passed from generation to generation. *Kokeshi* dolls, sized from 1.5" "pencil toppers" to fine 8" examples were plentiful in postwar souvenir shops throughout the country. Pictured dolls from 1953 include a 6" plainly decorated doll, and a more elaborate 5.5" chubby *Kokeshi*. $5-30 depending upon decoration and size.

A doll festival, *Hina Matsuri*, is celebrated on March 3 each year. Children exhibit elaborate displays of *Hina* dolls based upon the old Imperial Court of Kyoto. On May 5th of each year, Boys Day is celebrated. Dolls, *Musha-ningyo*, dressed and armed as warriors and heroic figures are displayed. Both standing and seated *Hina* dolls, 4-24" tall, dressed in more elaborate kimonos made from finer fabrics, were sold just after WWII in glass-sided lacquer display cases as souvenirs. Musha warriors were often purchased by servicemen stationed in Japan as well. The pictured doll is 5.25" tall with a clay face finished in a *gofun* style. $20.

The postwar occupation opened a market for traditional dolls purchased by servicemen and their families stationed in Japan. A favorite souvenir was boxed sets, inferior copies of similar sets made for domestic consumption in the 1920s-30s, of 5-7" dolls with interchangeable kimonos, wigs, or masks. $30-50/set depending on age.

China

Christian missions had long been a fixture in China, but the 19th and 20th centuries saw a great increase in mission activity reaching a high point in the 1920s. Missions shifted to providing education and practical support, especially to China's poorer classes. Shanghai's famous Door of Hope Mission founded by the Englishwoman, Cornelia Bonne, in 1901, opened its doors to primarily protect homeless girls and young women from life-long entrapment in prostitution. Recognizing that the children, not only lacked basic education, but also knowledge of practical skills to support themselves, Cornelia enlisted the aid of other like minded individuals. She opened a school and factory where, not only reading, arithmetic, religion and writing, but also cooking and sewing was taught. Students practiced their sewing, making costumes for small wooden head, cloth-bodied dolls dressed traditionally as everyday Chinese. The dolls were sold, providing income for the young women and additional support for the donation dependent mission. Dolls were imported to the United States by mission societies, churches, and by Kimport Dolls, until the mission was burned in 1937 during the Japanese occupation of China. The Mission restarted after the war but relocated to Taiwan after the Chinese Communist government came to power. Its production of dolls ceased soon thereafter. About 25-28 distinct styles of dolls have been catalogued, but they are too large to be considered dollhouse sized, ranging from 6.5" for a baby, 8" for an older child and 12" for an adult.

The influence of the Door of Hope dolls is clearly seen by the number of missions that used dolls for teaching tools as well as fundraisers. Lynn Murray, in her well researched May 2007 *Antique Doll Collector* article, attributes some look-alike dolls possibly to the Florence Crittenton Association for Rescue. A number of doll families were produced by other missions: the Baptist Industrial Mission Of Shaoshing, the Chefoo American Presbyterian Mission, the "Robins Nest" of the Tientsin Mission, and the Industrial Mission of Shanghai. They differed significantly from Door of Hope Dolls in size, quality, and scope.

In 1952, the Chinese government expelled all foreign missionaries, and, faced with persecution, most missions either closed their doors or relocated to Taiwan or Hong Kong. There is little evidence that Chinese mission dolls in any quantity were made thereafter, although the Lutheran World Federation sponsored a doll making project in Hong Kong in the 1960s to assist mainland refugees.

A 5 member family 2 ¼" – 3 ¼" made by the Baptist Industrial Mission of Shaoshing in Chekiang Province in the late 1930s or between 1946-1952. Each finger was separately formed from fine covered wire. Shaoshing's small dolls are often found in families of 5, although grandparents and amahs were not uncommon. They had wire frames wrapped in fabric with fabric heads. Facial details were hand painted. Women's hair was fine thread, but men had painted hairlines. They were dressed in every day dress without the fine fabric and detail of the larger Door of Hope dolls. Dolls are often found still attached to a piece of cardboard, which may, or may not be printed with the mission source. $50/5 member family.

56 regional dolls of China represent the vast array of minorities in China. Molded in un-fired clay with hand-painted detail, the dolls, 2" tall, are modern souvenirs made since the opening of China's borders. $15/set.

Asia

Not all dolls sold as souvenirs were made in Western Europe. Dolls were offered on every continent. Asian countries celebrated their rich heritage with beautifully costumed figures. Among the most authentic and well crafted were the dolls made by Thailand's Tongkorn Chanavimol through her firm, Bangkok Dolls. Having studied doll making in Japan after the war, Mrs. Chanavimol's first doll was a character doll made in 1956 to present to Thailand's Queen on her birthday. The Queen encouraged her to start a business to make dolls that reflected and honored Thailand's heritage.

Tongkorn Chanavimol designed and produced dolls, operating first in the mid-1950s as a home industry. She relocated to a workshop in Bangkok, which now also houses Bangkok Doll Museum. Dolls are authentically dressed in historic Thai costumes, the clothes of every day people, dancers, and members of Thailand's royalty. Doll bodies are cloth with wire armatures, stuffed with straw. Heads are cloth glued over a plastic form. Facial details are painted on. Dolls range in size from about 8" to 17" with most 10" to 12", oversized for dollhouses. The clothing is the most striking feature utilizing fine silks, brocades, and satin with hand sewn sequins, jewels, and other details. Although in her mid-70s, Mrs. Chanavimol continues to make dolls today along with a long-time staff of more than 20 women. $20.

Even remote Asian countries produced nationality dolls for export. The pictured 6.25" wood carved dolls are Nepalese. $15.

Mid-East & Latin America

Dolls from the Mideast hint at past similarities in culture and ethnicity. Dolls from Latin America and the Caribbean islands display the area's great ethnic and cultural diversity.

A collection of dolls from the Mideast reflect similarities of cultural styles, dress, and ethnic heritage that cross borders. A 6" Jordanian woman on the left, balancing a water jug on her head, had wooden legs and shoes, plastic covered wire arms, and a hand-painted baked clay face. The 5.5" Lebanese couple in the center were made in Beirut in 1967. They each had baked clay bodies and heads. Their shoulders were jointed and they were mounted on wooden stands with their ethnic origin stamped on the front. The padded wire framed bodies of the traditional Israeli pair on the right stand 6.75". Their heads were painted, baked clay, and their leather hands held a drum and water jug. They were marked "handmade by Sabra." $15/pr.

Nationality dolls, quite naturally, were often made of materials common to the craft workers of that country. Two all-leather Uruguayan dolls, with hand-painted features and yarn hair, were purchased in Montevideo in 1964. $15/pr.

The island of Barbados produced this 4″ cloth-covered wire framed guitarist in straw hat, serenading sun-worshiping tourists. $7.

Latin American dolls differed dramatically from country to country and doll maker to doll maker. A Guatemalan couple in the center represents the cities of San Martin and San Antonia. Each, about 4.5″, was made from a brown tape covered wire frame. Heads were stuffed heavy cloth with embroidered features. Clothes were made of burlap. The Honduran fisherman and mother with child were wire framed covered with burlap. Embroidery provided the facial detail to these 5.5″ dolls. $15/pr.

Kimport Dolls

No discussion of international dolls in the United States can take place without mention of Kimport Dolls of Independence, Missouri. Kimport was founded in 1933 by Ruby and Arthur McKim. After returning from a vacation trip to Europe, they were unable to find foreign dolls to supplement collections they had started for their daughters. The McKims were marketing geniuses, scouring the world for sources of unique dolls that could then be made available through direct mail catalogs to individuals unable to travel abroad. The McKims had survived through the war, shifting their emphasis to American folk dolls and selling inventory that had been stockpiled before the war. As soon as the war ended, they recontacted their previous overseas sources and established new ones. They sponsored tours of their 1000 doll collection to many of the major department stores in the United States, again building interest for dolls in general and their offerings in particular. The McKims sold their business to their son, Kim, in 1957 and moved into semi-retirement. The business continued successfully until 1985 when Kim closed the business after unsuccessfully searching for a buyer.

American isolationism had ended with WWII, and the United States market was hungry to learn more about overseas cultures. A number of companies imported dolls from all over the world, often appealing to adult collectors, as opposed to children. An October 1957 *House and Garden* ad from World-Wide Dolls offered pairs of dolls from 15 countries at $5.50 a pair. Many of these dolls are commonly found today. $15/pr.

Kimport Dolls helped introduce United States collectors to dolls of foreign lands: Door of Hope, Lenci, Jay of Dublin. Many collections contain "international dolls" today that found their way to this country through Independence, Missouri. Kimport created its own demand, forming the Doll Hobby Club. The $1 membership fee entitled a member to the company's catalogs and a one-year subscription to the club newsletter, Doll Talk. Every doll came with a sheet of paper describing its background and provenance, sometimes in fanciful, but accurate terms. Doll Talk had a feature to answer collectors' questions. Books were reviewed and a column on antique dolls was added. These background papers and the Doll Talk magazine filled a void for information at a time before the special interest magazines of today. The company established a doll-of-the-month plan, tailored to the budget and interests of individual collectors. The pictured 6" Italian pair was offered in the early 1940s. $65.

Molded Plastic Dolls of the World

Commonwealth Plastics Company of Leominster, Massachusetts, played an interesting role in the "international" doll market. Commonwealth, whose origins trace back to 1922 as Independent Lock & Key, moved into notions, novelties, and household items as New England Novelty Company around 1930 under the direction of two brothers, Harry and Louis Levine. In 1935, the company moved to a new location in Leominster, renaming itself, Commonwealth Plastics Company, Inc. Commonwealth was one of the pioneers in injection-molded plastics, after commissioning the well regarded engineer and later founder of Pyro Plastics Corp., William Lester, to design a revolutionary new machine molder in 1934. The hydraulic based Lester machine could produce a plastic part in quantity in six seconds. With this equipment Commonwealth was able to mold acetate dolls for Vogue Doll Company. They prospered throughout the war making plastic parts for the military, and by the end of the war they were well placed to continue their novelty business, and also supply toys compatible with the commercially produced dollhouses and miniatures of the time.

Capitalizing on heightened awareness of American children to the world around them, in September, 1950, Commonwealth introduced 12 small dolls molded in solid flesh-colored plastic. The set later grew to include 32 dolls, 24 women and 8 men. A New York based customer of Commonwealth had originally suggested that the dolls be made and which countries should be represented. Designing was done in-house by the talented team of Louis Charpentier, the head of the model shop, and his assistant, Zigmund Olbrys of Clinton, Massachusetts. Mr. Charpentier, a talented sculptor, demonstrated his wood carving at the Smithsonian Institute in 1987, and his tableaus and life-sized Crucifix decorate his parish church in Leominster. The talent of the two men helped create real life-like detail in the dolls. Mr. Charpentier designed many of the toys produced by Commonwealth as well as many of their more utilitarian products, but he maintained that the dolls were his most difficult assignment. A 47 year employee of Commonwealth, Mr. Charpentier was a friend and contemporary of George and Christina Bauer, who had assisted Ethel Strong in the design and production of her Twinky dolls.

Originally retailing for $1.75 per set of eight dolls, boxes were printed with scenes highlighting "famed landmarks throughout the world." The Levines were good marketers and continued to repackage the dolls and find new outlets for them. Dolls were sold through dimestores but also were used as giveaway premiums by local businesses. The author's original tin dollhouse was inhabited by dolls supplied by her aunt, an employee of Pittsburgh's Dimling's Candy Shops. Commonwealth was sold in 1978 and its assets sold a few years later when it ceased manufacturing.

A similar series of 32 different 2" international dolls is often found in white or cream hard plastic. Made in the same time period, the dolls were included as premiums in boxes of cereal sold by Van Brode Milling Company of Clinton, Massachusetts. The fact that the dolls bear a striking resemblance to the Commonwealth Dolls of Our World is explained in part by the fact that their designer was the artist Zigmund Olbrys, Mr. Charpentier's assistant at Commonwealth. Olbrys was apparently freelancing for Van Brode. Commonwealth itself was not involved with the Van Brode dolls, and since Van Brode did have plastic molding capability, used for the production of plastic table utensils, it is likely that Van Brode made its own dolls. Dolls were not sold separately, only as premiums in cereal boxes. The job of inserting the doll in each box was one of the most sought after in the Van Brode plant. A woman would sit with a large plastic bag filled with dolls and slide them into a filled cereal box using a special funnel.

Each Commonwealth Plastic "Doll of our World" figure, about 2" high, was molded in its native costume and posed differently in what Commonwealth called an "action pose." Costumes were brightly painted. The doll's nationality, ethnic origin, or time period was marked on the base, and two diamonds were molded into the bottom of the base, perhaps for stability. First introduced as twelve dolls in September 1950, the line was expanded in February 1951 with a second set of 12 dolls and a suggested retail price of $1.89. The first three sets were costumed females, but in 1952, Commonwealth added eight male dolls to complete the series of 32. $3/each unboxed.

In 1952, the 32 dolls were each attached to a separate card containing "interesting" (and somewhat naïve) facts about the doll's background or country of origin (front row, left, and center). Dolls could also be bought unpainted on an ivory or jade colored plastic base for 10¢ (front row). In 1953 Commonwealth divided the 32 dolls into four sets selling for 98¢ and packaged them with a large chart showing all 32 flags corresponding to the dolls' country or origin (back row). In 1958 the dolls were reboxed and advertised by Doll Bodies, Inc., a Commonwealth distributor, as "32 Dolls of Faraway Lands." The set, including seven paint pots, sold for $2.98 (center row, left). Finished figures could be attached to round decorated plastic bases that were included. Apparently, Commonwealth either sold the molds in the early 1960s or produced the dolls for others, as the dolls can be found in bright hard plastic colors (front row, right), in packages of various sizes and combinations marked with company names such as Jak-Pak, Toy Shop Toy Manufacturing, and Tiny Teen (center row, right). Small ¾" charms have been found that are perfect replicas of the Commonwealth dolls (front row). Boxed sets generally sell for $4 times the number of included dolls.

2" plastic dolls, similar to Commonwealth's, were made by Van Brode Milling Co. Inc., as premiums included in their cereal boxes. Two of the 32 dolls, the Dutch boy and girl, were molded to represent the Van Brode trademark, and they were simply marked Van on the boy's base and Brode on the girl's. $3.

The international dolls of Commonwealth and Van Brode are among the most endearing examples of dolls fostering Baby Boomers' growing awareness of the world around them.

Van Brode's series was comprised of a male and female from each of 16 countries, about half of which overlapped with Commonwealth dolls. They were molded in white, ivory, and cream colored plastic. $3

The dolls are easy to differentiate from Commonwealth's series. While well carved, they were made of lighter-weight plastic. The country name was on the front and the Van Brode name on the back of each base. There were no diamonds on the bottom of the bases, and the word "Clinton" occasionally appeared. $3.

Section 4
Barbie and the Television Era
1960-1990

As the Baby Boomer Era ended in the late 1950s, a number of factors coincided, leading to the decline in popularity of commercially produced dollhouses and their inhabitants. Television was the obvious cultural change for adolescent Baby Boomers. Children no longer had to depend on imaginative play to occupy their time. Television programming aimed at families and children filled every waking hour. *The Today Show* saw you off to school; the *Mickey Mouse Club* and *American Bandstand* were just airing as you got home. After dinner you might watch *Father Knows Best, Wagon Train*, or *77 Sunset Strip* with Ed "Kookie" Byrnes. The family probably was tuned in Sunday nights to *Disney's Wonderful World of Color* and *Ed Sullivan*, and on Saturday mornings you got up early to watch a solid block of cartoons: *Rocky and Bullwinkle, Yogi Bear, Mighty Mouse, Bugs Bunny*. In the United Kingdom, televisions might have been tuned to the *Watch with Mother* series or *Camberwick Green*. Canada contributed *Tales of the Riverbank*. As mothers returned to the workforce in the 1960s, 70s, and 80s, television became a child's "baby-sitter." Programming for children was expanded, especially as animation techniques improved.

Most American families had automobiles, and with gasoline selling between 25-50¢ a gallon, they took the opportunity to travel. In Europe train systems had all been repaired and improved. Beach resorts and destination theme parks became summer vacation targets, further cutting into the need for toys that occupied a child's time. As boys and girls sports leagues grew, and anxious parents insisted upon after school music, dance, and karate lessons, less unstructured playtime was left.

Children's tastes changed as well, in no small part a result of the 1959 introduction of Ruth Handler's Barbie doll. Produced in 1:6 scale known as "playscale," there was no interchangeability between Barbie, Skipper, and Ken and the common dollhouse scales. Wardrobes, accessories, cars, dream houses, and beauty parlors were produced for Barbie, competing directly for children's interest in doll play. Boys were introduced to play sized GI Joe in 1964, further weakening manufacturers' interest in producing miniature playsets. Interest in science increased as a result of the "space race." Toys with electrical and electronic components became more prevalent.

Toy marketing changed as well throughout the 1970s and 1980s. Toys tied to television shows and movies like the *Smurfs, My Little Pony,* and *Garfield* pushed demand away from traditional toys. *Sesame Street's* complete line of toys appealed to younger children and to parents searching for some educational component for playtime activity. Many small high-quality toy stores closed, as did the toy departments of urban department stores. They were replaced by the mass market offerings of large specialty toy chains like Toys-r-Us and Kay-Bee Toys, and discounters like K-Mart and Wal-Mart. High-quality miniature dolls were found at doll and toy shows, through mail-order catalogues, and in specialized shops dealing with miniatures.

Dollhouses became a toy market niche. There were certainly commercially produced dollhouses, although the choice was restricted to a few larger, well-known manufacturers. Plastic was the material of choice for houses, dolls, and accessories. The commercial dollhouse market shifted its target to pre-schoolers, because older siblings found other interests. A parallel development was the increase of fine scale dollhouses, primarily 1:12. Plywood kits and finishing materials in a vast array of materials became very popular during this period. Furnishings, accessories, and dolls became works of art. These modern fine scale dollhouses were sometimes meant more for display, than for play, reminiscent of their 19th century counterparts.

The 1960s, 70s, and 80s were a turbulent time politically. While current events such as the assassinations of the Kennedy brothers and Martin Luther King, the Vietnam War, the Peace movement, Watergate, Civil Rights awareness, Cold War tensions, and the drug culture were well reported and were part of children's consciousness, world conditions did not result in fewer or drastically different toys being made or sold. Social factors, particularly television, created the change. Children no longer had to amuse themselves.

Chapter 11

The Space Age 1957-1969

The space race began when the Soviet Union launched *Sputnik* in October 1957. Children all over the globe awoke to hear the satellite's beeping communications from space, played over radio and television. Manned travel followed in 1961. Presidents Kennedy and Johnson authorized the Apollo program aimed at putting a man on the Moon. The concept captured the imagination of the world, and the goal was reached in June 1969. The space race changed much for American children. Schools emphasized the teaching of math and science. Gender barriers lessened and girls and young women were encouraged to study fields seen as critical to the recovery of American technological leadership. New inventions and discoveries easily translated into everyday life and encouraged children both to understand and improve on new technologies. We learned of things like permanent press clothes, non-dairy creamer, food processors, hand held calculators. Small transistor radios could be purchased for less than $20; electric typewriters were common, and "portable" televisions found their place in America's bedrooms.

Many toy makers viewed this focus on science as the single biggest change the industry had seen. No longer was there a gradual evolution in childhood interests and playthings. Toys changed rapidly, as did children's fickle tastes. Traditional toys still had a place, but they competed with a larger array of playthings, and with children's ever increasing structured activities. European manufacturers like Lundby and Erna Meyer tended to stay with more traditional concepts, although the fashions worn by their dolls were kept very up-to-date.

No discussion of the period is complete without a mention of the role of "school toys" or "learning toys." Dolls and dollhouses found their way into schools and psychologists' offices long before the 1960s, but starting in the 60s, toys sometimes won a spot in a classroom or in a battle at home with television, if a parent or teacher could justify the time spent as "educational." Dollhouses, furniture, and dollhouse figures were simply and solidly made to withstand the daily play of many children. They were advertised in educational magazines and catalogues to parents intent upon creating an "educational experience." Companies like Flagg directly marketed their dollhouse dolls to schools, social workers, and mental health professionals, highlighting the fact in their consumer advertising.

Sizes of "small" dolls changed, and companies were quick to copy a competitor's success. Dolls like *My Merry*, *Liddle Kiddles*, *Flatsy's*, *Dolly Darlings*, and Remco's *Pocketbook Dolls*, each about 3"-5.5" tall, were similarly conceived and sized, but never aimed at nor proportioned for the dollhouse market, although some were sold in playsets with room-boxes, furniture, and accessories. Cindy Sabulis' two *Collector's Guides to the Dolls of the 1960s and 1970s* clearly identify and picture the variety of these small dolls.

My Merry's 4" doll was typical of the "small dolls" of the 1960s. Packaged with dollhouse like accessories, it was not scaled for the dollhouses of this era, but could have been used as such by a creative child. $10.

Liddle Kiddles became a toy genre of their own, and they were never advertised as dollhouse dolls. They were intended as "pocketbook dolls" that could be carried around by their young owners. $10-15.

Doll artisans continued their craft into the 1960s. This wooden 3-5" pipe cleaner family was made by an unknown Columbus, Ohio, artist in her home. She made similarly sized nationality dolls as well. $10/each.

Major toy makers continued to make some dollhouses and dollhouse sized dolls. Marx continued making tin dollhouses until his business was sold. The company tried to create new interest with its Little Hostess/Amanda Ann lines in 1964, which featured fully molded, hard plastic figures. Marx introduced their *Twistoys* and *Brown/Jones* family bendable dolls in 1962 and 1966. Ideal Toy's 1963 *Petite Princess/Princess Patti* lines featured a bendable family, with nicely molded faces. Interestingly, Sears sold Marx dolls with later versions of the *Petite Princess/Princess Patti* miniatures. Some companies offered room box type settings made from lithographed cardboard or molded plastic, together with inexpensive miniature furniture and dolls. Other companies offered dolls packaged to go with existing dollhouses of others, or in playsets that were complementary to dollhouses. With limited exception, mass-produced miniature dolls made during the 1960s were either extensions of the molded plastic figures of the 1950s, or were made with pipe cleaner frames and solid heads, hands, and feet. New plastics were used, but quality and detail often suffered.

Auburn

Tire manufacturers possessed the necessary knowledge to produce small products from rubber, and some like Sun Rubber and Seiberling Tire turned their attention to making dolls and toys. Another manufacturer, originally known as the Double Fabric Tire Co. of Auburn, Indiana, and later as Auburn Rubber Company, made a similar shift, adding industrial rubber accessories to their tire products. In the mid-1930s the Company's principal stockholder, A.L. Murray, brought back lead soldiers from a trip to England, thinking it might be a venture for Auburn to pursue. His idea proved profitable for Auburn as they began making inexpensive, rubber figures and eventually vehicles. After World War II, they reentered the toy market and continued to use rubber for their products until 1952, when they began using vinyl plastic. They made an assortment of figures including farm sets with barns and animals, Indians and pioneers with cabins, cowboys with wagons, soldiers, policemen, and firemen.

Auburn's six dollhouse figures measured between 2.5 to 3". All of the figures were molded in seated positions except one girl, who was on a stand. Their facial features, hair, and clothing were very nicely molded, possibly by Ferriot Brothers. It is possible to see the tiny detail on their shirt collars and belts. Auburn figures were frequently packaged in sets, sold in 5 & 10¢ stores. Packages for dollhouse play included swing, patio, and picnic sets, a Bar-B-Q and a Suburbanite set. The patio set (pictured) was sold in a header bag with furniture and figures for 59 cents. Dolls, $5/each.

For young girls, Auburn made unbreakable polypropylene rooms with furniture. There were four rooms: living room, utility room, kitchen, and bedroom/bath that could be attached to one another to form a ranch style house. In the dollhouse figure line Auburn made a set of six dolls, three boys and three girls. At first they were made of a rubber-like vinyl, molded in pink. Later they were red, soft polypropylene plastic. The boy figure pictured on their advertising was "Little Aubie." The toy division of this company was purchased by the city of Deming, New Mexico, in 1960, but was unable to overcome years of poor management and inadequate investment. Auburn went out of business in 1969.

Blue Box

Blue Box Holdings Ltd. of Hong Kong was founded in 1952 by its current company chairman, Peter Chan Pui. The company's first factories were in Kowloon, later expanding to Singapore. In the 1980s manufacturing was consolidated on mainland China. The company makes toys and collectibles for all ages. Blue Box made plastic dollhouses and room settings called "Dream House" in the late 1960s through early 1970s. Both contained their 1:24 scale plastic dollhouse furniture and families. Over time Blue Box added other figures and animals to complement their original sets, sometimes changing paint colors. They also made a "Summer Resort" with small-plastic swimming pool figures on stands. Blue Box was available through Wards catalogs and in variety stores.

Blue Box dollhouses contained four- to nine-member hard plastic, non-flexible families, 2.25" and smaller. Their facial features and clothing were hand-painted. Six figures: father, mother, grandfather, grandmother, boy, and girl were offered in a Q.T. Novelty catalog of the 1960s for $1. Dolls were marked Hong Kong. $2/each.

Irwin Corporation

Irwin Cohn began his highly successful company in New York in 1922, focused on the production of housewares, but by the 1940s he had established their niche in the toy business. Rising to the top of the plastic toy industry during the 1950s, Irwin had a showroom in the Fifth Avenue building in New York City and factories in Fitchburg and Leominster, Massachusetts, and Nashua, New Hampshire. Their long list of offerings, from the 1940s to the 1960s, included celluloid and plastic dolls, roly-polys, infant toys, seasonal holiday items, mechanical toys, tea sets, hula hoops, die cast cars and trucks, guns, and banks. They made dolls ranging from 1" to 20" in height, and produced a number of small dolls suitable for dollhouse play.

Irwin did not enter the dollhouse market until 1964 when they introduced a 230-piece Interior Decorator set and a 164-piece Studio Apartment with interlocking furniture pieces. While not a true dollhouse, it included decorated wall panels and floors that held furniture, accessories, and family. It was offered in the fashionable color palette for real houses as suggested by *House and Garden* magazine. Irwin was sold through popular catalog houses and in toy stores. The company was sold to Miner Industries in 1973.

Irwin's 2.5" soft plastic seated girls dressed in sunsuits painted in various primary colors with painted details. They appeared on many Irwin toys, such as its wind-up carnival ride. $3.

3.75" hard plastic "Brother and Sister Dolls" had painted outfits in a variety of colors. Hair and facial features were painted. Dolls were marked "Irwin." They were originally sold on a cardboard card resembling a cozy living room. A 2.25" hard plastic baby, marked "Irwin", with jointed arms and legs wore a cloth diaper with a safety pin. Eyes and mouth were painted. Brother and Sister, $8/each. Baby, $5.

The doll family to accompany Irwin's Interior Decorator sets was a five-member, flexible plastic family made in Hong Kong. Mother (4") and son (3") were molded on stands. Father (3.25") and daughter (1.875") were molded in a sitting position. There was also a 1.75" Spaniel dog. This family was not marked. Shoes and clothes were spray painted, along with facial features. They were sold by Sears in a cardboard box as a set of five figures for $1.33. $35/set MIB.

Jenny's Home

Jenny's Home dollhouse line, made by Spot-On in Northern Ireland for the English firm of Triang, was produced in conjunction with their *"Homes and Gardens"* magazine in 1965. The line included Jenny and her friends. Furniture, in 1:16 scale, was plastic. One could assemble the various clear plastic rooms to make "Jenny's Home" large or small.

Jenny, the actual namesake of Triang's "Jenny's Home" line, was a vinyl, poseable 3.5" doll marked "Made in Hong Kong." She had molded hair with painted features. She could also be purchased wearing a wig. A complete family, including Jenny, her 4.5" tall father and mother, smaller brother, and babies, was also available for the house. Pictured is a mother, Jenny with a blonde wig, and Jenny with molded hair, much easier to find. Dolls, $20/each.

Miner Industries

Miner Industries was a diversified toy maker and marketer with offices in New York. They entered the dollhouse miniature market in the mid-1960s with products that were a good illustration of the decline in the commercial dollhouse market. In 1964 Miner offered individual room-boxes furnished with 1:24 scale wood furniture made in Japan. They later sold a "Fold Away" cardboard dollhouse, which had room settings filled with soft plastic furniture by MPC. Their next "dollhouse" was a snap together plastic room with a sliding picture window in typical 1960s style. It was called "Bend-A-Family's Model Home." It was sold with plastic furniture and dolls for $1. Two additional versions of the dolls were sold by Miner.

The "Bend-A-Family" was a series of dolls continuously made by Miner in the 1960s and 70s. The first "Bend-A-Family" made sometime after 1963, was a flexible, rubbery family of four dolls (bottom left). Father and Mother were 4.5"; boy and girl, 2.5". Dolls had molded hair and painted shoes and facial features. They wore simple cloth clothing of felt and cotton with modest trim for decoration. The family, as well as being included in Miner's Model Home, was packaged in a cardboard box and sold through the Sears catalog in 1967 for 99 cents. A later edition of "Bend-A-Family" was labeled "Bend-Me-Toy Play Family" (bottom right). The dolls were slightly shorter: father, 4"; mother, 3.75"; boy and girl, 2.25". They wore different cloth costumes. Shoes, hair, and facial features were painted on all dolls. Dolls were made in Hong Kong and a boxed set sold for $2.99. Miner sold a larger family in which the father and mother were almost 6" and the toddler girl, 3.25" (top row). This family was also sold in a cardboard box with a header card, lithographed as a room, to be used as a backdrop. They were flexible rubbery dolls with painted shoes and facial features. The box carried Miner's name. $10/set MIB.

In later years other manufacturers sold sets of look-alike or "bendy" dolls. On the left, the "Shape-Me-Family" look-alikes distributed by Baroco Enterprises. "Bend-a-Family" made of a soft vinyl with molded vinyl clothes and painted shoes and facial features, and a similar "Bendy Family" by Kingsway borrowed the name from Miner (middle and right). $5/set MIB.

Norstar Corporation

Norstar Corporation of the Bronx, New York, was another broad scale toy manufacturer/distributor in the 1950s. In addition to action games and housekeeping toys, in the mid-1960s the company made a folding, heavy cardboard, lithographed dollhouse supplied with 1:18 scale soft plastic furniture. In 1969 they added a boxed set of dollhouse figures, made in Hong Kong. Their packaging bore the message: "Fun to play with in your dollhouse or by themselves."

Norstar's dollhouse dolls (right) measured: Father, 5"; mother, 4.5"; boy, 2.75"; girl, 3"; 2" baby. Dolls, with wire limbs covered in flesh-colored vinyl extending from hard plastic torsos, were bendable and flexible. They had a vinyl head, but hard plastic hands and shoes. Hair was molded and faces painted. They wore cloth clothing in assorted fabrics: jersey, felt, and nylon. Seams unraveled easily, as they were not finished. The line was expanded to include a grandfather, grandmother, doctor and nurse, all similarly made (left). $10/set MIB.

Wolverine

Wolverine Supply & Manufacturing Company was founded on Pittsburgh's Northside in the early 1900s by Benjamin Bain. Over the years it underwent a number of name changes. It changed from Wolverine Toy Company to Today's Kids in 1986 after its 1968 acquisition by Spang and Co. and its 1971 move of manufacturing operations to Booneville, Arkansas. A tool and die maker, Wolverine entered the toy business in 1913 when its customer The Sand Toy Co. went out of business. Wolverine decided to manufacture Sand Toy's "Sandy-Andy." Wolverine continued to make different versions of this gravity action sand toy over the years, and went on to utilize its lithographed sheet metal capability, making housekeeping toys, action games, mechanical merry-go-rounds, dishes, and adding machines.

Wolverine was one of the first companies to see the benefit of plastics as a dollhouse furniture material. A lithographed tin bathroom room-box with injection-molded Lumarith bathroom fixtures was introduced less than a year before the War. Wolverine had converted 100% of its production to military products by the end of 1941.Wolverine was one of the last companies to make a metal dollhouse in the postwar style. In 1968, it introduced two lithographed steel houses with plastic windows, doors, chimneys, and trim. They came furnished with 1:24 scale soft plastic dollhouse furniture in assorted, solid, very 60s colors. A few of the dollhouses came with figures. In the early 1980s, Wolverine introduced four dollhouses and furnishings in 1:12 scale made from fiberboard, metal, and plastic. Known as "Rite-Scale," the line also featured the three-member "Bender Family."

A few of Wolverine's dollhouses came with white, unpainted, standing male and female figures. Approximately 3.5" tall, they were molded onto a base and can easily be identified by their hollowed out backs. Figures had nice detail and were not marked. $10/each.

Wolverine's later Bender family sold with its Rite-Scale line measured: 6.25", father; 5.5", mother; and 2.875" baby. Adult dolls were uniquely designed. Their legs were hard plastic spindles with jointed knees covered by their vinyl slacks. Dolls were also jointed at the shoulders and hips. They had a hard plastic upper body and head. Dolls had plastic shoes, painted hair, facial features, and shirt decoration. Marked "Wolverine, Taiwan", dolls could be purchased separately for about $3. $25/set MIB.

Emenee

Emenee Industries, Inc., had its beginnings in 1949-1950 as a toy and novelty manufacturer. Headquartered in the toy building on Manhattan's Fifth Avenue, with a plant in Long Island City in Queens, New York, Emenee was best known for its Arthur Godfrey Ukulele. In 1951, Emenee introduced fairytale figures made from Vinylite. Each set was packaged in a decorated window box with plastic accessories. Soon after they introduced a ten member Play Family.

In 1964, Emenee introduced a set that allowed a child to create his or her own dollhouse family. Easy to make using the company's Formex 7 formula, which melted over an electric light bulb, a child poured the hot liquid into molds. When cooled, the figures were ready to paint. Additional molds were available including "Dolls of Other Countries," a schoolroom, and a military casting set for boys. The doll set, pictured in the 1964 Sears catalog, sold for $4.99.

Emenee's 1964 "Little Doll Family" came with enough Formex 7 to make over 26 figures. When molded, mother and father were 3.75"; older boy and girl, 3 1/4", young girl, 2 1/2". A child could also mold the family pets, a dog and a cat. Although these were stationary figures, they would be very suitable for dollhouse play. $20/set MIB.

Emenee's early 1950s fairytale like vinylite "The Play Family" was advertised as appropriate for dollhouses, although, at 1-2", dolls were not well scaled even for the tin 1:24 houses of the time. $15/set MIB.

MPC

Multiple Products, Inc., was headquartered in the Bronx in the early 1960s. They were a division of Loral Corporation. They produced a wide range of boys and girls toys: farms, dollhouse miniatures, fire fighting toys, and spacecraft. The company sold a cardboard dollhouse, called a Fold-A-Way, filled with 1:18 scale soft plastic furniture in solid colors. MPC furniture was often supplied in cardboard houses and plastic room-boxes made by Miner Industries. MPC made a line of 3.5" teenage male and female dolls to appeal to teens and pre-teens. MPC, like Marx, was purchased by General Mills as part of their ill-conceived toy diversification strategy in the late 1960s or early 1970s.

MPC's "Teenettes" were molded in standing and sitting positions in flesh-colored and other solid colored soft plastic. Some dolls were hand-painted. Standing dolls were molded on bases. There were pleats, ribs, and checks molded into some of their clothing, giving texture and interest to the dolls. Pictured dolls were sold with a "shake shack" backdrop. $40/set MIB.

Teenettes were packaged with fashion accessories that could be held by the ring hands of the dolls. Sets like the pictured boxed grocery or beauty parlor added play value, although little attention was paid to the scale of the toys accompanying the sets. $40/set MIB.

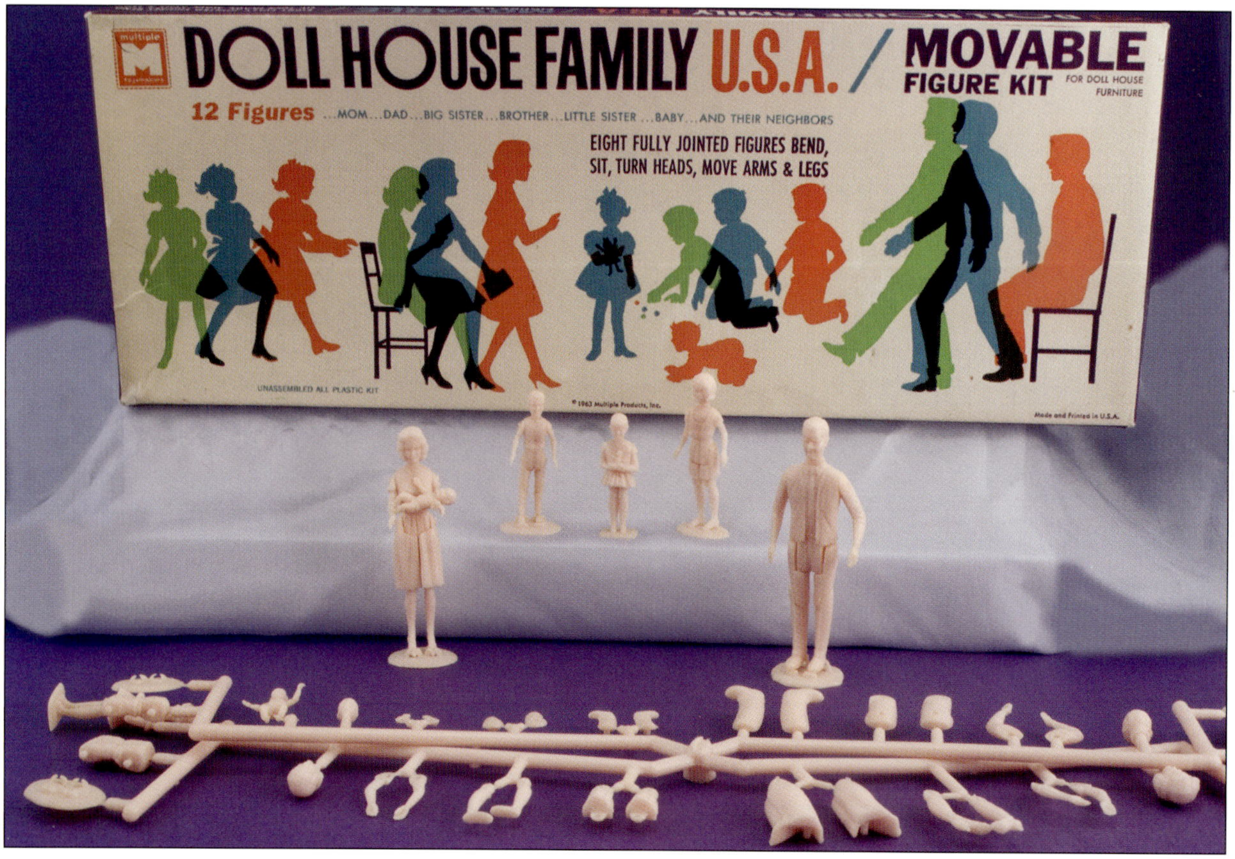

MPC figures included a family of put-together figures similar to Marx' "Flexible Joint Dollhouse Family." Packaged in a box with figures' parts on sprues, they had to be assembled and put on their stands. MPC figures were made of a slightly softer plastic than Marx. $15 MIB.

Farmers and Firemen

A number of companies made figures to accompany their farm vehicle and barnyard playsets or their fire and rescue trucks. While such figures are very common in the postwar era they are not the subject of this book. Two companies, particularly, made figures, however, that are often found in and around Baby Boomer dollhouses and buildings because of their 1:18 scale.

Hartland, dating back to the late 1930s or early 1940s, is well known today for its Western figures. Hartland Plastics had its beginnings in Hartland, Wisconsin, a decade before World War II as a maker of steering wheels. After the war, the company made plastic crèche sets and religious figurines, sold by large mail-order retailers. In 1954 they began to produce a line of large western figures and horses that capitalized on televised westerns and frontier series. In the late 1950s the company added plastic baseball and football figures decorated in favorite team colors. Looking for ways to spread production out past the Christmas rush, the company introduced cake toppers and other decorative figurines. In 1964, it introduced the "Sunny Acre Farm" Series. After the mid 1960s, Hartland was sold and re-sold. It is now known as Hartland Collectibles, and owns the molds for the Sunny Acre Farm series.

Ny-Lint Tool & Manufacturing Co. of Rockford, Illinois, was founded by Bernard Klint and David Nyberg in 1937. After the war, Nylint shifted its focus to producing wind-up action toys. By the 1950s they were making a large variety of heavy-gauge rolled edge steel vehicle toys. Nylint's "Fun-On-The-Farm" set, including figures, was pictured in a March 1964 *Playthings* magazine.

Hartland's "Sunny Acre Farms" figures were first packaged as eight different carded sets. Each set included a well painted molded figure, either a 4.25" mother, 4.5" father, 3.375" boy, or 3" hard plastic girl and a sampling of their farm animals, pets and farm tools. Three Hartland figures are pictured on the left. Nylint's 1964 "Fun on the Farm" set included a 1:18 scale plastic boy and girl, animals, tools, and pick-up truck for $3.49. Mother and father figures were also available. These figures were the same molds as the Hartland "Sunny Acre Farm" series, touching off a debate of "who copied who." Facial features as well as hair and clothing were painted, but not nearly as well as Hartland's figures. The paint often chipped. Nylint's plastic was slightly lighter in weight. Nylint's figures were marked Nylint, Hong Kong, but Hartland's were unmarked. *Figures from the collection of Geraldine Scott*. Hartland figures, $15/each. Nylint figures, $10/each.

Hartland introduced "cake-toppers" to help spread its production beyond the Christmas rush. Pictured is a capped and gowned figure meant to decorate a graduation cake. Nylint also made a fireman and construction worker, based on its farm boy figure and an EMT based on its father figure, sold with its construction and emergency vehicles. *Figures from the collection of Geraldine Scott*. Hartland figures, $15/each. Nylint figures, $10/each.

Playful Molded Children

Children, molded in action poses from various soft plastics, were also available on the market as part of playsets or individually as complements to dollhouses and playsets offered by others. Primarily 1:24 scale, dolls are reminiscent of the figures sold by Marx for his schoolhouse, zoo, and dollhouse playsets.

Tim Mee began in the late 1940s as a sideline of the Anchor Brush Company of Aurora, Illinois. A friend of the owner, John Baumgartner, thought Anchor could make use of machine downtime by making toys from plastic, leftover from the manufacturer of brush handles. Their first offering was a set of cowboys. Timmy, the nephew of Mr. Baumgartner's secretary, became the namesake for the toy line as well as the proud owner of its very first toy. In 1965 Processed Plastic Company purchased the Tim Mee lines. Processed Plastic made numerous well-detailed vehicles and figures appropriate for dollhouse play. They hold the record for producing the most miniature army men of any United States toy maker.

Tim Mee's 1:24 scale figures suitable for dollhouse play: Man with hammer, woman gardener, boys playing sports, girl cheerleader, girl jumping rope. $5/each.

Schoolchildren and school bus by Gay Toys, a southeastern Michigan maker of vehicles and figures. Figures were approximately 2", molded from soft plastic. Unmarked, the figures have a hole molded in the base. $5/each.

"Educational" Dollhouses

Among the leading proponents of educational toys were Frank and Theresa Caplan, founders of Creative Playthings. Their goal was to create educational toys for infants and young children. Building on a firm belief in starting a child off on the right foot, the company proclaimed that the early years were the most important, and the time when a child achieved the majority of his intelligence. Their toys, made to encourage creativity, included wood blocks, trains, puppets, wheeled toys, easels, dollhouses, miniature furniture, and dollhouse dolls. The company promoted housekeeping toys for kids to enable them to take on family roles and learn to share. Since many of the wood items were timeless and withstood years of play value, they became a best buy for schools.

At first a retailer, the company's roots were in New York City. In 1949 Edith and Bernard Barenholtz merged interests with the Caplans, and, in 1950, incorporated a new company, also known as Creative Playthings. By 1952, the company's shop offered more than 500 toys, nearly half of them made by Creative Playthings and their affiliate School Interiors, Inc. In June of 1964, Creative Playthings opened a new facility, the Learning Center, at One Rockefeller Plaza. In 1966, Creative Playthings was sold to CBS. Frank Caplan remained for a while as director of the Learning Center. Initially, Creative Playthings toys were sold through direct mail-order or in better retail stores like Bloomingdales and Neiman-Marcus. By 1963, they were not sold in stores, only through school and parent catalogs.

Frank Caplan talked about his dollhouse dolls in an October 5, 1948, *New York Times* article. He was concerned about the lack of mother and father dolls designed for very young children. His company rectified the situation by creating an entire family of dolls, both in miniature and larger size. A famous Swiss sculptor, Antonio Vitalli, created a wood family of 1:12 scale dolls and pets introduced in 1954 by Creative Playthings.

The company introduced its "Sta-Put" wired rubber family in 1960 when it opened a manufacturing facility in New Jersey. Figures were made with weighted feet, enabling them to be easily positioned.

A Hutterite community in Clarkesville, Georgia, conceived Community Playthings in the late 1940s. The Hutterian Society of Brothers adheres to traditional values, leading simple lives. The community supported itself by making wooden products, starting with hassocks and moving to children's blocks. Unlike the Amish, they used modern equipment to create their inventory. Their catalog of items was sent to preschools and kindergartens. In 1954, they joined another Hutterian Brotherhood community in Rifton, New York, and brought their crafts with them. Their first shop was an old barn with no heat. By 1964, they demonstrated their skills in the third floor showroom of FAO Schwarz.

Community Playthings initially offered a wide range from blocks to riding toys to play structures, all well made and designed to withstand years of continuous use. With a goal of making products that were safe and free of details so that children would be encouraged to use their imagination, dollhouses were a natural addition. Made from the 1950s until 1995, wooden houses, furniture, and figures were offered. Interestingly, in 1961, Community Playthings also sold a family of Flagg dolls in their catalog for use in their dollhouse.

Creative Plaything's early dolls (catalog picture on right) were internally wired for flexibility and covered with a spongy rubber material and then a layer of felt material was added. Their clothing, handmade, was also colorful felt. Heads of the dolls snapped on and off. Dolls were made in approximately 1:6 and 1:12 scale. The 1960 "Sta-Put" wired rubber family (catalog picture top left) measured 3-6". Wooden 1:12 scale dolls abstractly designed by Antonio Vitalli, gave children a full range of imaginative play, as they could become anyone or anything. They could be dragged and dropped and withstood rough play. These dolls were still available as late as 1963 and at that time, sold as a set of seven for $5.50 (catalog picture bottom left). Cloth dolls, insufficient examples to establish value. Rubber dolls, $10/each. Vitalli dolls, $45/set.

Creative Playthings' "Sta-Put" wire-framed rubber dolls had painted features and clothing that was sprayed with a plastic coating for long-lasting protection. The company thought them suitable for children 2-8 years old. There were initially five family members in 1:12 scale that sold for $6.25. Grandmother and grandfather were listed in their 1963 catalog for $2.95 a set. Eventually the five family members were available with white or brown skin. Community workers like a mailman, policeman, fireman, laborer, conductor, captain, and policeman were also available The dolls are pictured at the bottom of the photo. A confusingly similar set, unknown manufacturer, is shown at the top. The arms of most of these dolls are molded against their bodies. $10/each.

Other educational toy suppliers made large scale rubber doll families. This set was made by Marvel Education to appeal to classroom teachers. $5/each.

Community Playthings made families to inhabit its solidly constructed dollhouses, favorites of preschool teachers. The dolls at 1.25" thick, easily stood, and were suitable for block play. A family consisted of an 8" man, 7.75" woman, 5.5" boy and 5" girl. Community workers included firemen, conductors, and milkmen. Figures were made of solid maple or beech. Facial details and clothing were silk-screened onto the wooden shapes. $10/each.

Chapter 12

Hippies, Yuppies, and the Start of Another Era

The 1970s and 1980s saw considerable social change around the world. The global economy experienced unparalleled growth. Spendable income increased in all developed countries, and some undeveloped countries began to benefit from industrial development, expanding their consumer base. The Vietnam War came to a close, and the "less materialistic" communal philosophies of the Hippies quickly gave way to the voracious consumption of the Yuppies – generally the same people who had shed their bell-bottoms and donned corporate attire. Baby Boomers began to have children, and birth rates increased in most countries. Women began to enter the workforce at all levels in numbers never before seen, except during World War II. Increased divorce rates led to more single families. While more children were left to spend time alone or in the care of non-family members, the dominant entertainment provider was television. The first video games were introduced in 1972 and computers found their way into homes starting in the early 1980s, further turning children's attention away from traditional toys.

Economic conditions probably did more to influence toy and doll makers than any other factor. Families were affluent. They could afford the new electronics. Children no longer had to care for their toys in the same way that their grandparents did. If toys broke, they could be discarded and replaced. Especially in the United States, quality was not the object of toy manufacturers. Toys were designed to fit constantly changing fads and fashions.

Trends that had affected dollhouses and miniature dolls since the 1950s, continued through the next three decades. Collectors were still able to obtain fine display dolls and dollhouses, but the market for children was, in large part, mass-produced toys, often made in developing countries. The material of choice for toys was plastic, and considerable advance was made in material science, allowing for better molded detail and realism, but not necessarily longevity. Commercial dollhouses had abandoned concerns of scale and either "gone small" and cartoonish, as seen with Fisher Price's *Little People*, and Kenner's *Treetots*, or "gone large" and pastel as seen in the late 1980s and early 1990s in offerings by Little Tikes, Playskool, and Fisher Price. Both trends were aimed at children younger than the traditional dollhouse market, because older children had abandoned the "traditional." Appealing to older children, and further changing the market, were "playscale" houses and accessories compatible with *Barbie*. Mattel's *Sunshine Family* and Mego's houses and dolls based upon *The Walton's* television series, are examples of the trend.

Except for a few European producers like Erna Meyer and Caco, there was not significant choice in good quality dollhouse dolls. The market began to be served by doll artists producing very high-quality dolls. Using sophisticated clays and plastics, and with great attention to costume detail, these dolls surpass all but the finest dolls produced over the previous 100 years. These dolls are outside the scope of this book. The subject is left to be chronicled by others, as their artistry deserves thorough description.

B. Shackman & Co.

B. Shackman & Co. sold foreign and domestically made dollhouse miniatures, games, toys, and gifts beginning in 1898. In 1975, B. Shackman's catalogue advertised a family of four dolls. Dolls were packaged in a cardboard box advertising that they were fully bendable and hand-dressed. The dolls were found in Sears' 1979 catalog for $4.99 a set. Sears called their grouping of five dolls, which also included a 2.25" baby, *The Brown Family*. They appeared in a 1990 "Concord Miniatures" catalog for $18.99 a set. Another set of dolls, imported by B. Shackman and pictured in their 1975 catalog, was advertised as "sturdy, non-toxic and perfect for dollhouse play". Dolls were a pliable vinyl with hip and arm joints attached by wire to assist in their positioning. They were also advertised in the 1979 "Federal Smallwares" catalog selling undressed for $5.75, and $10.50, dressed.

Shackman's 1975 family included a 5.5" father and mother and a 3.5" girl and boy. Dolls had painted plastic swiveling heads and hard plastic hands and feet. Their bodies were wire frames with thread wrapping. Their molded hair and facial features were painted. They wore colorful, cloth clothing, with unfinished seams and hems. Dolls were labeled, "Copyright Shackman - Made in Hong Kong." Over the years, these dolls were dressed in various styles depicting an old-fashioned era as well as modern times. $30/set MIB.

Another 1975 Shackman four-member family was made in Hong Kong. Father was 5.5"; mother, 4.75"; brother, 3.875"; sister, 3.5". Dolls were a pliable vinyl with hip and arm joints attached by wire to assist in their positioning. They had painted hair, facial features, and shoes, and wore hand-made clothing. In the Shackman catalog they were available in regular clothes, *Kate Greenaway* costumes, nightclothes, or unclothed, to be dressed by the owner. $30/set MIB.

Sidney A. Tarrson Co. ("Tarco")

Sidney A Tarrson made plastic crib toys, pull-toys, and games to entertain infants through young adults. Tarco made two different series of dollhouse figures, contemporary and old fashioned. Figures were packed as sets in a cardboard box and also were sold individually. The cardboard box pictures a dollhouse, although it is not known if Tarco, in fact, made it.

Tarco's old fashioned family contained solid vinyl figures that measured: father, 5.5"; mother and maid, 5"; older girl, 3.75"; younger boy, 3.5". Hair, facial features, clothes, and shoes were molded into the figure and then colorfully painted. $30/set MIB.

The contemporary Tarco family was a vinyl family of five: father, mother, older boy holding a football, younger sister, and little brother. Father stood 5.5"; mother, 5.125"; older boy, 4"; younger sister, 3.5"; little brother, 2.75". $30/set MIB.

School Toys

A line of red, soft-plastic toys thought to be manufactured in the 1970s, were most probably used in kindergartens and elementary schools like flash cards to help develop English language skills, or in foreign language study.

School Toy's three inch boy and girl figures in various poses would be suitable for dollhouse play. Hair, facial features, clothes, shoes, socks, and accessories were all molded. $5/each.

Right:
The bodies of Fisher Price's "Little People" were of different heights and some were molded or turned to suggest clothing. The early dolls were made of wood; a second major version was plastic and wood, and eventually the dolls were made entirely of plastic. Fisher-Price settled on a basic base shape in 1965, which they continued to make until 1990. The very first all wood figures have higher value in today's market. $3-10/each.

Fisher-Price

In 1930, four people living in East Aurora, New York, all involved in the toy industry, formed Fisher-Price. Herman Fisher was the former president and general manager of "All-Fair" toy & games. Irving Price, a former employee of F.W. Woolworth Co., supplied financial background. His wife, Margaret Evans Price, an illustrator and writer of children's books, helped with art design on toys. Helen Schelle, owner of Penny Walker Toy Shop, was able to provide management and retail expertise. They began their company making quality wood toys with very colorful lithography, eye-appealing to young children. Employing just over a dozen employees, making 25¢ an hour, their studio was an old farm. Their hard work and love of their craft paid off. By 1950, they were considered a leader in the world of toys. Fisher-Price was purchased by Quaker Oats in 1969, and by Mattel in 1993.

In 1959, Fisher-Price sold a school bus with removable little wood figures shaped to fit into the holes drilled as bus seats. Aimed at preschoolers aged 1-4, many other manufacturers like Illco, Playskool, and Kenner made their own versions and styles, firmly establishing the genre. Fisher-Price kept expanding their line of pre-school playsets utilizing the figures and, in 1969, introduced the *Play Family House,* followed in 1974 by the *Play Family A-Frame*. Popularly known as *Little People,* dolls were similarly shaped with a spherical head, generally sitting on a cylindrical base, without arms or legs. The dolls, introduced in 1965, continued to be made until 1990. The full array of this type doll is beyond the scope of this book.

In 1978, Fisher-Price made a modern 3-story dollhouse with eight sets of furniture and three figures, man, woman and baby. The baby was also was sold with the "Baby's Room" of furniture. In 1979, a 3.25" girl and a collie dog were added to a slightly modified family. In 1981 a lighted Victorian styled dollhouse was introduced. The doll family, however, was new. There were four figures. Father was 4"; mother, 3.875"; girl, 3.375"; boy, 3.125". They were chubbier, plastic dolls with movable heads, painted hair and eyes. They wore molded, painted clothing and painted shoes. In addition to shoulder and hip joints, their knees were flexible. Dolls were sold as dollhouse accessories in boxed sets for $7.99, or individually. The collie dog continued to be sold with this set. In 1983, a family of four dollhouse neighbors was added to the line, dressed in different colored outfits. The family's clothing was modified in 1985. In 1993 Fisher Price introduced its large-scale pastel *Dream Dollhouse*. The large-scale dollhouses of Little Tikes and Playskool competed for a share of this market, aimed at small, not so dexterous hands.

Fisher Price's first scale doll house, introduced in 1978 came with 4" man and woman made of hard plastic, jointed at the arms, waist, and legs. Their heads were movable. With painted hair, eyes, and eyebrows for facial detail and painted shoes, they had clothing of vinyl and hard plastic. A 1.75" hard plastic baby with molded, painted pajamas also accompanied this set. The dolls' clothing was slightly modified in this 1979 set. A 3.25" girl and a collie dog were added to the family. $10/each.

By 1985, Fisher-Price was calling its lighted Victorian dollhouse a "deluxe version." Four family members look very similar to the 1981 versions, with some color changes in the clothing of the father, mother, and daughter. $10/each.

Dream Doll House

Ages 3 and up

Three fun levels for realistic play.

Easily folds for storage.

A.

A. Fisher-Price® Dream Doll House
3 yrs. and up. Little girls' dreams will come true with the Fisher-Price Dream Doll House, the place where fun unfolds. The two-story house has Victorian styling and features easy access to each of the rooms from the front or back. The doors open and the doorbell really works. A 12-piece accessory set and family of three are included. When play time is over, the entire house and accessories fold away for quick storage.
Approx. retail price $99.99.

B.

B. Families
3 yrs. and up. Families of custom-designed figures of Asian American African American,or Hispanic heritage Each family includes mom, dad, little sister and baby. Each family sold separately .
Approx. retail price $12.99 ea.

40

In 1993 Fisher Price introduced its large-scale pastel "Dream Dollhouse." Four-member families were completely redesigned. Asian American, African American, and Hispanic heritage families were also offered. $15/set MIB.

Little Tikes competed in the large-scale toy dollhouse market and featured a vinyl, jointed family of 4. $15/set MIB.

Playskool's large scale dollhouse offering included not only two families of different racial origin, but also neighbors and profession dolls. $7.50/each.

The Littles

In 1980, Mattel introduced a plastic, ½" scale Victorian style dollhouse, together with a full line of metal and plastic furniture and accessories to fill it. The three-member family that inhabited it was *The Littles*. The dolls' plastic heads were oversized, not unlike Mattel's *Liddle Kiddles*, first introduced in 1966. Their family grew to include five daughters and one son. Becky Littles, a very rare doll, was not introduced until 1982, and may not have been sold in the United States.

Mattel's "Littles" had jointed, plastic arms and legs, and their heads had painted features with various eye colors. They ranged in size from 2.5" to 3", except for the 1" baby. Female dolls had rooted hair in various colors and styles. Father and Kenny Littles had painted hair, and baby had molded, unpainted hair. Clothing was a mix of fabric and vinyl. The dolls, frustratingly unable to stand alone, were made in the Philippines until they were discontinued in1983. Mother, father, and baby were packaged in a cardboard box and called the Littles Family (pictured by the front stairs). They were available with light and dark skin. Mattel produced six more dolls, most of which were sold boxed with a complete room of furniture or with a single piece of furniture, e.g. Flossie was packaged with the complete bedroom set, but also available with just the bed. Becky Littles, probably not made for the United States market, is missing from the picture. $10/each.

Tomy

Tomy Corporation was founded in 1924 by Eichiro Tomiyama in Tokyo, Japan. The company is well known for its strong toy innovation and its long history of trade with the United States and other countries. They were Japan's third largest toy company before their 2006 merger with Takara, Japan's second largest toy maker. Now known as Tomy Company Ltd. it is led by its global president and CEO, Kantaro Tomiyama, grandson of the founder.

In 1980, Tomy Corporation advertised a new dollhouse with the heading "It's for little decorators with big ideas." Perhaps the last of the "traditional" commercially made scale dollhouses, the playset was called *Smaller Home and Garden.* The house, designed for the United States market, was contemporary and made of plastic and fiberboard. A full line of attractive up-to-date furnishings and accessories, as well as a family of four plastic dolls, completed the line. It was manufactured in Japan in 1:18 scale.

The dolls accompanying the Tomy "Smaller Homes" line had molded painted hair, facial features, and clothing, except for the mother's cloth skirt. Mustached father stood 4.5"; mother with sandals, 4"; girl, 3.5"; boy, 2.375". Dolls had jointed arms and legs. In 1982, a nursery and baby was added to the playset. The plastic 1.25" baby, in a molded yellow diaper, had jointed arms and legs. The nursery with baby is harder to find today. The family of four sold for $9.99. Four-member family, $40/set MIB. Baby $20.

Appendix

Doll Variations of Certain Post-War Doll Makers

Twinky Dolls
- Bo Peep
- Little Red Riding Hood
- Peter Pan
- Little Lord Fauntleroy
- Mom Beck
- Colonel
- Little Colonel
- Walker
- Large and Small Witch
- Fairy Queen
- Small Clown
- Large and Small Santa
- Holy Family (4)
- Male Indian
- Female Indian w/ papoose
- Pilgrim Family (4)
- Colonial Family (4)
- Scots Family (4)
- Russian Family (4)
- Spanish Family (4)
- Dutch Family (4)
- Swedish Family (4)
- Swiss Family (4)
- Mexican Family (4)
- Hawaiian Family (4)
- Western Family (4)
- Large and Small Arab
- Coronation Couple
- Dollhouse Family (4)
- White Baby, Black Baby
- Aunt & Uncle
- Grandfather
- Bride and Groom
- Formal Lady
- Butler
- Chef
- Maid
- Cook
- Nurse
- Army Man and Woman
- Navy Man and Woman
- Yachtsman
- Nun (2 different)
- Baseball Player
- Football Player
- Majorette
- Ski Girl
- Girl Scout
- Brownie

Winsor Wooden Head Dolls
Dollhouse Dolls
- Mother
- Father
- Boy
- Girl
- Toddler
- Baby
- Grandma
- Grandpa
- Infant
- Swaddling blanket
- Infant in cradle
- Toddler in high chair
- Toddler in long dress in high chair
- Child in sleepers (various colors) holding a stuffed animal
- Child on rocking horse
- Children in Dr. Dentons
- Children in snowsuits with hoods (various colors)
- Girl in long dress holding a bouquet
- Girl with straw basket
- Girl jumping rope
- Girl holding a matching doll
- Girl in blue jeans
- Girl in jacket with plaid skirt
- Kate Greenaway Girl
- Choir Girl holding music folder
- Little Red Riding Hood
- Boy in shorts
- Baseball player
- Cowboy
- Bunny Children
- Children at a birthday table with crepe paper hats
- Woman in long winter coat, hand muff, hat
- Door-to-Door Market Researcher
- Frontiersman
- Baker
- Sea Captain in yellow slicker
- Grandma in long white apron
- Grandma in wooden rocker, knitting
- Grandma sitting in a wing chair, long shawl
- Grandma with a plate of apples & knife
- Grandpa in wooden rocker, reading NY Times
- Grandparents in overalls with terrier dog
- Bridal Party
- Pilgrim Family
- Carolers
- Angel
- Santa
- Santa on antlered reindeer
- Elf on small reindeer
- Mr. & Mrs. Santa Claus with tree & presents
- The Long Sermon-woodenhead grandma & girl seated in wooden pew
- Driftwood Boys
- Crèche, Jesus, Mary & Joseph
- Puritan Kitchen - Diorama
- Schoolroom with plastic desks – Diorama
- Original Cohasset schoolroom – Diorama

Tiny Town Dolls
Series Names
- Kiddies
- Ballerinas
- Nationalities
- Story Characters
- Moderns
- Maids of Yesteryear
- Specialties
- Teacher and 3 Pupils
- Family Set (4)
- Elves
- Tiny Town Tots

Dolls
- Linda
- Mary
- Pat
- Betty
- Ann
- Jean
- Chickie
- Honey
- Blondie
- Mickey
- Peggy
- Cathy
- Judy
- Sally
- Nancy
- Laurie
- Jeanie
- Jessie
- Suzy
- Elena
- Babs
- Heather
- School Girl
- Sister
- Brother
- Mother
- Cowgirl & Cowboy
- Lazy Daisy
- Buttons & Bows
- Little Peasant
- Folk Dancer 1 & 2
- Little Artist
- Outdoor Girl
- Fiesta Girl
- Sailor
- Ballerinas with choice of hair color & tutu
- Irish Colleen
- Scotch Lass
- China Girl & Boy
- Chinese Princess
- Dutch Girl & Boy
- Indian Girl & Boy
- Irish Girl & Boy
- Scotch Girl & Boy
- Spanish Girl & Boy
- Swiss Girl & Boy
- Queen of Hearts
- Red Riding Hood
- Goldilocks
- Pretty Milkmaid
- Marjorie Day
- Alice
- Bo-Peep
- Cinderella
- Thumbelina
- Snow Queen
- Miss Muffet
- Hansel & Gretel
- Polly Flinders
- Farmer Boy & Farmerette
- Bride
- June Bride (a special)
- Groom
- Bridesmaid
- Clown
- Majorette
- Nurse
- Abagail
- Ermaline
- Belinda
- Deborah
- Clarissa
- Matilda
- Colonial Girl & Boy
- Puritan Girl & Boy
- Eton Girl & Boy
- Valentine Girl
- June Graduation
- Easter Girl
- Prissy
- Halloween Witch
- Ball Player
- Mother's Day Grandma
- Christmas Doll
- Baby
- Teacher & 3 Pupils - hair color variations
- Family Set of 4
- Elves
- Tiny Town Tots, girls & boys - hair color variations

Flagg Dolls 1:18 scale
- Father
- Mother
- Girl
- Boy
- Baby
- Twin Babies
- Grandfather
- Grandmother
- Maid
- Colored Mammy
- Chef
- Doctor
- Nurse
- School Teacher
- Nun
- Minister
- Gardener
- Policeman
- Postman
- Fireman
- Crossing Guard
- Bride
- Groom
- Bridesmaids-costumed in 4 colors
- Flower Girls-costumed in 3 colors
- Puritan Man/John Alden
- Puritan Woman/Priscilla
- Puritan Boy
- Puritan Girl
- Indian Brave

Indian Maiden
Cowboy
Cowgirl
Farmer
Farmerette/Milkmaid
Clown
Pixie
Tiny Cherub with wings
Ballerina-costumed in 3 colors
Tiny Boy Partner
Senorita
Mother Goose Dolls:
Bo Peep
Bunny Girl
Cinderella
Davy Crockett
Frontier Woman
Jack & the Beanstalk
Jack-Be-Nimble
Little Boy Blue
Mistress Mary
Peter Pan
Wendy
Tinkerbell
Pied Piper
Red Riding Hood
Grandmother Wolf
Robin Hood
Maid Marion
Friar Tuck

Grecon Dolls
Father
Mother
Boy-older and younger
Girl-older and younger
Baby
Toddler Twins
Kids dressed for indoors, outdoors, in pj's
Grandfather
Grandmother
Maid
Chef
Nurse
Chauffeur
Postman
English Policeman
Minister
Ballet Dancer
Clown
Cowboy
Cowgirl
Equestrian
Gardener
Hiker
Pianist in Evening Dress
Tennis Player
Golliwogs
Pixies
Bride
Groom
Bridesmaid
Flower Girl
Austrian, Male and Female
Dutch, Male and Female
Scotch, Male and Female
Swiss, Male and Female
Scots Guard, Bag Piper
Grenadier Guard
Household Cavalry Life Guard
Beefeater Tower of London Guard
Royal Navy Dress Uniform
Royal Navy W.R.E.N.
Queen Elizabeth II, Philip, and Charles

Tomac Dolls
Father
Mother
Girl with Cat
Girl with Dog
Doll in Snowsuit
Maid
Bride
Groom
Boy Scout
Girl Scout
Guide
Golfer
Hiker
Soccer Player
Cowboy
Indian
Elves
Pirates
Black Island Women in various costumes
Black Island Men in various costumes
Bermuda Bobby
Dutch Male & Female
Scots
Swiss
Queen
Beefeater
Royal Guard
Little Red Riding Hood

Dol-Toi Dolls – Plaster/Plastic Heads
Father
Mother
Boy-older and younger
Girl-older and younger
Plastic Baby
Family in Coats
Riding Family
Wedding Party
African Heritage Family
Indian Sub-Continent Family
Maid
Nurse
Chef
Mailman
Brownies/Scouts/Troop Leader
Cowboy
Snow Fairy
Father Christmas

Dol-Toi Dolls – Nation's Dolls
Bulgarian
Cornish
Dutch
Eskimo
Mexican
Persian
Rumanian
Scottish
Tyrolean
Welsh

Baps Dolls
Fairy Tale Characters
Alice in Wonderland and the White Rabbit
Baa Baa Black Sheep
Beauty and the Beast
Cinderella and Prince Charming
Chimney Sweep
Goldilocks & the Three Bears
Goosey Goosey Gander
Hans Brinker and Sister
Hansel, Gretel, and Witch
Heidi and her Grandfather
Huck Finn & Bessie
Jack and Jill
Little Black Sambo, Mambo & Jambo, Tigers
Little Bo Peep
Little Jack Horner
Little Miss Muffet
Little Red Riding Hood
Mary had a Little Lamb
Mary, Mary, Quite Contrary
Peter Cottontail
Peter Pan and Tinkerbell
Peter, Peter Pumpkin Eater
Puss in Boots
Queen and Knave of Hearts
Rain, Rain Go Away
Ride a Cockhorse
Rumpelstiltskin
Simple Simon and Pieman
Sing a Song of Sixpence
Snow White and the Seven Dwarves
Three Little Kittens
Three Little Pigs
Wynken, Blynken, & Nod

Nationality Dolls
Bavarian
Black Forest
Hessian
Hungarian
Norwegian
Sicilian
Spanish
Spreewald
Swedish
Yugoslavian

18th century Court Dolls

Commonwealth Dolls of the World
Girls
American Indian
China
Cowgirl
Cuba
Czechoslovakia
Denmark
Early American
Egypt
Eskimo
Finland
France
Germany
Haiti
Hawaii
Holland
Italy
Japan
Mexico
Norway
Portugal
Scotland
Siam
Sweden
Switzerland

Boys
Argentina
Austria/Switzerland
China
Cowboy
India
Java/Japan
Korea
Spain

Van Brode Dolls of the World Pairs
Bali
Burma
China
Cuba
Egypt
England
Hawaii
Hungary
Ireland
Italy
Mexico
Scotland
Spain
Turkey
Dutch "Van" & "Brode"
West Indies

Bibliography

Ackerman, Evelyn. **Dolls in Miniature**. Annapolis, Maryland: Gold Horse Publishing, 1991. First published 1983.

———. "Grecon Miniature Dolls." *Antique Doll Collector*, August 2006.

———. "Modern Miniatures." *Dolls*, June-July 1992.

"American Made Celluloid Dolls." *Playthings*, March 1940.

"American Toys are Doing Very Well." *New York Times*, December 19, 1920.

Angione, Genevieve. *All Bisque and Half-Bisque Dolls*. Rochester, New York: Thomas Nelson & Sons, 1969.

Anne Beate Design. "History." http://www.annebeatedesign.dk.

Antiques Digest. "Wax and Composition Dolls." Old and Sold: Antiques Auction and Marketplace. http://www.oldandsold.com/articles01/article582.shtml.

Antique Doll Advisors. "Bru Dolls, The Quintessential Image..." The Antique Dolls Collectors Online Advisors. http://www.antiquedolls-collectors-onlineadvisors.com/Bru-Dolls.html.

Arkins, Dian C. "Just Like Mom's." *American Country Collectibles*, date unknown.

Armistead, Judith. "Tynietoy's Elusive Cloth Dollhouse Dolls." *Antique Doll Collector*, April 2008.

Arndt, Jessie Ash. "Doll Groups Become Decor." *The Christian Science Monitor*, January 19, 1956.

Axe, John. *Effanbee: A Collector's Encyclopedia, 1949-Present*. Grantsville, Maryland: Hobby House Press, Inc., 1996.

Bateman, Thelma. *Delightful Dolls, Antique and Otherwise.* Grantsville, Maryland: Hobby House Press, 1976.

Blue-Box Toys. "About Us." http://www.blueboxtoys.com.

Bouchard, Zendelle. "Bisque and China Dolls." Vintage Doll Collector.com. http://www.vintagedollcollector.com/bisque.htm.

Brean, Herbert. "Top Toymaker's Buying Guide." *Life*, November 23, 1959.

Brett, Mary. "Ideal Plastic Dollhouse Furniture." *Miniature Collector*, July-August 1994.

———. "1950's Dollhouse Accessories by Irwin." *Miniature Collector*, September 1997.

———. *Tomart's Price Guide to Tin Litho Dollhouses & Plastic Dollhouse Furniture*. Dayton, Ohio: Tomart Publications, 1997.

Bright, Virginia. "Cohasset Mother All Dolled Up." *Boston Daily Globe*, June 20, 1957.

Brooke, Bob. "Parian Ware-Affordable Art for the Masses." *The Antiques Almanac*. http://www.theantiquesalmanac.com/parian.htm.

Butler Brothers Catalog. Various issues. Chicago, IL: Butler Brothers, 1920-1930.

Callicott, Catherine Dorris, and Lawson Holderness. *In Praise of Dollhouses*. New York: William Morrow & Company, Inc., 1978.

Coleman, Dorothy S., Elizabeth A. Coleman, and Evelyn J. Coleman. *The Collector's Encyclopedia of Dolls*. New York: Crown Publishers, 1968.

———. *The Collector's Encyclopedia of Dolls*. Vol. 2. New York: Crown Publishers, 1986.

Coleman, Evelyn J., ed. *1914 Marshall Field & Co. Kringle Society Dolls*. Cumberland, Maryland: Hobby House Press, 1980.

Coleman, Evelyn J., and Dorothy S. Coleman. "American Dolls' Shoes, 1860s to 1880s." *Doll Reader*, August-September 1984.

Cook, Cathy. "Wolverine Toys: Tin Litho Stars." *Collectibles Flea Market Finds*, Spring 1997.

Diehl, Fred. "My Merry." *Dollhouse Toys n' Us*, June 2001.

The Doll Collectors of America, Inc. *Doll Collectors Manual 1956-1957*. Boston: The Doll Collectors of America, Inc., 1956.

Doll Reference. "Armand Marseille Doll Co.-Dolls 1885-1950s Germany." http://www.dollreference.com/marseille_armand_dolls.html.

———. "Celluloid Dolls 1869-1950s." http://www.dollreference.com/celluloid_dolls1869_1950s.html.

———. "China Head Dolls 1840-1940." http://www.dollreference.com/china_head_dolls.html.

———. "Jne Bru & Cie-Dolls 1866-1899 French." http://www.dollreference.com/jne_bru_cie.html.

Donovan, Charles, Jr. "Renwal! And Sometimes Other Stuff!" *Dollhouse Toys n' US*, October 2001.

Earnshaw, Nora. *Collecting Dolls Houses & Miniatures.* Tampa, Florida: Pincushion Press, 1993.

Edward, Linda. *Cloth Dolls from Ancient to Modern*. Atglen, Pennsylvania: Schiffer Publishing Ltd., 1997.

———. "Crepe Paper Dolls." *The Museum Doll Shop*. http://www.dollmuseum.com.

———. "Doll Treasures of Italy." *Doll News*, Spring 1999.

———. "Tynietoy and the Toy Furniture Shop." *Antique Doll Collector*, April 2005.

87th Scale. General information about Ari. http://www.87thscale.info/ari.htm.

Ellenburg, M. Kelly. *Effanbee, The Dolls with the Golden Hearts.* North Kansas City, Missouri: Trojan Press, Inc., 1973.

Elster, Barbara. "The Art of Toymaking (The Bodo Hennig Story)." *Dollhouse Miniatures*, June 2000.

"Emenee Toys." *Playthings*, March 1951, August 1952, and March 1964.

Erna Meyer. General information. http://www.erna-meyer.com.

"Experts See Toys in Stimulant Role." *New York Times*, October 5, 1948.

F.A.O. Schwarz 1930 Christmas Catalog. Reprint, Evanston, Illinois: Jeanne Breslin Vintage Catalogs, 2004.

Ferguson, Candee. "Colleen Moore Doll Castle Reigns at Toy Museum." *Antique Trader's Collector Magazine*, December 2001.

Fisher, Judy. "Lenci Miniatures from the Regions of Italy." *Antique Doll Collector*, September 2006.

Foreign Folk Dolls. Catalog. Independence, MO: Kimport Dolls, 1944.

Formanek-Brunell, Miriam. *Made to Play House: Dolls and the Commercialization of American Girlhood, 1830-1930*. Baltimore, Maryland: Johns Hopkins University Press, 1988.

Foulke, Jan. "All-Bisque Dolls by Kling & Co." *Doll Reader*, October 1990.

———. *14th Blue Book of Dolls & Values*. Grantsville, Maryland: Hobby House Press, 1999.

———. *Kestner King of Dollmakers*. Grantsville, Maryland: Hobby House Press, Inc., 2000.

———. *16th Blue Book of Dolls & Values*. Grantsville, Maryland: Hobby House Press, 2003.

———. "A Study of Käthe Kruse Doll I." *Doll Reader*, December 1991-January 1992.

———. *12th Blue Book of Dolls & Values*. Grantsville, Maryland: Hobby House Press, 1995.

Fredge, Frederique. "Dolls by Milwaukee Artist Help Reclaim 'Bad Children'." *Milwaukee Journal*, September 23, 1944.

"The Friendly Folks Motel Checkout Time: 11 a.m." *Plastic Figure & Playset Collector*, April 1993.

Geppert, T. J. "Auburn Educational Safe-Play Toys." *Plastic Figure & Playset Collector*, August 1996.

Gervais, Cherie. "The Jay Dolls of Ireland." *Doll News,* Summer 2004.

Goldstein, Elaine Dann. "Shopper's World; In Folk Dress or Fine Brocade, Handmade Dolls of Thailand." *New York Times*, July 28, 2007.

"Grecon Dolls." *International Dolls House News*, Winter 1974/75.

Griffin, Peni R. "The Peni Doll Page." http://users.idworld.net/griffin/doll.htm.

Grimshaw, Susan. "Between Friends." *Antique Doll Collector,* December 2006.

Grout, Jean. "BAPS." *Doll News*, Spring 2003.

Guyette, Barbara. "Remember the Littles." *Doll Reader,* February 2004.

Hanlon, Bill. "Dr. Islyn Thomas." *U.S. Dimestore*, Bill Hanlon Enterprises. http://www.prestostore.com/cgi-bin/storefront.pl?ref=americandimestore.

———. "Peco" and "Premier Products Co.," *Collecting Toy Soldiers*, No. 2, by Richard O'Brien. Florence, Alabama: Books Americana Inc., 1992.

———. *Plastic Toys: Dimestore Dreams of the 40s & 50s*. Atglen, Pennsylvania: Schiffer Publishing, Ltd., 1993.

Hardwick, Kay. "A Discussion of Plastic Toy Molds with Islyn Thomas." *Playthings*, October 1953.

Hartland Collectibles. General information. http://www.hartlandcollectibles.com.

Haug, Melissa. "The English Poured Wax Doll." *Victoriana*. http://www.victoriana.com/antiquedolls.antiquedoll.htm.

Herbst, Penny. "Käthe Kruse Dollhouse Dolls." *Doll Reader*, May 2005.

"Here's the Artistic Doll---That's the Latest." *New York Times*, February 6, 1910.

Holz, Loretta. *The How to Book of International Dolls*. New York: Crown Publishers, Inc., 1980.

History of Bridgeport and Vicinity. Vol. 2. New York-Chicago: The S. J. Clarke Publishing Co., 1917.

How It All Began, Celebrating 50 Years: 1948-1988. Brochure. Rifton, NY: Community Playthings, 1997.

"It's a Wonderful Toy... It's Ideal." *Plastic Figure & Playset Collector*, October 1994.

Izen, Judith. "Doll Talk-Don't Overlook Irwin Toys as Today's Collectibles." *Toy Shop*, May 24, 1996.

Jacobs, Flora Gill. *Dolls' Houses in America*. New York: Charles Scribner's Sons, 1974.

Jensen, Don. "Patsy The Ageless Imp." *Collector's Showcase,* December 1989-January 1990.

Johl, Janet Pagter. *The Fascinating Story of Dolls*. Watkins Glen, New York: century House, 1941. Reissued with additions, Watkins Glen, New York: century House, 1969.

———. *Still More About Dolls*. New York: H. L. Lindquist Publications, 1950.

———. *Your Dolls and Mine*. New York: H. L. Lindquist Publications, 1952.

Johnson, Judy M. "History of Paper Dolls." *The Doll Sourcebook*, December 2005.

Judd, Polly, and Pam Judd. *European Costumed Dolls*. Grantsville, Maryland: Hobby House Press, Inc., 1994.

Kämmer & Reinhardt. "My Darling" *Dolls 1927 Catalog*. Reprinted with introduction and editing by Dorothy S. Coleman. Des Moines, Iowa: Wallace-Homestead Book Co., 1972.

Katz, A. M. "Ideal Plastics' Future Plans." *Playthings*, June 1951.

Kern, Rusty. "Inside Marx, Part I: The Real Louis." *Plastic Figure & Playset Collector*, February 1998.

———. "Inside Marx II: The Playset Kings." *Plastic Figure & Playset Collector,* April 1998.

———. "Inside Marx III: The Playsets." *Plastic Figure & Playset Collector,* June 1998.

———. "Inside Marx IV: The Figures & Figureheads." *Plastic Figure & Playset Collector,* August 1998.

———. "Inside Marx V: Memo from Louis." *Plastic Figure & Playset Collector*, October 1998.

———. "Inside Marx VI: Christmas to Christmas-The Assembly Line." *Plastic Figure & Playset Collector,* December 1998.

Kernon, Gillian. "Dol-Toi Dolls." *International Dolls House News*, Autumn 1991.

———. "Dol-Toi Products (Stamford) Ltd." *International Dolls House News*, Spring 1987.

King, Constance Eileen. "Art in Porcelain." *Doll Reader*. http://www.dollreader.com/tutorials.php?id=85.

———. *The Collector's History of Dolls' Houses, Doll's House Dolls, and Miniatures*. New York: St. Martin's Press, 1983.

Koch, Rick. "Rick's Pix." *Plastic Figure & Playset Collector*, February and April 1996.

Korbeck, Sharon. "A Tale of Little People: Collecting Modern Fisher-Price." *Toy Collector,* December 1995.

Krombholz, Mary Gorham. "Identifying German Chinas and Parians-Part One." *Antique Doll Collector,* June 2007.

———. "Identifying German Chinas and Parians-Part Two." *Antique Doll Collector*, September 2007.

———. *Identifying German Parian Dolls*. Cumberland, Maryland: Reverie Publishing Co., 2006.

———. "Under This Roof." *Doll News*, Spring 1995.

Leopard, Dave. *Rubber Toy Vehicles*. Paducah, Kentucky: Collector Books, 2003.

Lavitt, Wendy. "Innovative Importers." *Dolls,* August 1995.

Lewis-Smith, Anne. "Mrs. Ibotson Fashions Dolls' Furniture." *Lincoln, Rutland & Stamford Mercury*, January 29, 1965.

Linden, Gary J. "Marx Nursery." *Plastic Figure & Playset Collector*, October 1989.

Lipinski, Angelika. "Celluloid and the Doll Industry In Germany—1896-1960." *Doll Reader,* September 1988.

———. "Celluloid Dolls by Bushow & Beck." *Doll Reader*, September 1992.

"The Little King." *Time,* December 12, 1955.

Lobel, Carl. "Jaymar Wood Figures." *Collectors' Showcase*, November-December 1993.

Lotz, Jean D. "Miscellaneous European Wood Dolls." *The Lotz Doll Pages*. http://www.lotzdollpages.com/leuro.html

"Louis Marx Toy King." *Fortune*, January 1946.

MacKay, Ruth. "White Collar Girl." *Chicago Daily Tribune*, September 14, 1943.

Marshall, Michiko. "About Dolls." *EastWestCrafts.Com*. http://www.eastwestcrafts.com/about-doll/about-doll.htm.

McEvoy, J. P. and Peggy McEvoy. "Talk with a Toy King." *Reader's Digest*, January 1955.

Millsap, Cheryl-Anne. "Look at my Treasures!" *The Spokesman-Review*, March 9, 2006.

"Miniatour III." *Nutshell News*, Summer 1997.

"Miniature League of Nations." *Games & Toys*, July 1960.

Morse, Sue Garbill. "My Quest for More Lundby," *Dollhouse Toys n' Us*, September 1999.

Murray, Lynn. "From the World of Flowers through the Door of Hope," *Antique Doll Collector*, May 2007.

_____. "Käthe Kruse Dollhouse Dolls." *Doll News*, Summer 2004.

Museum of Science and Industry/Chicago. *Colleen Moore's Fairy Castle*. Milwaukee, Wisconsin: Ideals Publishing Corporation, 1981.

Musser, Cynthia E. "China's Door of Hope Mission Dolls." *Dolls*, April 2007.

_____. "Dolls in Foreign Costume: Souvenirs of Travel." *Dolls*, November 2007.

My Dream Dollhouse. "Fisher-Price" and "Dollhouse Fugure ID 2001-2007." http://mydreamdollhouse.com.

Nisbet, Peggy. *The Peggy Nisbet Story*. Cumberland, Maryland: Hobby House Press, Inc., 1988.

"Now It Can Be Told." *Playthings*, November 1945.

"Ny-Lint Adds to Extensive Line of Scale-Model Scale Toys." *Playthings,* March 1963.

O'Brien, Richard. *Collecting Toy Soldiers*. No. 2. Florence, Alabama: Books Americana Inc., 1992.

O'Neill, Eleanor. "The Littles by Mattel." *Dollhouse & Miniature Collector's Quarterly*, October 1990.

Orgeron, Cynthia. "Julie Ann, a Louisiana Original." *Doll News*, Summer 1998.

Osborne, Marion. *Bartons "Model Homes."* Chilwell, Nottingham: privately printed, 1988.

Palka, Kurt. "Schildkrot, King of Celluloid Dolls." *Doll Reader,* May 2006.

"Paper Dolls." *Collectibles Flea Market Finds*, Spring, 1996.

Pennegues, Dominique. "French Celluloid Dolls, Societe Industrielle de Celluloid." *Doll Reader*, December 1991-January 1992.

Pinsky, Maxine A. Greenberg's Guide to Marx Toys. 2 vols. Sykersville, Maryland: Greenberg Publishing Company, Inc. 1988-90.

Planton, Patricia S. "Grecon Little People." *Doll Reader*, February 2004.

Preh GmbH. "Company History." General information about PlasticBaby. http://www.preh.com/rw_nlmm/main.asp?WebID=preh2_e&PageID=505.

Plastics Academy Staff. "Islyn Thomas, O.B.E.-Hall of Fame Entry." *The Plastics Academy's Hall of Fame*. http://www.plasticshalloffame.com./articles.php?articleld=129.
Processed Plastic. "About Us." General information about Tim Mee. http://www.processedplastic.com./aboutus.html
Redgate, Russell J. "Even Wall Street Brokers Play with 'Wubba Dollies'-The Kind Ted Braitling's Shop Makes for Santa's Sack." *Bridgeport Sunday Post,* December 3, 1939.
Reed, Robert. "The Fisher Price Story." *Treasure Chest*, December 1995.
———. "The World of Marx Toys." *Treasure Chest*, April 1995.
Reed, Sonja. "China Heads and Parians." *National Doll World*, September-October 1989.
Ridenour, Glenn F. "Meet Mr. Schuck Tim Mee Employee." *Plastic Figure & Playset Collector,* August 1992.
Robinson, Julie P. "History of Collectible Plastic Materials." *Celluloid Forever!* http://www.celluloidforever.com/HistoryofCollectiblePlasticMaterials.html.
Roeder, Nancy. "The DMCQ Mailbox." *Dollhouse & Miniature Collector's Quarterly*, Spring 1996.
Sabulis, Cindy. *Collector's Guide to Dolls of the 1960s and 1970s*. Paducah, Kentucky: Collector Books, 2004. Orig. pub. 2000.
Schmuhl, Marian. "Pliant Playthings of the Past." *Dolls*, December 1993.
Shorrock, Eugenia S. "Celluloid Dolls." *Doll Collectors Manual 1973*. Boston: The Doll Collectors of America, Inc., 1973.
Siccardi, Rosita. "The Destiny of 'Una bambola e altre creazioni.'" Translated by Patricia Hayes. *The Lenci Doll Collector.* http://www.lenci-dolls.net/History_of_Lenci_felt_dolls.html.
Smith, Michelle L. *Marx Toys Sampler.* Iola, Wisconsin: Krause Publications, 2000.
Smith, Patricia R. *Effanbee: Dolls That Touch Your Heart*. Paducah, Kentucky: Collector Books, 1983.
———. *Doll Values*. 5th series. Paducah, Kentucky: Collector Books, 1987.
Snyder, Dee. "Colleen Moore's Doll Castle - by Rich Toys." *Nutshell News*, February 1988.
———. "England's ¾" Dol Toi." *Nutshell News*, January 1981.
———. "Flagg Folks." *Nutshell News*, May 1991.
———. "Grecon Dolls." *Nutshell News*, February 1989.
Sprecher, Kent. *General information about MPC.* Toy Soldier HQ, Inc. http://www.angelfire.com/biz/toysoldierhq/MPC1.html.
St. George, Eleanor. *Dolls of Three Centuries*. New York: Charles Scribner's Sons, 1951.
"Stamford Museum." *Dolls House & Miniature Scene*, October 2003.
State of Illinois. "Dolls in the Looking Glass: The Joy E. Orozco Collection." Illinois State Museum. http://www.museum.state.il.us/exhibits/changing/orozco/france.html.
"The Story of Ny-lint Toys." *Playthings*, September 1949.
Story Land Park. Where Fantasy Lives. Brochure, 1992.
Stover, Carol J. *Small Dolls of the 40s & 50s*. Paducah, Kentucky: Collector Books, 2002.
Stuecher, Mary Rickert. "Paper Palaces." *International Doll World,* October 1992.
Sura, Agnes J. "Edith Flack Ackley, Dolls to Make for Fun and Profit." *Doll News*, Fall 1996.
———. "Edith Flack Ackley, Dolls to Make for Fun and Profit." *Antique Doll Collector,* June 2006.
"Susy Goose." *Plastic Figure & Playset Collector*, June 1994.
Theriault, Florence. *Hertwig & Co. Archives, 1890-1937*. Annapolis, Maryland: Gold Horse Publishing, 2000.
Theriault's. Coming to America. Doll auction catalog. Annapolis, Maryland: Theriault's, September 2, 1995.
Timpson, Anne. "Tynietoy: The Toy Furniture Shop of Providence, Rhode Island—Part II." *International Dolls House News*, 1997.
Tomy Corporation. "About Tomy." http://www.tomy-usa.com/history.php.
Topher. "Van Brode Company International Figurines." *Topher's Castle*. http://www.lavasurfer.com/prizenside/pi-vanbrode.html.
Tubbs, Marcie, and Bob Tubbs. "C'mon, Let's Play! Acme/Thomas Dollhouse Toys." *Miniature Collector*, May-June 1995.
———. "Dollhouse Families of the 40s, 50s, & 60s." *Miniature Collector,* October 1998.
———. "Twinky Dolls—Postwar Gems." *Miniature Collector,* March 2003.
Turnersan, D. "Antique China Dolls - dating and detecting repros." eBay. http://reviews.ebay.com/Antique-China-Dolls-dating-and-detecting-repros_W0QQugidZ10000000000851149.
"UFDC Special Exhibit: The Hand Follows the Heart." *Antique Doll Collector,* January 2005.
University of Navarra. "Straight from the Herat." *IESE Business School Alumni Magazine 96* (January-March 2005). http://www.ee-iese.com/96/ingles/agrup1.php.
Van Patten, Denise. "A Brief History of Antique Dolls: Part I, Early Dolls through Paper Mache and Wax, and Part II, Chinas and Parians through German Dolly Faced Dolls." About.com: Doll Collecting. http://collectdolls.about.com/library/weekly/aa011503a.htm.
———. "Bru Dolls." About.com: Doll Collecting. http://www.collectdolls.about.com/od/dollprofiles/p/brudolls.htm.
———. "Composition Dolls." About.com: Doll Collecting. http://collectdolls.about.com/od/dollprofiles/p/compositiondoll.htm.
———. "Wax Dolls." About.com: Doll Collecting. http://collectdolls.about.com/od/dollprofiles/p/waxdolls.htm.
Weizel, Richard. "Given Their Daily Bread by the Hand of Technology." *New York Times*, August 30, 1992.
Wentzlau, Sylvia. "Hersteller anliker Puppen und ihre Markungen." General information about PlasticBaby. http://www.sylvias-puppenhaus.de.
Whorton, Judith. "Sewing Doll Sets." *Doll News*, Spring 1980.
Newcomen Society of the U.S. *Winds of Imagination*. Brochure about the history of the Morrell Corporation, September 14, 1990.
Zillner, Dian. *American Dollhouses and Furniture from the 20th century*. Atglen, Pennsylvania: Schiffer Publishing Ltd., 1995.
———. *International Dollhouses & Accessories, 1880s to 1980s.* Atglen, Pennsylvania: Schiffer Publishing Ltd., 2003.
_____ and Patty Cooper. *Antique & Collectible Dollhouses and Their Furnishings*. Atglen, Pennsylvania: Schiffer Publishing Ltd., 1998.
———. *Furnished Dollhouses 1880s-1980s.* Atglen, Pennsylvania: Schiffer Publishing Ltd., 2001.

Index

4
DOLLY DRESS
PATTERNS
H

J